REENTRY
ESSENTIALS, INC.

LIFE SKILLS SERIES

Basic Skills for Lifelong Success

CONTENT

ACTIVE PARENTING PRE AND POST RELEASE

REENTRY
ESSENTIALS, INC.

Life Skills Series
Basic Skills for Lifelong Success

Please read:

This workbook provides general information only. It does not supersede or replace any court orders that are in effect regarding your rights relative to contacting your child or your child's caregiver.

Reentry Essentials, Inc.
2609 East 14 Street, Suite 1018
Brooklyn, NY 11235-3915
P: 347.973.0004
E: info@ReentryEssentials.org
I: www.ReentryEssentials.org

This workbook belongs to:

_____

You may find it helpful to keep important names and phone numbers handy.

Write them below.

Child's caregiver

Name_____

Phone_____

Probation officer

Name_____

Phone_____

Parole officer

Name_____

Phone_____

Social services

Name_____

Phone_____

Child support office

Name_____

Phone_____

Other important numbers

_____

_____

_____

_____

_____

_____

IF YOU ARE A PARENT CURRENTLY IN PRISON OR WERE RECENTLY RELEASED, THIS WORKBOOK IS FOR YOU.

It can help you:

Stay connected with your child

You can do this by:

- staying in regular contact
- keeping track of your child's education

Become more involved in raising your child after release

- It will be a new chance for you to be there
- for your child as he or she grows up.

Work on being the best parent you can be

There are many skills involved in parenting. You can work on the skills you have, and learn new ones. All it takes is effort and commitment.

You can still play an important role in your child's life.

CONTENT

CAN YOU BE AN EFFECTIVE PARENT WHEN YOU ARE IN PRISON?

The answer is yes. But you will face some challenges.

Being away from your child is a challenge.

You won't be able to provide for your child. You also won't be able to see him or her every day. You won't be able to be there to celebrate accomplishments and help your child learn and grow. But you can still be a part of your child's life. This involves:

- making the most of the contact you do have with your child
- being honest with him or her
- sharing thoughts and feelings
- learning all you can about
- what's going on in your child's life
- staying involved in your child's education as much as you can

Your child is being raised by someone else.

The caregiver may be your current partner, a former partner, the child's grandparent or a foster parent. You may or may not currently have a good relationship with the child's caregiver.

To be an effective parent in prison, you will need to:

- set aside negative feelings you have for the caregiver, if any
- treat him or her with respect
- ask for the caregivers help to stay in touch with your child
- work with the caregiver on what's best for your child

Your sentence affects your child, too.

He or she will miss you. But your child may also face teasing from other children about your prison term. This could lead to many feelings, such as anger, in your child.

Your child may not want to have much to do with you at first. But if you respect your child's feelings and work on his or her terms, you can take steps to improve your relationship.

Pledge to make any changes needed to be a better parent. Your child needs you!

YOUR CHILD WILL HAVE QUESTIONS.

Be as honest as you can in your replies. Here are some common questions children ask, with tips on answering them.

"What is prison?"

If your child is young, he or she may not even know what prison is. Explain that prison is a place some adults have to go to when they break the rules (law).

"Why are you there?"

Explain that you made a mistake, and that you are taking responsibility for your actions. Don't get into details about your crime for younger children, but give a brief explanation. For example, "I hurt someone," or "I sold something that is not allowed." If your child is older, he or she may have more questions. Answer them as honestly as you can.

"How long will you be there?"

Tell your child when your sentence is scheduled to end. If you will be eligible for parole, explain that you may be able to come home earlier. But don't make any promises. Don't say you'll be home "soon," if you still have a lot of time left in your sentence.

"Are you OK?"

It's important for your child to know that you are safe. If your child visits you, he or she will be able to tell it's not a nice place to be. Don't give your child the idea that you are in a good place. But reassure him or her that you are safe there.

"What is prison like?"

You can tell your child:

- what you eat
- what you wear
- where you sleep
- about the facilities in the prison (for example, TV room, library, showers and the yard)
- when you wake up and go to bed
- when you exercise
- how you spend your day, including any jobs you do or classes you take

"Is it my fault?"

Children may feel guilty that you are in a corrections facility, and think that they made it happen somehow. Help your child understand that you are not in prison because of anything he or she did. Make it clear that you are the one who did something wrong, and nobody else.

"Will I go to prison when I grow up?"

Children may be afraid that they will end up in prison just like you. Explain to your child that only people who break the law have to go to prison.

"What will happen to me?"

Your child may wonder what things will be like when you are not around. Explain:

- what your child's living arrangements will be
- who his or her caregiver will be
- any changes this involves (such as moving to a new place)

Reassure your child that he or she will be OK.

STAY IN TOUCH WITH YOUR CHILD REGULARLY.

Take responsibility for staying in contact with your child.
Don't wait for your child to contact you.

Write to your child often.

- Always mention how much you love and miss him or her.
- Encourage your child to write back to you. Ask him or her to send along photos, drawings and copies of schoolwork.
- Ask questions when you write— for example, about your child's school, friends or pets.
- Send younger children many short letters or notes. Print with large, clear letters. Ask the caregiver to read the letters aloud, if needed.
- If your child can't write, ask the caregiver to write out your child's messages to you.
- For an older child or teen, share memories—about your child, or about when you were his or her age.
- Be sure to write before any special occasions, such as your child's birthday.
- Consider a drawing activity if your child is young. Start a drawing and mail it your child. Ask the child to add to the drawing, and then send it back.
- Be sure to follow all the rules at your facility for sending and receiving mail (including e-mail, if your facility allows it).

Make phone calls when you can.

- Arrange a time when you can use a phone and your child will be home.
- Ask your child questions, but don't push any topics that he or she doesn't seem comfortable talking about.
- Ask about getting a prepaid inmate calling card, to avoid calling your loved ones collect.
- Be sure to follow all the rules at your facility for making phone calls. These may include limits on when you can use the phone and for how long. There may also be rules about what you can discuss.

If possible, arrange for your child to visit you.

Work out the details with your child's caregiver. Remember, your child may find your facility a scary place. He or she may not feel like talking much. But that's OK—the important thing is that you get to spend time together.

Don't give up!

Even if you don't hear back from your child, keep trying to get in touch. It helps show you care.

WRITE DOWN CONTACT INFORMATION FOR YOUR CHILDREN HERE.

	Child #1	Child #2	Child #3	Child #4
Name				
Caregiver				
Address and e-mail				
Phone number				
Best time to call				
Birthday				
Notes				

KEEP THE CONVERSATION GOING WITH YOUR CHILD
Here are some tips on interacting with your child in letters, phone calls and visits.

Talk about your child's interests.

For example, you can talk about his or her:

- favorite TV show
- favorite book
- friends
- family members

Ask about your child's day.

For example, you can ask about:

- what your child did
- what your child ate
- places your child went
- events your child attended

Talk about your day.

Let your child know how you spent your time. You can tell him or her about:

- any classes you take
- what you had for lunch
- what you did for work

Share experiences.

- Watch the same TV show or sporting event.
- Read a book your child is reading.
- Read short passages from a favorite book to him or her over the phone.

Play games.

- Start telling a story, and ask your child to continue it.
- Use letters to play a game by mail—such as tic-tac-toe.

Take part in parenting programs.

Some facilities have programs that allow parents to record audio or video messages for their children. Ask if your facility has any programs like this.

Make the most of visits.

- If your child is an infant, play games such as peek a- boo or patty-cake.
- If your child wants to talk, be a good listener.
- Draw pictures together.
- Read your child a story.
- Play a game together, such as "I spy." Or play a game your facility lets families use during visits.
- Ask about things that are going on in your child's life.
- Tell your child you love him or her.

Write some other ideas below:

_____
_____
_____
_____
_____
_____
_____
_____

Be sure to follow your facility's rules for interacting with visitors.

KEEP A JOURNAL.

This can help you cope with the separation from your child.
You can write about whatever you want, including:

Thoughts and feelings

These may include:

- thoughts on your situation
- feelings toward your child
- feelings about being separated from your child
- your daily life in the facility
- lessons you've learned
- regrets for how your child has been affected by your actions

Ways you can stay connected

These could involve:

- ideas on what to talk about with your child
- questions you want to ask your child
- conversations you want to have with your child's caregiver

Future plans

These may include:

- things you want to do with your child after your release dreams you have for your child (such as watching him or her graduate from college)
- completing your education
- ways you can be a better parent

Practice right now.

Write down what's on your mind below. (Later, you might want to start keeping your journal in a bound notebook. Follow facility guidelines for the type of notebook allowed.)

_____

_____

_____

_____

_____

_____

_____

_____

_____

_____

_____

_____

_____

_____

_____

_____

_____

_____

_____

_____

GET STARTED TODAY.

Use this form to write a letter to your child. Start by writing about something you thought of today (for example, something you and your child did together in the past).

Date: _____

Dear _____

Today, I

_____

_____

_____

_____

_____

_____

_____

_____

_____

_____

_____

_____

_____

_____

_____

_____

_____

_____

_____

Here is something I want to share with you.

I though it was

_____

_____

_____

_____

(Attach a cartoon or photograph from a newspaper or magazine, for example.)

RESPECT YOU CHILD'S FEELINGS.

Your child loves you, but he or she may be having trouble coping with your sentence.

Your child may have many different feelings.

He or she may feel:

- angry
- abandoned
- sad
- worried
- confused
- frustrated
- guilty
- tense
- afraid
- ashamed

All of these feelings are normal.

Talk with your child about these feelings.

Encourage him or her to share these feelings with you. Explain that it's OK to have those feelings. Reassure your child that you love him or her no matter what. And remind your child that he or she is not responsible in any way for your being in the correctional facility.

Encourage your child to find an outlet for these feelings.

For example, to manage feelings, he or she can:

- draw
- keep a diary or journal
- listen to music
- talk to a trusted adult

For feelings of anger or frustration especially, suggest counting to ten, or taking several slow, deep breaths.

Share your feelings, too.

For example, you can talk about how you feel about what you did. Or you can tell your child that it makes you sad when you can't see him or her. And you can remind your child that you love him or her very much.

Talk with your child's caregiver.

Ask him or her to watch for signs that your child is having trouble managing feelings.

These signs may include:

- withdrawal from people or activities
- bed wetting (after child has learned to stay dry)
- lack of interest in other people
- low self-esteem
- falling grades
- frequent or severe temper tantrums
- fighting
- physical problems (such as trouble sleeping, headaches or stomachaches)

Encourage your child's caregiver to talk to your child about feelings often. Ask him or her to consider talking to your child's health-care provider or school counselor if these signs seem severe or last a long time.

STAY INVOLVED IN YOUR CHILD'S EDUCATION AS MUCH AS YOU CAN.

You can't be with your child every day. But you can still help him or her be successful in school.

Always ask your child about school.

You can start the conversation by asking, "How's school?" But don't stop there. Ask about your child's assignments, report cards and how he or she did on tests. Other questions you could ask:

- "What were the best and worst parts of your day?"
- "Which subject do you like the most (and least)?"
- "What did you do in class today?"

Encourage good study habits.

Talk with your child's caregiver about setting rules for your child's homework. Encourage him or her to set up a study space and a time for doing homework each night.

Talk with your child about the importance of homework and always doing his or her best. Encourage him or her to ask the caregiver or a teacher for help, if needed.

Help build your child's self-esteem and confidence.

For example, you can:

- encourage him or her to get involved in school activities
- give praise when your child does well on a test

If your child doesn't do well on a test, don't criticize. Talk about ways he or she can do better next time.

Try to get copies of your child's work.

Ask your child's caregiver if he or she will make copies of:

- graded tests
- assignments
- other projects

If you want to learn more about a subject your child is taking, check your facility's library.

Help your child set goals.

Ask your child what he or she would like to do in the next few months. For example, he or she might want to:

- get a better grade
- join a club
- try out for a play

Talk about steps your child can take to reach these goals.

Stay on top of your child's school schedule.

Use the space on the next page to keep track of this information. (Ask the child's caregiver for help.) Learn about your child's:

- teachers
- friends
- schedule
- homework assignments
- tests, including standardized tests

USE THIS CHART TO KEEP TRACK OF YOUR CHILD'S TIME IN SCHOOL.

School information:

- Name of school:

  _____

- Address:

  _____

  _____

- Child's teacher(s):

  _____

  _____

  _____

- School principal:

  _____

Notes (friends, activities, etc.)

_____

_____

_____

_____

_____

_____

_____

_____

_____

_____

Grades:

Subject	Date	Description	Grade

Standardized Tests/State Tests:

Name	Date/Time	Score

WORK ON A GOOD RELATIONSHIP WITH YOUR CHILD'S CAREGIVER.

It's important if you want to stay connected with your child and be an involved parent.

Remember, the caregiver is your connection to your child.

He or she is responsible for raising your child and providing for your child's needs. Always keep that in mind, whether the caregiver is your:

- current spouse or partner
- former spouse or partner
- parent
- other relative
- foster parent

Whatever has happened between you and the caregiver, leave the past in the past. Focus on what's best for your child.

Always treat your child's caregiver with respect.

In general:

- Treat the caregiver the way you would like to be treated.
- Don't yell or raise your voice.
- Don't bring up things that happened in the past.
- Don't blame or criticize the caregiver.

Ask the caregiver to treat you with respect.

The caregiver may have negative feelings toward you. Encourage him or her to discuss those feelings, and listen. Explain that you understand those feelings, but that you just want to do what's best for your child.

Be polite to each other in front of your child.

If you are having a conflict with the caregiver, talk about it in private. Discussing it in front of your child will only make things more stressful for him or her. Don't display any negative feelings toward the caregiver, even if you are angry.

Don't use your child as a messenger.

If you have anything to say to the caregiver, say it directly to that person. Don't ask your child to pass along a message.

Don't say bad things about the caregiver to your child.

If you have negative feelings toward the caregiver, there's no need to tell your child. Doing so will only make him or her upset. Remember, your child lives with the caregiver. It's important for your child to feel that everything is OK between you.

Make your intentions clear.

- Tell the caregiver that you want to stay involved in your child's life as much as possible.
- Make it clear that you are willing to work with the caregiver to do what's best for your child.
- Consider taking a parenting class, if your facility offers one.

Ask for the caregivers help.

- Ask him or her to encourage your child to respond to letters you send, and to take your phone calls.
- If your child is very young, ask the caregiver to help him or her write letters to you.
- Ask the caregiver for photos of special events your child is involved in.
- Ask to be told about any developments or problems involving your child—at school or at home.

Agree that your child's needs come first.

Be willing to set aside any differences you have with the caregiver to focus on what's best for your child. Also be willing to make any changes needed.

How can you improve your relationship with your child's caregiver?

Write your ideas below.

_____
_____
_____
_____
_____
_____
_____
_____
_____
_____
_____
_____
_____
_____
_____
_____
_____

Even if you are in a positive, loving relationship with your child's caregiver, you still need to make the effort to be involved in your child's day-to-day life.

WHEN YOU ARE RELEASED
Take steps so you can be there for your child.

Think of your release as a new beginning.

This is a chance to rebuild your life and to be a better parent for your child. Building a new life means making changes. This could involve giving up old habits and even old friends.

Take it slow.

It will take time to put your new life together. You won't be able to do everything at once. Focus on one thing at a time, one day at a time.

Stay positive.

Starting over may seem challenging. But lots of people have done it, and you can, too. Remember, everybody has setbacks and bad days. But if you keep working on making positive changes in your life, it will pay off. Keep yourself busy for example, with school, work and volunteering.

Remember that your actions are important.

They could determine your visitation rights and whether or not you get custody of your child. If you are paroled, taking the right steps is very important.

Follow your pre-release plan.

- If you are paroled, make sure you understand the conditions, and follow them. Stay in contact with your parole officer.
- If you've had problems with alcohol or other drug use, consider a treatment program or support group.

Build a support system.

- Reach out to friends and family members who are positive influences.
- Stay away from old friends who are negative influences, or who take part in criminal behavior.
- Get involved in a community or church group.

Write down things you'll need to do first after your release:

_____

_____

_____

_____

_____

_____

_____

_____

_____

_____

_____

_____

_____

_____

_____

_____

_____

_____

_____

_____

_____

_____

KEEP YOUR EXPECTATIONS REASONABLE.

Being released is something to feel good about! But don't expect things to go back to the way they were before you went to a correctional facility.

Your child may have mixed feelings.

Remember, your child has been used to limited contact with you. He or she may be happy you are out, but may also wonder what's going to happen. (See page 20 for some common reactions children have after being separated from a parent.)

You may have mixed feelings, too.

Things may not seem the same as before you went into prison. That's because things aren't the same. Your loved ones have changed during that time—and so have you.

Resist thinking about the time you've lost or the things you don't have. Instead, focus on the opportunity to start over. This includes the opportunity to become more involved in your child's life.

Take things slowly with your child.

Arrange for regular visits, but don't try to change your child's routine too much. If you are seeking custody, keep in mind that it may take some time.

Be honest with others and yourself.

- Accept that spending time in prison may limit the opportunities you have for jobs and places to live. Make the most of the opportunities you do have.
- Don't make promises you can't keep.
- Ask for help if you need it.

Give things time.

It will take a while for your family, including your child, to adjust to your being out of prison. It will take time for you to adjust, too.

What are your expectations after release?

Write them below.

_____

_____

_____

_____

_____

_____

_____

_____

_____

_____

_____

_____

_____

_____

_____

_____

_____

_____

_____

_____

SET SOME GOALS.

Keep them practical and realistic. Make a plan for reaching the goals you set.

Personal goals

These may include:

- building a better relationship with your child
- spending time regularly with your child
- becoming a better parent
- joining a church or support group

Practical goals

Some examples include:

- finding a place to live
- getting a car

Professional goals

For example, you may want to:

- get a steady job as soon as you can
- enroll in a training program

Educational goals

You may want to:

- take classes
- work toward getting a degree

Short-term goals

(things I want to do in the next few days or weeks)

_____

_____

_____

_____

_____

Medium-term goals

(things I want to do in the next few months)

_____

_____

_____

_____

Long-term goals

(things I want to do in the next few years)

_____

_____

_____

_____

_____

_____

ADJUSTING TO CHANGE CAN BE CHALLENGING.
But it's also an opportunity to improve yourself.

Your child has been living with someone else.

Depending on your situation, this may continue to be the case. Avoid criticizing your child and his or her caregiver. They did the best they could while you were serving your time.

While you were away, your child looked to the caregiver for guidance and support. You can play a greater role in your child's life, but you will have to earn back everyone's trust.

Your family has learned to live without you.

If you were the head of the household before, don't expect to step right back into that role. You have to prove that you have changed and are dependable.

If you won't be living with your family, it will take time for you to become part of their lives again.

Remember that things won't go back to the way they were.

You may want things to get back to normal after your release. That's not likely to happen, but that's OK You'll find a "new normal." You may get a new:

- job
- place to live
- partner

But your child can be a big part of your new life.

Take steps to help you stay out of prison.

Avoid old habits and old friends that had anything to do with the crime that landed you in prison. There's a very good chance they would help send you back. See page 30 for sources of help, if you need them.

What are some changes you've noticed?

Write down anything that seems different to you since you've been out:

_____

_____

_____

_____

_____

_____

_____

_____

_____

_____

_____

_____

_____

_____

_____

_____

_____

_____

_____

HOW YOUR CHILD REACTS TO YOUR RELEASE

Depends on your relationship with him or her, and how long you were away. But here are some common reactions you can expect.

Infants

Even if your sentence was short, and your child is still an infant, he or she will not recognize you. In fact, your child may react as if you are a stranger. He or she may:

- cry
- not want you to hold him or her
- cling to the caregiver

Toddlers

If your child is a toddler, he or she may:

- act shy around you (especially if he or she was unable to visit you)
- seem to not recognize you
- cry
- throw tantrums
- cling to the caregiver

Preschoolers

A child this age may:

- seek all your attention
- be angry with you for going away
- blame him or herself for your prison term
- test limits
- be eager to tell you about things that happened while you were away

Older children

If you had a good relationship with your child before, he or she will likely be happy to see you. Your child may seek all your attention. He or she may want to talk to you about school or other topics.

If you didn't have a good relationship with your child before, he or she may seem withdrawn.

Teens

A child this age is already going through a lot of changes. He or she may:

- have mixed feelings about your being back
- seem excited to see you, or act withdrawn
- wonder what's going to happen now that you are out
- feel uncomfortable expressing feelings

How did your child react?

Write down what happened:

_____

_____

_____

_____

_____

_____

_____

_____

_____

_____

_____

_____

_____

_____

SPEND TIME WITH YOUR CHILD.

The more time you spend with your child, the closer you will become.
Here are some tips for developing a closer relationship.

Infants

Hold and touch your baby. Play simple games, such as peek-a-boo. If you live with your child, get involved with his or her daily care—such as feedings or changing diapers.

Toddlers

It's important to be gentle and loving. When talking with your child, sit or kneel down so that you are at eye level. This will seem less threatening.

Preschoolers

Reassure your child it wasn't his or her fault that you had to go away. Play fun games together. Avoid discipline at first.

(See pages 22 and 26 for more on disciplining your child.)

Older children

Give your child lots of love and attention. Continue to keep track of how your child is doing in school. Praise your child's accomplishments, and let him or her know how proud you are. Don't criticize your child, and avoid disciplining at first.

Teens

Teens are very sensitive to criticism and teasing, so it's best to avoid those behaviors. Your child may be withdrawn. Ask him or her questions about what's going on in his or her life. You can also ask about how he or she feels about your release. Accept your teen's feelings, whatever they are.

Do fun things together.

For example, you could take your child to:

- the park
- the library
- a museum
- a movie

Write down some things you can do with your child:

_____
_____
_____
_____
_____
_____
_____
_____
_____
_____
_____
_____
_____
_____
_____
_____
_____
_____
_____
_____
_____
_____

CONTINUE TO WORK WITH YOUR CHILD'S CAREGIVER.

Whatever your situation, talk about ways you can take on more parenting responsibilities.

Arrange times to see your child.

If you're not living with your child, don't drop by unannounced. Talk with your child's caregiver ahead of time about when you can visit or spend time with your child.

Work out financial responsibilities.

There are many costs involved in raising a child. As soon as you get a job, work out a family budget or a payment plan to help cover the costs of:

- clothing and food
- school supplies
- health care
- child care (day-care centers or baby sitters, for example)
- long-term savings (a college fund, for example)
- any child support you owe

Talk about making decisions.

It's important to be effective "co-parents" for your child's sake. Discuss how you will make decisions about your child. Some may be done together—for example, decisions about discipline. If you live apart from your child, other decisions may be made by the caregiver alone—mealtimes and study time, for example.

Discuss morals and values.

For example, you might want to talk about:

- how you will each teach your child important values (such as respect, responsibility and honesty)
- where and how your child will worship
- what forms of entertainment are acceptable for your child

Work out a plan for special occasions.

Make a schedule ahead of time. Talk about plans for:

- birthdays
- holidays
- vacations

Respect the caregivers' rules.

For example, he or she may have rules about your child's bedtime or diet. Support these decisions to help keep things consistent for your child.

Be ready for unexpected changes.

For example, your child may get sick or may need a ride. Be ready to help out when needed.

Take it slowly as you readjust to family life.

If you are living with your child and his or her caregiver, getting to know each other again will take some time. Be patient— and get help if needed.

IF YOU GET CUSTODY OF YOUR CHILD.

Here are some tips on learning to live together again.

Keep your child's caregiver involved in your child's life.

Work out times when the caregiver can visit your child or spend time with him or her. Invite the caregiver to birthday parties and other special occasions.

Don't be jealous of your child's time with the caregiver.

Your child may miss the caregiver and have mixed feelings about living with you again. Respect these feelings, and encourage your child to talk about them.

Transition your child slowly.

Remember, your child has been used to living in a different home, with a different set of rules. Consider following the caregivers rules at first. Work in rules you have little by little.

Let your child help with decisions.

This can help him or her feel responsible and part of the household. Depending on your child's age, he or she can decide on:

- what to have for dinner
- chores he or she can do
- a fun thing you can do together, such as going for a walk or reading

Be patient.

It will take time for you and your child to get used to living together again. Things won't always go smoothly. If you are having problems, reach out to your support system. (See page 16.)

What are some ways you can be a family again?

Write your ideas below.

_____
_____
_____
_____
_____
_____
_____
_____
_____
_____
_____
_____
_____
_____
_____
_____
_____
_____
_____
_____
_____
_____

IMPROVE YOUR COMMUNICATION SKILLS.

This can help you work with your child's caregiver more effectively. It can also help you be a better parent.

Know what good communication is.

Good communication means.

- sharing your own feelings
- listening to the other person
- solving conflicts and working out solutions to problems

Be willing to share your thoughts and feelings.

You may find it hard to open up at first. At times, it may seem as if nobody understands what you went through.

But remember that your time in the correctional facility affected the whole family, including your child. Your family had to learn to get by without you. And your child may have been teased at school. Your time in prison is something you all had to deal with.

Be a good listener.

Here are some ways to let a person know you are interested in what he or she has to say:

- Maintain eye contact.
- Ignore distractions while the other person is speaking.
- Don't interrupt.
- Don't overreact to anything the person says.
- Pay attention to the person's body language and tone of voice. They can give you clues on how he or she really feels.
- Restate what the person told you in your own words, to show that you understand.
- Ask open-ended questions, rather than questions that can be answered with "yes" or "no." For example, you could ask, "How do you feel about that?" instead of "Are you angry?"

Create win-win situations.

If you are having a conflict with the child's caregiver, try to solve it. First, figure out what the problem is. Together, think of different ways you could solve the problem. Come up with as many different possible solutions as you can. Choose the one you think will work best for both of you, then try it out. If it doesn't work, try another solution.

Don't make it personal.

Remember, the problem is not your child's caregiver. The problem is the conflict you are having. Keep the discussion focused on the conflict. Keep your feelings about the caregiver out of it.

Don't criticize or judge.

You may not approve of the way the caregiver handled certain things while you were gone. But criticizing won't help anything. It will only make the caregiver angry, and could make it more difficult for you to spend time with your child.

Accept that the caregiver did the best he or she could. Leave the past behind. Focus on decisions you need to make right now. If there is an unresolved conflict you'd like to talk about, deal with it another time.

Use "I" statements.

This is a way of telling someone how you feel without placing any blame. Placing blame only makes a person defensive, and gets in the way of communication.

For example, saying, "You never tell me anything!" places blame on the other person. A more effective statement is "I get upset when you don't tell me things that involve my child."

Practice using "I" statements.

Think of a conflict you are having with your child's caregiver. How can you phrase it as an "I" statement?

Write it below.

_____

_____

_____

_____

_____

_____

_____

_____

_____

_____

_____

_____

_____

_____

_____

_____

_____

_____

_____

_____

_____

_____

_____

_____

FOCUS ON BEING THE BEST PARENT YOU CAN BE.

It will take patience, planning and practice.

Express your love for your child often.

Tell your child regularly that you love him or her. You can also show your love by:

- holding him or her
- smiling
- sharing your time
- listening
- staying involved in your child's life

Help build your child's self-confidence and independence.

- Let your child try new things that are appropriate for his or her age.
- Give your child responsibilities, such as chores. For example, he or she can be in charge of feeding a pet, or clearing off the table after dinner.

Use loving discipline with your child.

Work with your child's caregiver on discipline and agree on the methods you'll use in general:

- Set some rules your child must follow. Also set consequences for breaking those rules. Make sure your child understands both.
- If your child breaks a rule, put the consequence into effect right away. Be sure to stay calm. Don't call your child names or yell.
- Be consistent and fair. Make sure the consequences fit the action. For example, if your child doesn't put a toy away, say he or she can't play with it for a short time.
- Praise your child when you see him or her being good. Be specific about the behavior you liked.
- Never spank your child or use any form of physical punishment.

Use discipline methods that are appropriate for your child's age.

- Hold your child and say "no" calmly but firmly. Don't yell. Or redirect children younger than 2 from unsafe or unwanted activity.
- If your toddler has a tantrum, stay cool and wait for it to pass. Don't reward the tantrum with your attention.
- Consider "timeouts" for children ages 3 and 4. Have your child sit quietly for a minute or two in a place where there are no distractions.
- If your child is between the ages of 5 and 10, explain the reasons for rules. For example, say "You have to go to bed at this time so you'll have enough rest for school tomorrow."
- Adjust rules as needed for preteens and teens. For example, you can set a curfew.

Be a good role model.

Your child learns a lot about how to interact with other people by watching you.

- Show respect for your child and for others.
- Treat other people fairly.
- Approach problems with a positive attitude.
- Demonstrate good values, such as honesty, responsibility and hard work.

Talk to your child each day.

Give your child at least 5 minutes of your undivided attention each day, if possible. If your child doesn't live with you, stay in touch each day through a short phone call. (Be sure to arrange this with the child's caregiver first.)

Be a positive influence in your child's life.

- Take part in your child's activities.
- Let your child know that you will always be there for him or her.
- Keep your child away from people in your past who were negative influences.
- If your child is old enough, talk about your prison term. Explain that what you did was wrong, and that you have learned from your mistake.

What are some things you will do to become a better parent?

Write them below.

_____
_____
_____
_____
_____
_____
_____
_____
_____
_____
_____
_____
_____
_____
_____
_____
_____
_____
_____
_____
_____
_____
_____
_____
_____
_____

TAKE CARE OF YOURSELF.
Follow these tips on staying healthy.

Find healthy ways to deal with stress.

- Recognize when you are feeling stressed. Common signs include tight muscles, headaches and getting upset over things that usually don't bother you.
- Continue to keep a journal of your thoughts and feelings.
- Set priorities, and focus on getting the most important things done first.
- Accept what you can't control. For example, if there's a long line at the store, there's nothing you can do about that. But you can control how you react. Stay calm.
- Try to think positively. Tell yourself you can handle the situation. Keep things in perspective.
- Spend some time each day on a hobby or other fun activity.
- Consider a relaxation technique, such as deep breathing. Take several slow, deep breaths.
- Try progressive muscle relaxation. Sit or lie down. Slowly tense, then relax, muscles in different parts of your body.

Find healthy ways to manage anger.

- Make a list of things that trigger your anger. For example, these could include feeling ignored, being criticized or being in traffic jams.
- Recognize when you are getting angry. Your muscles may get tense and your jaw may clench. You may start breathing faster, or raise your voice.
- If you feel yourself getting angry, stop what you are doing.
- Count slowly to 10 to try to calm down.
- Walk away from the person or situation that is making you angry, if you can.
- If possible, go for a walk and don't come back until you have calmed down. (Don't leave your child unsupervised).
- Call someone in your support network to talk it out. See page 30.

Get enough physical activity.

- Get at least 150 minutes of moderate—or 75 minutes of vigorous—physical activity each week.
- For greater health benefits, get at least 300 minutes of moderate—or 150 minutes of vigorous—physical activity each week.
- Try to spread your activity throughout the week, getting at least 10 minutes at a time.
- In addition, do muscle strengthening exercises at least 2 days each week.

Consult your health-care provider before starting an exercise program.

Create a healthy eating pattern.

- Know how many daily calories are right for your gender, age and activity level. Having more calories will lead to weight gain.
- Find out what's in your food and drinks—check Nutrition Facts labels and ingredients. Limit items high in calories, saturated or trans fats, sodium, cholesterol and added sugars. Choose more whole grains.
- Build a healthy plate—fill half with fruits and vegetables.
- Drink more low-fat or fat-free milk.
- Choose lean cuts of meat. Eat seafood at least twice a week.
- Limit sweetened drinks to help cut calories.
- Cook more at home so you are in charge of what's in your food. Use small amounts of vegetable oils, when needed, in place of butter or other solid fats. And add little salt or sugar.
- Avoid oversized portions, and don't eat in front of the TV you'll eat more.

Avoid alcohol and other drugs.

They don't help you cope with problems and only make things worse. In addition, they could land you back in prison. You could also be putting the time you spend with your child at risk.

- Follow any guidelines in your pre-release plan about getting treatment or support for substance abuse.
- If you think you might have a problem with alcohol or other drugs and would like to get help, contact the Center for Substance Abuse Treatment's Referral Service at
  1-800-662-HELP
  (1-800-662-4357) or visit
  www.findtreatment.samhsa.gov.

YOU ARE NOT ALONE.

Support and advice are available to help you be the best parent you can be while you're in prison and after you get out. Sources include:

Your support network

These are people who are trustworthy and dependable people whose judgment you trust. They are people you can turn to when you need help or advice. Members of your support network could include:

- friends
- family members
- community groups
- spiritual leaders

State and local services

These could include:

- health clinics or healthcare providers
- social and family services
- hotlines
- the extension service in your state

Check the community service number in the front section of your phone book.

Your probation or parole officer

He or she may be able to connect you to sources of help.

National organizations

- Administration for Children and Families U.S. Department of Health and Human Services www.acf.hhs.gov

- American Academy of Pediatrics www.healthychildren.org

- Childhelp® National Child Abuse Hotline
  1-800-4-A-CHILD
  (1-800-422-4453)

- Prevent Child Abuse America]
  1-800-CHILDREN
  (1-800-244-5373)
  www.preventchildabuse.org

- National Domestic Violence Hotline 1-800-799-SAFE
  (1-800-799-7233)
  (English and Spanish)
  1-800-787-3224 (TTY)

Who is in your support network?

List their names and phone numbers below

_____

_____

_____

_____

_____

_____

_____

_____

_____

_____

_____

_____

_____

_____

_____

_____

_____

_____

_____

_____

_____

_____

_____

_____

_____

_____

_____

_____

STAY INVOLVED ON YOUR CHILD'S LIFE.

Remember, a prison sentence doesn't stop you from being a parent.

Do what you can while in prison.

- Stay in regular contact with your child through letters and phone calls.
- Work on keeping a good relationship with your child's caregiver.
- If possible, ask the caregiver to bring your child for visits.
- Take advantage of any programs at your facility that let you record audio and video messages for your child.

Focus on being a better parent when you're released.

- Set goals for yourself, and make a plan to reach them.
- Spend as much time as you can with your child.
- Avoid old habits, friends and situations that could get you in trouble again.
- Build a support network and reach out for help when you need it.

It's never too late to make positive changes in your life!

ANGER MANAGEMENT AND YOU

REENTRY
ESSENTIALS, INC.

Life Skills Series
Basic Skills for Lifelong Success

Please read:

Talk to your health-care provider! This workbook is not a substitute for the advice of a qualified health-care provider.

Reentry Essentials, Inc.
2609 East 14 Street, Suite 1018
Brooklyn, NY 11235-3915
P: 347.973.0004
E: info@ReentryEssentials.org
I: www.ReentryEssentials.org

This workbook belongs to:

_____

You may find it helpful to keep important names and phone numbers handy.

Write them below.

Health-care provider

Name_____

Phone_____

Counselor

Name_____

Phone_____

Emergency contact

Name_____

Phone_____

Other important numbers

Name_____

Phone_____

Other important numbers

_____

_____

_____

_____

_____

_____

_____

_____

_____

_____

_____

_____

_____

_____

THIS WORKBOOK CAN HELP YOU MANAGE YOUR ANGER.

It can help you understand what causes your anger and the problems that can result if you're unable to control it. It will also help you learn ways to manage and express your anger.

Anger is a powerful feeling.

Everyone feels angry sometimes. And everyone has a right to feel that way. It's what you do with your anger that makes the difference.

Managing your anger appropriately is an important skill.

It involves:

- identifying what triggers your anger
- learning how to calm yourself
- finding healthy ways to express your anger without losing control and hurting yourself or others

CONTENT

WHAT IS ANGER?

Anger is a natural emotional reaction.

Anger affects your body.

When you get angry, your body creates energy. Here's what happens:

- Adrenaline and other chemicals enter your bloodstream.
- Your heart pumps faster.
- Your blood flows more quickly.
- Your muscles tense.

Everyone gets angry sometimes.

Handling anger well can help you:

- overcome problems
- reach your goals
- stay healthy
- feel better about yourself

But too much anger or uncontrolled anger can cause problems.

It can cause:

- problems in your relationships with family and friends
- problems at work
- legal and financial troubles
- physical and mental health problems

How can you tell when you are getting angry?

_____

_____

_____

_____

_____

_____

_____

_____

_____

_____

_____

_____

_____

_____

_____

_____

_____

_____

_____

_____

_____

_____

Anger isn't good or bad. It's what you do with it that counts.

WHAT CAUSES ANGER?

The causes vary from person to person and from situation to situation. Some common causes of anger include:

Stress

Stress related to work, family, health and money problems may make you feel anxious and irritable.

Frustration

You may get angry if you fail to reach a goal or feel as if things are out of your control.

Fear

Anger is a natural response to threats of violence, or to physical or verbal abuse.

Annoyance

You may react in anger to minor irritations and daily hassles.

Disappointment

Anger often results when expectations and desires aren't met.

Resentment

You may feel angry when you've been hurt, rejected or offended.

Think about a time you got angry due to one of the causes listed on this page. What was it that made you angry? Write about it here:

_____

_____

_____

_____

_____

_____

_____

_____

_____

_____

_____

_____

_____

_____

_____

_____

_____

_____

POORLY HANDLED ANGER CAN CAUSE MANY PROBLEMS.

Some people try to pretend they aren't angry. Other people feel as if their anger is out of control. They don't believe they can handle it. But ignoring or giving up control over it can lead to:

Physical health problems

These may include:

- headaches
- sleep problems
- digestive problems
- high blood pressure
- heart problems

Poor decision making

Anger can make it hard to think clearly. You may have trouble concentrating or may use poor judgment. This can lead to car crashes, injuries and other problems.

Problems with relationships

If you can't control your anger, you may end up insulting, criticizing or threatening those close to you. They may respond with anger or resentment. Getting angry may also keep you from telling your loved ones how you really feel.

Depression

Anger that's kept bottled up can affect your thoughts and feelings. You may begin to feel unhappy and lose interest in things you used to enjoy, such as hobbies, work, friends or sex.

Alcohol or other drug problems

You may use alcohol or other drugs to try to:

- dull anger and other strong feelings
- forget about the negative consequences of an angry outburst

But using alcohol or other drugs won't solve any problems. And it usually results in more anger and problems.

Low self-esteem

If you have trouble managing anger, you may feel bad about yourself. You may feel as if you have little control over what happens.

Problems at work

If you blow up on the job, coworkers, supervisors, and customers may develop a negative impression of you. Your career may suffer as a result.

Learning how to keep your cool can help you lead a happier, healthier life.

Has anger ever caused problems for you? Write about it here:

_____

_____

_____

_____

_____

_____

_____

_____

_____

_____

_____

_____

_____

_____

UNCONTROLLED ANGER CAN LEAD TO AGGRESSION.

The results of uncontrolled anger may include:

Verbal attacks or physical assaults

You may lose control and attack others physically or verbally.

For example, you may:

- throw or break things
- yell, insult or threaten
- slap, shove, kick or hit

Abuse

Tension and frustration may build. Family members may become your target, even if your anger has little to do with them. The abuse may be:

- physical
- verbal
- sexual

Other criminal behavior

Anger is often a driving force behind:

- destruction of property
- murder
- other violent crimes

But remember, you can learn to control your anger.

HOW ANGER CAN HELP YOU

Learning to recognize and express anger appropriately can make a big difference in your life.
Anger can help you:

Reach goals

Trying to reach a goal can be frustrating. Frustration can lead to anger, which in turn can motivate you to work harder.

Solve problems

Anger is a sign that something is wrong. It may serve as a warning for you to think about your feelings and attitudes.

Handle emergencies and protect yourself

Anger can cause an immediate burst of strength and energy. This allows you to react quickly if you're in danger.

Communicate with others

Talking about your anger can help keep it from building up. You may release tension and enjoy better communication with family, friends and co-workers.

You can find ways to help anger work for you - not against you.

IS YOUR ANGER HURTING YOU?

Think about how often you get angry and how you handle angry feelings. Complete the checklist below. It can help you decide if you need help managing your anger.

Am I prone to anger?	True	False
1. I feel tense a lot of the time..	☐	☐
2. People often tell me I need to calm down.......................................	☐	☐
3. I get angry quickly..	☐	☐
4. I stay angry for a long time..	☐	☐
5. Sometimes it seems like everything makes me angry	☐	☐
6. Minor troubles annoy me more than they do most people	☐	☐
7. I often blame my troubles on other people	☐	☐
8. When I feel wronged, I want revenge	☐	☐
9. Getting angry makes me feel powerful and in control	☐	☐
10. I am still angry about bad things that happened to me in the past	☐	☐
11. I get into a lot of arguments	☐	☐
12. I get very upset when things don't go my way	☐	☐

If you answered "true" to any question above, you may get angry more often than most people.

Too much anger can cause problems in your life. But you can take steps to reduce the amount of anger you feel.

How do I handle my anger?	True	False
1. I store up anger until I'm about to explode	☐	☐
2. I try to ignore my anger in the hope it will go away	☐	☐
3. When angry, I say or do things that I later regret	☐	☐
4. My anger:		
• frightens me	☐	☐
• frightens others	☐	☐
5. When I get angry, I:		
• yell or scream	☐	☐
• cry uncontrollably	☐	☐
• break things	☐	☐
• hurt myself	☐	☐
• hurt others (physically and/or verbally)	☐	☐
6. My anger has resulted in:		
• problems at work or school	☐	☐
• problems at home	☐	☐
• trouble with the law	☐	☐
7. I have tried to control my anger and failed	☐	☐
8. I use alcohol or other drugs to try to cover up angry feelings	☐	☐
9. I sometimes feel out of control when I'm angry	☐	☐
10. I want help managing my anger	☐	☐

If you answered "true" to any question above, you may have trouble handling your anger.

You can learn ways to keep your cool and stay in control when you get angry.

RECOGNIZING YOUR BODY'S ANGER WARNING SIGNS
is an important step in learning to manage your anger.

What are your warning signs?

Think about how you feel when you get angry. Check the warning signs you often have when you get angry. Write in signs that aren't listed.

My warning signs are:

☐ tense muscles

☐ tight fists

☐ clenched jaw

☐ sweaty palms

☐ racing heartbeat

☐ fast breathing

☐ trembling or feeling shaky

☐ feeling warm or flushed

☐ upset stomach

☐ loud or mean voice

☐ _____

☐ _____

☐ _____

☐ _____

☐ _____

☐ _____

☐ _____

☐ _____

Talk with your health-care provider.

Certain physical and mental health problems, such as Alzheimer's disease or brain injury, may increase your anger. And handling anger poorly can lead to other health problems. Talk to your healthcare provider about your anger and how it affects you. Have regular checkups.

WHAT SETS YOU OFF?

Different things can trigger a person's anger. Some common triggers are listed below. Check the ones that trigger your anger. Use the blank spaces to fill in your own triggers.

I feel angry when I:

- ☐ think I am treated unfairly
- ☐ am embarrassed
- ☐ feel ignored
- ☐ don't get credit for something I've done
- ☐ have to follow orders
- ☐ fail at something or don't do something well
- ☐ feel helpless or out of control
- ☐ get jealous
- ☐ _____
- ☐ _____
- ☐ _____
- ☐ _____
- ☐ _____
- ☐ _____

I feel angry when people:

- ☐ insult me
- ☐ criticize me or my work
- ☐ don't listen to me
- ☐ disagree with me
- ☐ don't work as hard as I do
- ☐ lie to me
- ☐ tell me what to do
- ☐ are rude or inconsiderate
- ☐ are late
- ☐ don't act or feel the way
- ☐ I think they should
- ☐ _____
- ☐ _____
- ☐ _____
- ☐ _____
- ☐ _____
- ☐ _____
- ☐ _____
- ☐ _____

I feel angry when faced with these events or situations:

- ☐ traffic jams and encounters with other drivers
- ☐ conflict at work
- ☐ family arguments
- ☐ child misbehavior or temper tantrums
- ☐ waiting in line
- ☐ financial problems
- ☐ yelling or loud noises
- ☐ mistakes or errors
- ☐ wasted time
- ☐ losing a game or a contest
- ☐ name-calling or teasing
- ☐ child abuse
- ☐ prejudice toward anyone
- ☐ mistreatment of animals
- ☐ _____
- ☐ _____
- ☐ _____
- ☐ _____
- ☐ _____

Once you're aware of your anger triggers, you can work to change the way you respond to them.

KEEP AN "ANGER JOURNAL".

Use these 2 pages to start your journal.
Over the next several days, keep track of things that trigger your anger.

Date and Time	Trigger	My Anger Warning Signs	My Anger Rating 1 = mild 2 = moderate 3 = severe	What I Did In Response	How I Felt Afterwards

Do you notice patterns in your anger? For example, do minor triggers often set you off? Does your anger rating seem out of proportion to the trigger? Are you satisfied with the outcome?

Date and Time	Trigger	My Anger Warning Signs	My Anger Rating 1 = mild 2 = moderate 3 = severe	What I Did In Response	How I Felt Afterwards

BE AWARE OF HIDDEN ANGER.

Sometimes what triggers your anger isn't the only thing causing angry feeling.
When you get angry, ask yourself:

Are my level of anger and my reaction out of proportion to the trigger?

Do you seem to overreact to minor annoyances? Perhaps there is something else on your mind that's making you angry.

Am I directing my anger at an innocent person?

Are really angry with the person who triggered your feelings? For example, suppose you have a disagreement with your boss. It bothers you all day, but you say nothing. Later, you let your anger out by blowing up at your partner or child.

Am I taking something personally?

Learning to deal well anger means learning not to take problems or arguments personally.

Is this how I usually respond in similar situations?

You may respond with anger in certain situations because that's what you've always done. You may have learned this behavior growing up. But you can change the way you react.

Am I trying to take charge with my anger?

Anger is a common reaction when a person feels as if he or she is losing control. But the best way to show control is to react calmly and manage your feelings.

SOME REACTIONS TO ANGER WON'T HELP.

Many people react poorly to anger. Their reaction doesn't help them control their anger. And sometimes their reaction can make things worse. Avoid negative reactions, such as:

Not letting go

You may have trouble getting past your anger. You may remember events or hurts that occurred long ago. As time goes by, your anger may continue to grow. You may become obsessed with angry thoughts or hopes of revenge.

Keeping bottled up

This usually makes you feel worse. Sooner or later, your feelings will come out. And when they do, it may be in the form of an angry outburst. Holding angry feelings in may also contribute to health problems.

Blaming

Blaming others doesn't solve problems. You need to learn to take responsibility for your own feelings and actions— both positive and negative.

Responding to anger with anger

This may seem like a natural reaction, but it often makes a situation worse.

Think about a time you did not handle anger well. What happened?

Write about it here:

_____

_____

_____

_____

_____

_____

_____

_____

_____

_____

_____

_____

_____

_____

_____

_____

_____

_____

_____

_____

_____

_____

USING ALCOHOL OR OTHER DRUGS ONLY CAUSES MORE PROBLEMS.

They do little to get rid of angry feelings. They can make it harder for you to think clearly and solve problems. It's important to know that:

Alcohol or other drug use may increase anger.

Using alcohol or other drugs to dull anger doesn't work. These substances may mask angry feelings—but only for a short time. And they often make anger worse. Alcohol and other drugs play a major role in many cases of violence.

You shouldn't use alcohol or other drugs as an excuse for angry or violent behavior.

The truth is, there's no excuse for losing control in this way.

Treatment programs are available.

Some treatment programs are designed to help people recover from an alcohol or drug problem and learn to manage their anger.

Get help if you have a problem with alcohol or other drugs.

- Call the Center for Substance Abuse Treatment's National Helpline at

    1-800-662-HELP
    (1-800-662-4357)

- Look in the phone book for numbers of local self-help groups, such as Alcoholics Anonymous (AA).

Having a problem with alcohol or other drugs makes it harder to manage anger.

Look in the phone book for local sources of help for substance abuse.

Write down their contact information here:

Name_____

_____

Phone number_____

Name_____

_____

Phone number_____

Name_____

_____

Phone number_____

TAKE STEPS TO GET BACK CONTROL
When you're angry. Start by taking a "timeout":

Stop what you're doing

When you feel your anger warning signs developing and you start thinking angry thoughts, tell yourself to stop. This may help you calm down and think more clearly.

Try to relax

For example:

- Count to 10 or 100.
- Get a drink of water.
- Take a walk.
- Take several slow, deep breaths.

Leave if necessary

If you are angry with another person, tell him or her that you need to take a timeout. Ask someone to watch a child or an elderly or ill person for you, if necessary. Then go for a walk and calm down. Avoid driving.

Return when your calm

Once you've got your anger under control, go back and talk with the person or face the situation that triggered your anger.

Think about a time when you didn't lose control of your anger and handled it well.

What happened? Write about it here:

_____
_____
_____
_____
_____
_____
_____
_____
_____
_____
_____
_____
_____
_____
_____
_____
_____
_____

FIND HEALTHY WAYS TO EXPRESS YOUR ANGER.

Don't keep angry feelings locked inside you. Express them in ways that help you keep control—and won't hurt others.

Remember to calm down.

Think carefully before you speak. You're less likely to say something you'll be sorry for later.

Name the problem.

Calmly and clearly explain why you're angry or what the problem is. Don't yell, use insults or make threats. People will be less likely to consider your point.

Use "I" statements.

After you describe the problem use "I" statements to tell the person how you feel. These statements focus on you and your needs, wants and feelings. They also help the listener avoid feeling blamed or criticized. (See the next page for examples.)

Identify solutions.

Say what you would like to change or see happen in the future. If you're having a conflict with another person, try to find a solution together.

Get help if you need it.

Talk with a family member or friend if you're having trouble expressing your anger constructively. Or consider seeing a counselor or other mental health professional. He or she can help you learn ways to express your feelings through role-playing and other methods. (See page 61.)

Don't hold a grudge. After a disagreement, be willing to forgive the other person— and yourself.

PRACTICE USING "I" STATEMENTS.

When you're angry, it's easy to blame someone or something for your problems. Getting comfortable using "I" statements can help you learn to take responsibility for your feelings. Fill in the statements below to practice talking in terms of yourself and your feelings.

I feel _____

When_____

Next time I would like

_____

_____

_____

_____

_____

_____

I feel _____

When_____

Next time I would like

_____

_____

_____

_____

_____

_____

I feel _____

When_____

Next time I would like

_____

_____

_____

_____

_____

_____

I feel _____

When_____

Next time I would like

_____

_____

_____

_____

_____

_____

I feel _____

When_____

Next time I would like

_____

_____

_____

_____

_____

_____

I feel _____

When_____

Next time I would like

_____

_____

_____

_____

_____

_____

HOW DO YOU TALK TO YOURSELF?

You may say things silently to yourself every day. This is called self-talk.

Avoid negative self-talk.

This includes criticizing yourself and blaming yourself or others for your problems. Negative self-talk can add to your anger and make it harder to manage.

Learn to use positive self-talk instead.

Try to stop negative self-talk as soon as it pops into your head. Replace the negative thought with a positive one. For example:

- Instead of saying, "I can't handle this traffic. I'm going to explode," you could say, "Relax. I can handle it. This happens to everyone sometimes. It won't last long."
- Instead of saying, "That jerk, she embarrassed me on purpose," you could say, "It's OK she probably didn't mean anything by it. Maybe she's just having a bad day."

Learning to identify negative messages and change them to positive ones can help reduce the amount of anger you feel

PRACTICE YOUR POSITIVE SELF-TALK.

In the space below, write down several problems or situations that made you angry. Did you give yourself a negative message? What positive message could you give yourself if the problem or situation happens again?

Situation	Negative Message	Positive Message
1. _____	_____	_____
_____	_____	_____
_____	_____	_____
2. _____	_____	_____
_____	_____	_____
_____	_____	_____
3. _____	_____	_____
_____	_____	_____
_____	_____	_____
4. _____	_____	_____
_____	_____	_____
_____	_____	_____
5. _____	_____	_____
_____	_____	_____
_____	_____	_____
6. _____	_____	_____
_____	_____	_____
_____	_____	_____

With time, it will get easier to replace your negative messages with positive ones. You may even find that you automatically think of positive messages.

PHYSICAL ACTIVITY IS A GREAT OUTLET FOR ANGRY FEELINGS.

It lets you quickly and safely let out strong feelings. And regular activity can improve your overall health. Here are some tips:

Talk with your healthcare provider.

Be sure to consult your healthcare provider before starting an exercise program.

Choose moderate activities.

Good choices include:

- walking
- swimming
- tennis
- dancing
- yoga

Just about any activity—even household chores—can be an effective outlet for your anger.

Don't overdo it.

Slowly increase the amount of activity you do. And be sure to warm up before you begin and cool down afterward.

What activities will you try to help manage you anger?

Write them here.

_____

_____

_____

_____

_____

_____

_____

_____

_____

_____

_____

_____

_____

_____

_____

_____

_____

_____

MORE WAYS TO HELP GET A HANDLE ON ANGER.
When things start heating up, try these methods to cool down:

Have a sense of humor.

For many people, having a good sense of humor helps them avoid getting angry. Try to find the humor in minor troubles and annoyances.

Do a hobby.

For example, try gardening, learning a musical instrument or making crafts. A hobby can be a productive outlet for tension and energy. And it can serve as a welcome distraction from angry feelings.

Write about your feelings.

Consider recording your thoughts and feelings in a journal or diary. Or write a letter. (You don't have to send it.) Writing can help you work through situations and problems calmly and at your own pace.

Get plenty of rest

Most people need about 6-9 hours of sleep each day: When you're angry, you may have trouble falling asleep. In tum, this lack of sleep may leave you telling more irritable. If you have trouble sleeping:

- Go to bed at the same time each night.
- Avoid having caffeine at least 8 hours before going to bed. It can keep you awake.

LEARNING TO RELAX CAN HELP YOU STAY ON CONTROL.

Using relaxation techniques regularly can help you reduce stress and stay calm.

Meditation

This can help calm you and clear your mind of anger. Follow these steps:

1. Find a quiet place. Wear loose, comfortable clothing. Sit or lie down.
2. Close your eyes. Take slow, deep breaths.
3. Concentrate on a single word, object or calming thought.
4. Don't worry if other thoughts or images enter your mind while you are doing this. Just relax and return to what you were focusing on.
5. Continue until you feel relaxed and refreshed.

Deep-breathing exercises

These can help keep anger from getting out of control. Follow these steps:

1. Sit comfortably or lie on your back.
2. Breathe in slowly and deeply for a count of 5.
3. Hold your breath for a count of 5.
4. Breathe out slowly for a count of 5, pushing out all the air.
5. Repeat several times until you feel calm and relaxed.

Progressive muscle relaxation

Tense and relax each muscle group, starting at your head and working your way down to your toes. Here's how:

1. Wear loose, comfortable clothing. Sit in a comfortable chair or lie down.
2. Tense the muscles in your face for 5-10 seconds. Then relax them for about 20 seconds.
3. Tense the muscles in the back of your neck for 5-10 seconds. Then relax them for about 20 seconds. Notice the difference in how your muscles feel when relaxed.
4. Move down to your shoulders. Tense and relax the muscles the same way you did in step 3.
5. Repeat the same steps with the other muscle groups in your body—in your hands, arms, chest, stomach, lower back, buttocks, thighs, calves and feet—one at a time.

Visualization

This technique uses your imagination to help you relax and reduce your anger.

1. Sit in a comfortable chair or lie down.
2. Imagine a pleasant, peaceful scene, such as a lush forest or a sandy beach. Picture yourself in this setting.
3. Focus on the scene. Continue until you feel refreshed and relaxed.

Make an appointment to relax.

Write down a relaxation technique you'd like to try, then schedule a time when you can try it during the next week

Relaxation technique:

_____

_____

_____

_____

_____

_____

When I can try it:

_____

_____

_____

_____

_____

_____

_____

_____

_____

Your health-care provider or local library can provide more information on these and other relaxation techniques.

DEALING WITH SOMEONE ELSE'S ANGER
Here are some tips:

Keep your cool.

Don't answer anger with anger. Remember that anger can lead people to say things they don't really mean. Criticism, threats or name-calling won't help resolve the situation.

Don't take it personally.

Try to understand why the person is angry. His or her feelings may have little or nothing to do with you.

Listen to the person.

Sometimes an angry person just needs to "blow off steam." Let the person express his or her feelings. Don't interrupt. Maintain eye contact to show you are listening.

Think of solutions together.

If you're having a conflict with someone, try to find solutions that you can both agree on. Do this only when you are both calm.

Don't take chances.

- If you're worried about your safety, get help right away. Try to leave yourself an escape path.
- If the person has a weapon, seek safety at the first opportunity. Don't confront or try to restrain him or her.

SOURCES OF HELP

You don't have to face your problems alone. Let others know that you want help controlling your anger. They can provide valuable support and encouragement. Consider contacting:

Your health-care provider

Your health-care provider can give you a physical exam and suggest relaxation techniques. He or she may also prescribe medications for related health conditions.

Mental health professionals and mental health centers

These provide a variety of services, including outpatient treatment and support groups.

Counselors, family therapists or social workers

They can help you learn ways to manage anger, control stress and solve problems.

Hotlines

Hotlines may provide emergency counseling to help you control angry feelings or behavior. Check your local phone book.

Employee Assistance Programs (EAPs)

These may offer referrals or counseling to help employees deal with issues like alcohol or other drug problems, job stress and relationship problems.

Religious leaders

They may offer advice and reassurance—or just listen when you need someone to talk to.

Asking for help is a sign of strength—not weakness.

DEVELOP AN ANGER MANAGEMENT PLAN.

Now that you've learned more about anger and how you respond to it, you can develop your own plan for managing your anger. Follow these steps:

1. Set positive goals and a time frame.

Your goals should address both a specific behavior and your reaction. For example, over the next month, your goal could be to communicate your feelings using "I" statements whenever you get angry at work.

You can set different goals for yourself. But don't try to meet too many at one time. You're less likely to reach them.

2. Get support.

Tell family, friends and coworkers about your goals. They can offer encouragement and advice. Seek out their help if you're having trouble with your anger. Or consider seeing a mental health professional.

3. Track your progress.

Consider keeping a daily log or journal. Make note of times when you avoid getting angry or handle anger well. Seeing improvement over time can keep you from feeling discouraged.

4. Reward yourself.

Treat yourself when you reach a goal or get halfway there. For example, go to a movie or enjoy a special meal.

MY ANGER MANAGEMENT PLAN

Goal:

_____
_____
_____
_____

My action plan:

_____
_____
_____
_____

Target date:

_____
_____
_____
_____

Reward:

_____
_____
_____
_____

People I can call one for help:

_____
_____
_____
_____

Learning to manage your anger takes time and effort. But you'll find the results are worth it

BEING A
SUCCESSFUL
EMPLOYEE

REENTRY
ESSENTIALS, INC.

Life Skills Series
Basic Skills for Lifelong Success

Please read:

Know and follow the policies and procedures where you work! This workbook does not take their place.

REENTRY
ESSENTIALS, INC.

Reentry Essentials, Inc.
2609 East 14 Street, Suite 1018
Brooklyn, NY 11235-3915
P: 347.973.0004
E: info@ReentryEssentials.org
I: www.ReentryEssentials.org

This workbook belongs to:

_____

You may find it helpful to keep important names and phone numbers handy.

Write them below.

Your workplace

Name_____

Phone_____

Address_____

Website_____

Your human resources (HR) or personnel department

Name_____

Phone_____

Your supervisors

Name_____

Phone_____

E-mail_____

Name_____

Phone_____

E-mail_____

Other important numbers

_____

_____

_____

_____

_____

_____

_____

_____

_____

IF YOU ARE NEW AT A JOB

or are about to start a new job, this workbook is for you.

You are the key!

It pays to make the best of every work opportunity. A positive attitude and can-do state of mind will help you get the most out of any job.

The basic skills for job success are the same.

You can use these skills if you:

- help provide a service or make a product
- do physical labor or work at a desk

Even if you've had bad work experiences before, you can learn the skills it takes to do well at this job!

Note: The term "supervisor" is used in this workbook. The person who supervises you may go by other titles, though, such as manager, team leader or crew chief.

CONTENTS

BEING A GOOD EMPLOYEE PAYS OFF.

Working hard can help you:

Earn a living

The money you earn from your job can help you:

- take care of yourself and your family
- pay your bills
- afford the things you want
- save for the future

Keep your job

That's obvious. But what if an employer has to make job cuts? Being a good worker may give you an advantage.

Get a raise or promotion

Most employers will reward hard work. No matter what kind of job you have, showing that you:

- can do it well may mean a raise
- are able to take on new responsibilities may mean a promotion. And promotions often mean more money

Work toward your dream job

Doing good work now can:

- teach you important skills
- give you experience
- help you get a good recommendation

These things can help qualify you for new work opportunities. They can also help turn a part-time or temporary job into a full-time position.

Feel good about yourself

When you do a good job, you can:

- take pride in your work
- feel confident in your abilities

What are some of your goals for your job?

Short-term goals

Example: I want to do well in my trial period.

_____

_____

_____

Mid-term goals

Example: I want a good review and raise at the end of the year.

_____

_____

_____

Long-term goals

Example: I want to become a supervisor.

_____

_____

_____

_____

HOW ARE YOUR WORK HABITS?

Think about this job and any other jobs you've had recently. Check the box that best describes each of your habits. (Be honest with yourself. Would your supervisors agree with your answers?)

	Always	Usually	Sometimes	Rarely
I show up on my scheduled work days.	☐	☐	☐	☐
I'm on time for work and meetings.	☐	☐	☐	☐
I get tasks done by the date and time asked for.	☐	☐	☐	☐
I do my best.	☐	☐	☐	☐
I follow instructions well.	☐	☐	☐	☐
I stay busy.	☐	☐	☐	☐
I'm honest.	☐	☐	☐	☐
I have a positive attitude.	☐	☐	☐	☐
I'm confident in myself.	☐	☐	☐	☐
I'm a team player.	☐	☐	☐	☐
I get along with people.	☐	☐	☐	☐
I put customers or clients first.	☐	☐	☐	☐
I follow the rules at work.	☐	☐	☐	☐
I'm willing to learn new things.	☐	☐	☐	☐
I'm organized.	☐	☐	☐	☐
I'm a good communicator.	☐	☐	☐	☐

These are just some of the qualities that are important to employers. Use this workbook to build up your weak areas—and build on your strengths. We all have room for improvement!

WHAT MAKES A GOOD EMPLOYEE?
Here are some basics.

Be dependable.

Your supervisor and co-workers should be able to count on you to:

- show up for work
- be on time
- do your best

Work hard, and be honest.

Your supervisor should be able to trust you. You should:

- put in a full day's work
- admit when you make a mistake—and work to fix it
- not lie, cheat, steal or break the rules

Meet the needs of customers or clients.

You should do your part to make sure customers or clients are satisfied. Even if you don't deal with them directly, your work still supports that goal down the line.

Be a team player.

You should:

- do your fair share
- help others
- work at getting along with others
- work for the success of the group, as well as your own

Be "professional."

Your words, actions and appearance should make you and your employer look good. They should tell people that you're smart and capable.

Have a positive, upbeat attitude.

You should:

- believe in yourself
- take pride in yourself and in your work
- focus on solving problems—not complaining
- keep your cool in tough situations

Aim for good communication.

You should be able to:

- listen and follow instructions
- share information and ideas

Be open to improvement and change.

You need to be willing to learn new things throughout your work years.

What other qualities

do you think your employer or supervisor values?

_____

_____

_____

_____

_____

_____

_____

_____

_____

_____

_____

_____

_____

_____

_____

_____

_____

FIRST IMPRESSIONS

Can set the tone for how you're treated at work. The way you look should show that you belong at the job and have pride in yourself.

Know the "dress code."

Ask about it ahead of time.

- For some jobs, you'll wear a uniform. For other jobs, suits be what's normal. Some jobs allow casual clothing.
- Some items may not be allowed, such as sneakers or jeans. Others may be required, such as safety gear.
- Whatever the dress code, make sure your clothes are neat and clean and fit well. Avoid very tight clothes or those that show a lot of skin or cleavage.

Be clean and well-groomed.

In general:

- Bathe daily. Brush your teeth regularly. Use deodorant. Keep your skin, hair and mouth clean and fresh-smelling.
- Avoid using perfume, cologne or other products with strong scents.
- Wear a neat hairstyle.
- Men should be neatly shaved. If facial hair is allowed, keep it neatly trimmed.
- Women should generally avoid too much makeup and jewelry.

Get off to a good start.

Beforehand:

- Plan to be there on time. Early is better. (See page 74 for tips.)
- Know where to report and who to report to.
- Know the routine for meal breaks and other breaks.

Once you're there:

- Introduce yourself. Give a firm (not hard) handshake.
- Smile. Be friendly, polite and upbeat.
- Listen and learn. There will be lots to take in.

Before you start your job, find out:

What types of clothes and shoes are OK to wear? _____

_____

What items are required (such as ties or safety gear)? _____

_____

What's not OK to wear? _____

_____

Are there other policies on appearance (facial hair, piercings or tattoos) that affect you? _____

_____

If a uniform is required, how will you get it? Do you launder it yourself?_____

_____

KNOW THE OTHER RULES, TOO.

Read your employee manual. Ask your supervisor about anything you have questions on. For example, know rules and policies for:

Missing work

It's your responsibility to show up. When you're out, co-workers have to pick up the slack. You may lose pay. You could even be fired for missing too many days.

Once in a while, you may have to miss work suddenly. For example, you may be sick or have a family emergency. (Bad excuses include a hangover or not feeling like working. Don't abuse sick leave!)

Follow the right steps. In general, you'll need to call your supervisor before you're scheduled to start.

You also need to understand how to ask for time off for vacation or appointments. You may need to put in for this weeks in advance.

What are the steps to take if you can't come in?

_____

_____

_____

How can you request time off?

_____

_____

_____

Taking breaks

Get to know the rules on breaks for using the restroom, eating meals, resting and smoking. Stick to your scheduled break times. It helps keep the workplace running smoothly.

List any special steps you need to follow before taking a break.

(For example, should you ask someone to cover your area?)

_____

_____

_____

_____

_____

_____

When and for how long are your rest breaks?

_____

_____

When and for how long is your meal break?

_____

_____

_____

Using equipment and supplies

Using workplace equipment and supplies costs your employer money. Doing things like downloading files online can also slow down the Internet connection for co-workers. Taking office supplies for personal use is stealing! Know the policies for using:

- phones
- copiers and fax machines
- computers and e-mail
- other office supplies and equipment

If some personal use is allowed, don't abuse the privilege.

Notes on these policies:

_____

_____

_____

_____

_____

_____

_____

_____

_____

_____

Alcohol, tobacco or other drugs

- Never use alcohol or other drugs on the job. It can lead to bad decisions, accidents, injuries and getting fired.
- Many employers limit where you can smoke. Some don't allow it at all.

Describe any drug testing policy at your workplace:

_____

_____

_____

Is smoking allowed? If so, where?

_____

_____

_____

Using personal cell phones or other devices

If these are allowed at your workplace, it's usually best to:

- Turn ringers or other sounds off. They can interfere with others' work.
- Avoid using these devices when you're on the clock. Wait for your break.

Notes on these policies:

_____

_____

_____

_____

_____

_____

Confidentiality

There may be rules about what you can and cannot share with others. For example, you may not be allowed to discuss:

- the personal information of your customers or clients
- a special way goods or services are created at your job

Things to keep confidential:

_____

_____

_____

_____

_____

_____

Don't cheat your employer out of time.

Wait for your breaks to do personal business. That includes calls, e-mail and texting. Save long chats with co-workers for when you're off the clock, too.

Don't count on privacy.

It can be tempting to use a work computer or phone for personal reasons. But be aware that your employer may be able to:

- track Web sites visited and calls made
- see e-mails you get or send at work—even if you delete them

What would you do?

A former co-worker sends Jade a flirty e-mail at work. Jade has always liked him and wants to reply.

If I were Jade, I would:

- ☐ Reply using my work e-mail, since it's faster and more convenient.
- ☐ Reply from work, but use a private online e-mail account.
- ☐ Reply from home using a private e-mail account.

Check your answer on page 90.

PLAN AHEAD.

This will help you avoid absences and lateness.
It will also help you balance work and family life.

Make a weekly schedule.

Use copies of page 75, a calendar or a planner. Write down:

- the days and hours you're scheduled to work
- any meetings or appointments
- any tasks that have to be done by a certain date or time
- the schedules of your children or other family members that affect you

Cell phones and other electronic devices often have calendars or planners you can use, too.

What would you do?

Lucy has a chance to go to her favorite team's playoff game. So, she asks Mia to switch days off with her. Mia says she'll think about it. Mia had to cover the morning rush alone twice this week because Lucy was late. And when Lucy called in sick last week, Mia had to pull a double shift.

If you were Mia, would you switch days?

☐ Yes. I might need a favor soon, too.

☐ No way. Why should I, after Lucy has made my life difficult?

Check your answer on page 90.

My plans for:

Getting to work on time

It's your responsibility. Remember, co-workers and customers are counting on you. To avoid being late:

- The night before, gas up and prepare your outfit and lunch or other meal.
- Check weather and traffic reports.
- Set your alarm for 30 minutes earlier than you think you need to.

Your main way to get to work:

_____

Your backup plan (for example, the name and phone number of a co-worker with a car):

_____

_____

To get out the door and to your desk or other work area, it takes you:

_____ minutes in traffic or bad weather

_____ minutes without traffic or bad weather

Dependent care

Try to avoid having to miss work because of children or relatives you care for. For example, childcare programs may not take a sick child. Or, a program may be closed on a day you have to work. Make note of the name and phone numbers of relatives, friends or co-workers who can help.

Weekday care:

_____

_____

Weeknight care:

_____

_____

Weekend care:

_____

_____

Backup plans:

_____

_____

See page 88 for more tips on managing your time.

MAKE A WEEKLY SCHEDULE.

	Sunday __/__/__	Monday __/__/__	Tuesday __/__/__	Wednesday __/__/__	Thursday __/__/__	Friday __/__/__	Saturday __/__/__
12-3 AM							
4-5 AM							
6 AM							
7 AM							
8 AM							
9 AM							
10 AM							
11 AM							
12 PM							
1 PM							
2 PM							
3 PM							
4 PM							
5 PM							
6 PM							
7 PM							
8 PM							
9 PM							
10 PM							
11 PM							

LEARN YOUR JOB WELL.

Take charge of the learning process.

Go to all training sessions offered.

Most jobs provide these when you start. More may be offered later. They'll help you:

- learn how your employer wants the job done
- learn to use equipment and to build skills needed for the job
- meet your co-workers
- understand how your job fits in with your employer's goals and mission

Watch, listen and learn.

- A mentor may be assigned to you. This is an experienced co-worker who will show you the ropes.
- If you're not assigned a mentor, look for an informal one. Befriend a co-worker who is good at his or her job. Model what you do after him or her.

Be sure to thank people for their help!

Ask questions.

- If you're unsure about how to do something, ask. Don't be afraid. Asking is much better than having to redo something. Build up your listening skills to help make sure the answer sticks! (See page 82.)
- Turn to your co-workers when you can. You don't have to ask your supervisor every time. He or she may be busy.
- Make note of the answers to your questions. Keep this information organized. (See page 88.)

Be patient.

- The tasks you get at first may not be very exciting. This may change once you get more experience.
- It's normal to sometimes wonder if you have what it takes for a new job. Don't get discouraged. Remember— you were hired because someone believed in you. So believe in yourself!

Scheduled training and orientation:

_____

_____

_____

_____

My main duties are:

_____

_____

_____

My minor duties are:

_____

_____

_____

My mentor is:

_____

_____

_____

Other co-workers who can answer questions:

_____

_____

_____

PUT SERVICE FIRST.

At many jobs, meeting the needs of customers or clients is the top priority.
If you serve customers or clients directly, here are some tips:

Know who you're serving.

Customers or clients are the people who buy or use the goods or services you help produce or provide. Without them, you'd be out of a job. At some workplaces, other departments may be treated like clients, too.

Be friendly and helpful.

- Greet each customer or client right away.
- Stop what you're doing and help.
- If you're already helping someone, let the other person know you'll be with him or her next.

Even if a customer is rude, use your words, tone and body language to show that:

- his or her needs are important
- you are listening and will do your best to help

Juggle in-person customers and phone calls with courtesy.

Follow your workplace policies. In general, if the phone rings while you're with a customer or client:

- Politely excuse yourself—" I'm sorry, please excuse me."
- Quickly find out the caller's needs. He or she may just need to be transferred, for example.
- If only you can help, let the caller know you're with someone. Ask if the caller can hold or call back later. Give him or her a time frame. (Or you may be able to return the call when you're done, if this is allowed.)
- Return to the first customer or client. Say, "Sorry about that. So you were saying that..."
- When you return to the caller, thank him or her for holding.

Be prepared.

Ask about what you should do in these tricky situations.

If I can't meet the customer's needs, I should:

_____

_____

_____

_____

_____

If the customer is getting abusive, I should:

_____

_____

_____

_____

_____

_____

Remember, even on breaks, you're representing your employer. Stay professional!

What would you do?

Juan is in the middle of telling a co-worker a funny story about his weekend when a customer comes up.

If I were Juan, I would:

- ☐ a) Finish my story—the customer can wait a few seconds.
- ☐ b) Help the customer now, and get back to my story later.

Check your answer on page 90.

BE A TEAM PLAYER.
Form good relationships with your co-workers.

It benefits everyone.

In general, when co-workers work well together:

- more gets done
- the workplace is more enjoyable

Get to know your co-workers.

Make this a top goal. But be patient. It may not happen overnight. For example:

- Say hello.
- Share meal breaks with them.
- Show an interest in their lives.
- Take part in social events. (Remember that what you say and do could affect your job, even if you're "off the clock.")

It can be hard to remember names when you meet new people. Repeat a name when you first learn it. Then use it once or twice in the conversation.

Work at getting along.

- Be friendly, polite and helpful.
- Be a good listener.
- Cooperate and share.
- Think about how your actions affect others. Be considerate. Respect coworkers' time, equipment, supplies and personal space.
- Respect differences. For example, you often find people of different races, ethnicities, physical abilities and religions in the workplace. Personality and work style can differ, too.
- Give feedback in ways that help people improve. Share ideas and suggestions—not just criticism. Choose your words carefully. Give sincere praise when it's due, too.

Workplace romances

Some employers have policies against them. Even if yours doesn't, be careful. If things don't work out, it could interfere with work. Also, remember that unwanted attention could be sexual harassment.

Avoid the pitfalls.

These include:

- sharing too much personal information
- gossiping
- bragging or being a know-it-all
- talking politics, religion or sex
- making insensitive jokes or remarks (such as those about race, ethnicity, gender, sexual orientation or physical abilities)
- making jokes or remarks of a sexual nature
- using crude or foul language
- letting work suffer due to too much socializing

It can be a serious offense to discriminate against or sexually harass someone. Know the policies where you work.

Earn the respect of your co-workers. Be dependable and pull your own weight.

GET ALONG WITH YOUR SUPERVISOR.

Build a positive relationship with him or her. It can have a huge impact on your job.

Your supervisor has a big say.

He or she will often make the call on:

- the tasks you're assigned
- whether you "pass" your trial or probation period
- whether you get a raise or get promoted
- the size of your raises
- whether you get disciplined— or fired

A good relationship with your supervisor generally means less stress for you and a more pleasant workplace.

Appreciate your supervisor's role.

You may not always see the work your supervisor does. But he or she is usually busy with many tasks, such as:

- overseeing the work of several employees
- paperwork
- scheduling and planning

Take note of your supervisor's style of managing.

For example, some supervisors tend to:

- give a lot of feedback and praise, while others focus on mistakes
- give you a lot of freedom, while others keep close tabs on you

Knowing your supervisor's style will help you know how to please him or her. It will also help you know what to expect.

You don't have to like your supervisor.

But if you want to keep your job, you do have to:

- treat him or her with respect
- do what is asked of you (unless it's illegal or unethical)

(See page 85 for tips on handling disagreements with your supervisor.)

Some tips:

Get assignments right.

Be sure you understand them.

- Repeat the instructions back in your own words.
- Ask questions if you have any.
- Take notes.
- Follow directions carefully.

Keep your supervisor informed at all times.

- Report on your progress whether it's good or bad.
- When you're done, ask for a new assignment. Don't sit around.

Keep things positive.

- Voice any concerns as questions or suggestions— not complaints.
- Discuss things when your supervisor is in a good mood and is not busy.

Remember—your supervisor wants you to succeed. (He or she spent a lot of time and money to hire and train you!)

BE A GO-GETTER.

Bring energy and initiative to the job. It will impress your supervisor.
It will also keep you from getting bored. You'll have a bigger sense of control, too.

Stay busy.

Show that you're responsible and self-motivated.

- If you finish assigned tasks, let your supervisor know right away.
- If you see that something needs to be done, do it. Don't wait to be told to do it.
- Go beyond what's expected.

Volunteer.

Take on new responsibilities. It can help you:

- build your skills
- show that you can handle bigger things. That can put you on track for a promotion

Look for ways to do things faster or better.

As a new employee, you're in a good position to spot them. Be creative! Just keep in mind that:

- There may be good reasons for doing things a certain way.
- Faster doesn't always mean better.

Look at the big picture before you suggest changes.

Lead.

Follow experienced co-workers, at first. Listen and learn. With time, though, look for chances to:

- Be a good role model with your skills, work quality, can do attitude and teamwork.
- Be the one others can turn to for help and know-how.
- Be a problem solver. Come up with ideas to get the job done.
- Show you can take charge and make good choices.

What would you do?

It's 20 minutes until the shift ends. Mark and Terrell have both finished their duties. As usual, Mark spends the time texting, while Terrell gets a head start on tomorrow's work.

You're the supervisor. A new position has opened up. It offers more challenges—and more pay. Do you promote:

- ☐ Mark?
- ☐ Terrell?

Check your answer on page 90.

Things I can do when I finish assigned tasks:

_____

_____

_____

_____

_____

My ideas for doing things faster:

_____

_____

_____

_____

_____

My ideas for improvements:

_____

_____

_____

_____

_____

_____

STAY POSITIVE.
Your attitude can make all the difference!

You choose how you look at things.

At work, there's a lot you can't control. You may be assigned tasks you don't like, for example. Or a co-worker may get on your nerves. One thing that is in your hands, though, is your attitude. It's your choice to focus on the negatives or the positives.

Why focus on the positives?

A bright, hopeful outlook has many benefits. For example:

- It helps you feel happier and less stressed.
- It signals to your supervisor that you can handle your job.
- Your co-workers will find you more pleasant to be around. (Listening to someone moan and groan gets old.)
- It helps improve the mood for everyone. A smile is contagious!

Get into the habit of positive thinking.

If you feel yourself getting negative, remind yourself to make a different choice.

- See the glass as half full—not half empty.

- Look for the silver lining. Bad situations often bring opportunities, too. For example, working hard as a team creates strong bonds.

- "Make lemonade" out of a "sour" situation. Look for the humor. Make things fun. Or learn the lesson and be stronger for it.

- Be optimistic that things will get better. Do your part to make it happen.

Use positive self-talk.

Instead of putting yourself down, tell yourself that:

- You're a worthwhile, capable person.

- Even if you do something wrong, you can learn from it and do better.

- There are lots of things you do right! Give yourself praise when it's due. And if you get a compliment, accept it!

What would you do?

Lee and Jared have been working lots of required overtime. Lee complains about this both at work and at home. Jared tries to think about how it won't last forever, it's good for the company and he's earning extra money.

Who are you more like?

☐ Lee
☐ Jared

Check your answer on page 90.

No matter what your job, you can take pride in doing it well!

BUILD ON YOUR COMMUNICATION SKILLS.

They can help you get your ideas across, get the job done right and avoid misunderstandings.

Be a good listener.

This may be the most important skill of all. Knowing how to listen well helps you get instructions and orders right. It also helps you get to know your coworkers. When someone talks:

- First, stop what you're doing.
- Focus on what's being said. Try not to think about what you'll say next.
- Don't interrupt.
- When they're done, repeat back what was said in your own words. ("So, what you're saying is...")

Afterward, write down important things you need to remember. Put listening and thinking before speaking!

Watch what you say and how you say it.

They can affect the way your co-workers and customers see you. Some tips:

- Speak clearly. Don't mumble.
- Watch your volume. Loud talking can disrupt others. Soft talking can make people strain to hear. Both can annoy.
- Use "good English." Avoid slang and foul language.
- Keep your tone friendly.
- Avoid a flat, boring tone.
- Avoid talking too fast. It can sound hurried and tense and be hard to understand.
- Avoid eating or chewing gum while speaking. It can make you hard to understand. Also, it doesn't look professional.

Be aware of your body language.

People don't just hear your words. They also "listen" to what they see. In general:

- Make eye contact. When you avoid this, people may feel that you are hiding something or aren't listening. (Holding eye contact for too long may make people uncomfortable, though. Take your cues from them.)
- Smile!
- Stand or sit up straight, but stay relaxed. You look disinterested or lazy when you slouch. Crossing your arms or being tense doesn't seem friendly, though.

What actions make you feel disrespected when you're talking? (Tapping a pencil, twirling hair, rolling eyes or scowling, for example?) Avoid doing these yourself!

_____

_____

_____

_____

_____

_____

_____

Keep messages brief, clear and to-the-point.

Remember that at work, "time is money." Your supervisor will be especially grateful if you respect his or her time.

Here are some tips. You can apply them to talking, writing (on paper or in e-mail) or leaving a voice message.

- Before you call, speak or write, stop and think. Get your thoughts in order. Know what you want to say. Also make sure you're going to the right person for the issue.
- State the main point of your question or comment in the simplest, clearest way you can.
- Clearly state what you need from the person. For example, does he or she need to answer a question? Take action?
- Clearly state the date or time you need a response.
- If leaving a message, clearly state your name and how the person can reach you.
- Be polite. Choose your words with care. Remember— the other person can't see your body language.

Work at writing well.

Good writing skills are important in the workplace. For example, you'll need them to:

- fill out forms
- write e-mails, letters, memos or reports Here are some more tips for business writing:
- Use good grammar, punctuation and spelling even for e-mail. It helps get your message across correctly. It also creates a professional image. E-mail and other computer programs can often help check your writing. (But they aren't perfect—watch out!)
- Keep sentences short and easy to understand. Organize them in a logical way. For example, group together those that have to do with the same thing.
- Avoid using all capital letters. It comes across as "yelling."
- Put the purpose of your message in an e-mail's subject line. Keep it brief.

Sound like a pro on the phone.

Your workplace may ask you to follow a script when answering phones. If not, it's helpful to come up with your own "script." In general:

- Answer the call quickly.
- Greet the caller. Smile— they will hear it.
- Identify your employer (unless you know the call is from a co-worker) and department.
- Identify yourself.
- Ask how you can help.

For example, "Good morning, this is ABC Rentals, Reservations Department. Hillary speaking. How can I help you?"

Remember that it's especially important to speak clearly on the phone.

How I should answer the phone:

_____

_____

_____

_____

_____

_____

_____

HANDLE CONFLICTS IN A SMART WAY.

Conflicts are a part of life. But it's the way you choose to handle them that makes the difference.

Criticism

It can be hard to hear that you made a mistake or fell short. But anger and denial won't get you anywhere. Instead, make criticism work for you!

Don't take it personally.

It's your supervisor's job to make sure you do well. That means correcting you sometimes. Stay calm. Remember, this is about the job—not about who you are.

Think long-term.

Criticism may be unfair or due to a misunderstanding once in a while. But pick your battles carefully. Challenging a supervisor or customer may come with a price— even if you're right. (See page 85 for tips.)

Grab the opportunity!

- Accept responsibility. It shows honesty, maturity and a desire to improve. Don't try to shift the blame or make excuses.
- Mistakes are a chance to learn! Ask questions. Understand what was wrong and what you should do differently. Take notes. Then make a plan to keep this from happening again.

Anger and frustration

Everyone feels them at times. But no matter who started it, letting your supervisor, co-workers or customers have a piece of your mind can risk your job. Getting physical can get you fired on the spot and cause legal problems.

Stop and think.

If you start feeling angry or frustrated, don't speak or write a response until you calm down. In the heat of the moment, it's easy to say things you'll regret.

Get under control.

To help yourself calm down:

- Take some slow, deep breaths.
- Count to 10 in your head.
- If possible, step away for a moment. Go for a quick walk. Or use your relaxation strategies. (See page 89.)

Solve the problem.

Find a way to express your anger or frustration in a productive way. It's not good to keep it bottled up! (See pages 85 and 86 for tips on solving problems.)

Use "I statements."

This means focusing on how you feel—not what you think the other person did wrong.

- Here's a "you statement": "Why can't you ever fill out your paperwork right?"
- Here's an "I statement": "I feel frustrated when paperwork isn't filled out right, because then I have to correct it."

Remember to be constructive. Offer a suggestion or solution. For example: "Would it help if we went over the steps again?"

Be assertive.

Always giving in to others is called being passive. Bullying people into doing what you want is called being aggressive. Neither of those will earn you true respect. To get that, find a point in the middle—be assertive.

- Say what you think, feel or need.
- Stand up for yourself, your ideas and your rights.
- Do both of these things in a respectful way.

Problems with a co-worker

Do your best to work the problem out yourselves first. Here are some tips:

- Point out that working things out is for the good of the team.
- Discuss the matter in private.
- Put all your skills for communicating and problem solving to work. (See pages 82, 84 and 86.)

If you can't work it out, go to your supervisor for advice.

Personal problems

Leave them at the door. If you can't, consider talking to your supervisor.

- It will help him or her understand a change in performance—and know that it's temporary.
- He or she may be able to help, (for example, by changing your duties for a while.)

Your workplace might also have helpful services, such as Employee Assistance Programs (EAPs). These often offer mental-health, financial and legal help. Your health insurance plan and health department may also be good resources. Remember, getting help is a sign of strength, not weakness!

Problems with your supervisor

It's normal to have disagreements with your supervisor once in a while. Handle them carefully. Here are some tips:

- Pick your battles. Is the issue worth it? If it is, discuss it with your supervisor in private.
- Stay calm. Share your ideas or opinions in a polite, respectful way.
- Provide suggestions or solutions to a problem— don't just complain.
- Remember that in the end, the supervisor gets to call the shots.
- If you can't make peace with how things end up, get advice from your human resources or personnel department or your union. You may be advised to go up "the chain of command" (that is, talk to your supervisor's supervisor).

Whatever you do, it's a good idea to keep records. Make note of all the steps you take and the responses you get.

Understand the discipline process at your job.

For example, you may get an oral warning first, then a written warning, then probation. You may then have to meet certain goals to keep your job.

If you're disciplined, be sure you understand:

- what you did wrong
- what you need to do to avoid getting into more trouble
- what will happen if you do something wrong again

Notes on the discipline process:

_____
_____
_____
_____
_____
_____
_____
_____
_____
_____
_____
_____
_____

BE A PROBLEM SOLVER.

At some point, your supervisor may ask you to find a solution to a challenge your team is facing, for example. Or you may need to solve a problem at home. Use this strategy:

1. Identify the problem

- Get down to the root of it. Don't focus on a symptom.
- State the problem in a clear, simple way.

For example, imagine customers complain about messy restrooms. The complaints are a symptom. Focus on the restrooms- "How can we make sure our restrooms are always clean and neat?"

2. Gather information

Spend some time learning about the situation. For example:

- What's the current policy for cleaning restrooms?
- Are other shift teams getting the same complaints?
- How do they check and clean restrooms?

3. Brainstorm

Make a list of every solution you can think of. Be creative. For now, don't worry about whether a solution is realistic or not.

4. Evaluate ideas

- Narrow down your list of ideas. Cross out those that aren't practical. Pull out those that seem most promising.
- For each promising idea, make a list of pros and cons. Pros are the good points or advantages. Cons are the bad points or disadvantages.

5. Try the best idea

- Pick the best idea by weighing all the pros and cons.
- Let your supervisor know what you picked and your plan for putting it in place.
- If he or she OKs your plan, put it into action.

6. Review the situation

- After a time, take a look at how things are going. Sometimes, even a really good idea won't work out.
- If things aren't working, look at why. Can you adjust the plan to make it work? If not, try the second best solution you came up with. Or run through the process again. You may come up with some better ideas using what you've learned so far.

Settling a dispute

Sometimes, a dispute or disagreement is the problem.

- Each party should have a chance to explain their side and what they need to get past the dispute.
- Negotiate. A solution can often be reached through give and take.
- Look for a compromise (middle ground). No one gets everything he or she wants. But no one loses everything, either. Being able to move on is often a "win" for everyone in the long run.

A group can also follow these basic steps together when tackling a problem as a team.

CONFLICT AND PROBLEM SOLVING WORKSHEET

Use this space to note any problems or conflicts you face.
Will you do things differently if you face the situation again?

Problem or Conflict	How I Reacted	The Effects of My Reaction	Things I Want to do Differently Next Time
Customer was rude to me	I was rude back.	Customer complained.	I will stay professional positive and helpful.

GET ORGANIZED.

Use skills and tools to help you avoid forgetting tasks, confusing dates or losing information.

Make lists of things you have to do.

- Include assignments or projects, duties, tasks, errands and chores.
- If things must be done by a certain date or time, add them to your schedule, too. (See page 75.)
- Check items off your to-do lists as you do them. This helps you track your progress.
- Save your to-do lists. They may be helpful later when you have a performance review. (See page 90.)

Prioritize.

When there's just not enough time in the day, tackle what's most important first.

- Divide your to-do list into things that have to get done today and those that can wait.
- Rank each item by how important it is (1, 2, 3...).
- Tackle the #1 item first, then the #2 item and so on.
- It's a good idea to run your prioritized list by your supervisor. He or she may think other items are more important.

Keep information organized.

Use a filing system. Find one that works for you. For example, you can group together similar how-to manuals and notes into binders of different colors.

Break big projects down into small steps.

Doing this can:

- make the project less overwhelming
- give you a clearer sense of the work ahead of you
- make it easier to track and report on your progress
- give you a sense of accomplishment as you complete each step

Remember to add the steps to your to-do lists and schedule.

Staying on the ball will show that you are dependable and can take on bigger responsibilities.

WORK AT STAYING HEALTHY.

So you can do your best at work (and home), learn how to prevent illnesses.
That includes managing stress. Every job has some.

Start with the basics.

- Get enough exercise. (Talk to your health-care provider before starting an exercise program.)
- Get enough sleep.
- Eat right.
- Stay at a healthy weight.
- Practice good hygiene, such as washing your hands often.
- Get regular medical and dental checkups.

Exercise is especially important. It's also a great way to blow off steam!

Don't rely on alcohol, tobacco or other drugs.

Using them can make problems worse. For example:

- A hangover can get in the way of your job.
- Having to take smoking breaks slows you down. And smoking makes you more likely to get sick.
- Using alcohol or other drugs on the job can lead to injury and getting fired. Many jobs do drug testing.

Learn to manage stress.

When stress gets out of control, you can suffer in body, mind and job! For example, stress increases the risks of heart disease, stroke and other health problems. It also robs you of energy and can mess up sleep and concentration. Even good things, like a promotion, can cause stress.

- Know what things cause you stress—your "triggers." Plan for how you can handle them.
- Take regular breaks. They will help you feel refreshed and recharged.
- Leave work at work when you go home.
- Do things you find relaxing, such as a hobby. Work some "me time" into your weekly schedule.
- Manage your time well. (See page 74.)

Practice relaxation exercises.
Here are a couple.

Deep breathing

- Get in a comfortable position.
- Close your eyes and place your hands on your stomach.
- Breathe in slowly and deeply. Feel your stomach rise.
- Breathe out slowly, for slightly longer than you breathe in. Feel your stomach fall.
- Repeat these steps several times.

Progressive muscle relaxation

- Get in a comfortable position.
- Tense, then relax, different muscle groups (muscles in your face, legs, arms, etc.) one at a time. Feel the tension let go.

WORK TOWARD A GOOD REVIEW.

Good reviews of your performance can lead to raises and promotions.

Know what's expected.

Many jobs will give you a review a few months after you start. Then, you may get a review each year. For a good review, you need to meet or go beyond what's expected of you. How do you know what's expected?

- Read your job description, or ask your supervisor. Also, make note of anything he or she asks you to work harder on.
- Talk to your co-workers. They can tell you how the reviews normally work and how long it usually takes people to get promoted, for example.

Ask for feedback.

You don't have to wait for a review. You can talk to your supervisor more often about how you're doing. Doing this can put you in a better position when your review rolls around. For example, ask about:

- any problems you're having— then take steps to fix them
- things you're doing well— build on these strengths
- anything else you can do to stay on track for a good review

Work to meet your goals.

- Make note of what's expected and any other goals you've been given.
- Post these where you'll see them. Review them regularly.
- Track your progress toward each expectation or goal.

Set goals for yourself, too! Take another look at the goals you listed on page 68, for example. Track your own performance. This will help you judge how well you're meeting your expectations and goals. It will also give you examples of your performance that you can share at your review. Your supervisor might not be aware of all that you do. Keep records of:

- tasks you were assigned or special projects you worked on (your to-do lists and schedules can come in handy for this)
- positive feedback, recognition or awards you got
- any noteworthy things you did, such as finding a faster way to do a task

Answers to What would you do? exercises

- Page 73: C—Jade's supervisor can access even deleted e-mails at work. Doing personal stuff on company time could also get Jade in trouble.
- Page 74: It's a tough call. It's also a good reminder that when someone puts his or her co-workers out, he or she may not be able to count on their help later!
- Page 77: B—Making the customer wait is rude. Plus, he or she could get you in trouble. Your employer may also lose this person's business.
- Page 80: B—Terrell's choices help show that he's up to a challenge and deserves a promotion.
- Page 81: A—Focusing on the negatives, like Lee does, can make a stressful situation even more stressful. B—Focusing on the positives, like Jared does, can help you feel less stressed in a tough situation.

Date of next review: _____

Goal Met	Goals for This Review Period	Notes
✓	Increase products made by 20.%	134 items made—34% more.

Other accomplishments
(Include compliments or positive feedback you've been given.)

_____

_____

_____

_____

_____

_____

_____

_____

BUILD YOUR SKILLS.

Improving on or learning new skills can help you keep your job—and position you to move up.

Make sure your basic skills are strong.

In almost any workplace, you'll need basic skills such as these:

- reading skills—to get information from instructions, signs and customer orders, for example
- writing skills—to fill out forms, write reports and share information, for example
- math skills—to make change, do inventory, measure things or work on budgets, for example
- problem-solving and critical thinking skills—to make good decisions and find solutions to problems, for example
- computer skills—to be able to input information, use e-mail and create professional looking letters, for example

Why build your skills?

It can help you:

- do better at your current job
- handle changes
- improve your chances of promotion
- compete in a global economy
- get qualified for another job, if you get laid off or you want a different opportunity

And remember—in general, people with more education earn more money.

Lifelong learning is the name of the game.

- Changes come to every job. You might need to take on new responsibilities. Or new technology may come along.
- The world is getting smaller. Learning another language can open many doors for you.

Learn to roll with the changes. Show your employer that you can be part of the future!

There are lots of ways you can build skills.

For example:

- Some workplaces offer continuing education classes or extra training sessions. (Some even pay all or part of the costs of outside classes.)
- There may be workshops or conferences held nearby.
- Local colleges offer many classes for people who want to continue learning, with or without seeking a degree.
- Local high schools or other community programs may offer classes to help you get a GED or improve your English.
- There may be many options online, such as distance learning and tutorials.

Find out what's available. It can help to read trade magazines. You can also ask at your local library.

HOW STRONG ARE YOUR SKILLS?

Rate them below. For those that are weak, make a note of how you could improve them. Consider doing that for those you rate as good, too. Add other skills that are important for your job—or the job you want to have.

Skill	Strong	Good	Weak	Plan for Improvement
Spoken English	☐	☐	☐	
Reading	☐	☐	☐	
Writing	☐	☐	☐	
Math	☐	☐	☐	
Problem Solving	☐	☐	☐	
Working with Computers	☐	☐	☐	
Teamwork	☐	☐	☐	
Other	☐	☐	☐	
Other	☐	☐	☐	
Other	☐	☐	☐	
Other	☐	☐	☐	

Options I have for building skills

Make note of upcoming workshops or nearby classes, for example:

WHAT BARRIERS GET IN THE WAY?

Make a plan to remove or work around them. Some common ones are listed below. Add others, such as those you described as other than "always" on page 69. Use the pages noted here and the problem-solving strategy on page 86 to help you make your plan.

Barrier	Page(s)	My Plan to Remove or Work Around Barrier
☐ I'm always late.	74	
☐ I don't have reliable transportation.	74	
☐ I don't have reliable childcare.	74	
☐ I have trouble managing time.	74, 88	
☐ Customers have complained about me.	77, 87	
☐ I'm having problems with a co-worker.	78, 85	
☐ I'm having problems with a supervisor.	79, 85	
☐ I've had a poor review.	80 - 81 90 - 91	
☐ I have trouble getting my point across.	72 - 73	
☐ My temper is causing problems.	84	
☐ Stress is causing problems.	89	
☐ I have weak skills in a certain area.	92 - 93	
☐ Other:		
☐ Other:		

SUCCESS AT WORK
Depends on you!

Learn what's expected of you.

That goes for your:

- performance
- behavior
- appearance

Then work to go beyond those expectations. Every job is important in its own way. Take pride in your work!

Work on creating good relationships.

That includes with your:

- customers or clients
- supervisor
- co-workers

If you have a conflict, work it out in a positive way. Put your communication and problem solving skills to work.

Stay positive and upbeat.

Your attitude and outlook will set the tone, no matter what your job. Remember to stay flexible and open to new ideas and ways of doing things. Lifelong learning is key!

Believe in yourself. You can do it!

BETTER
SELF-ESTEEM

REENTRY
ESSENTIALS, INC.

Life Skills Series
Basic Skills for Lifelong Success

This workbook belongs to:

_____

You may find it helpful to keep important names and phone numbers handy.

Write them below.

Primary health-care provider

Name_____

Phone_____

Other health-care providers

Name_____

Phone_____

Health plan

Name_____

Phone_____

Pharmacy

Name_____

Phone_____

An emergency contact

Name_____

Phone_____

Other important numbers

_____

_____

_____

_____

_____

_____

_____

_____

_____

Reentry Essentials, Inc.
2609 East 14 Street, Suite 1018
Brooklyn, NY 11235-3915
P: 347.973.0004
E: info@ReentryEssentials.org
I: www.ReentryEssentials.org

BETTER SELF-ESTEEM COULD HELP MAKE YOUR LIFE BETTER.

If you're looking to improve your self-esteem, this workbook is for you. It has information and activities to help you:

Learn what it means to have high self-esteem

—and why it is important.

See how your self-esteem is affecting your life

—and learn about changes you can make to improve how you feel about yourself.

Start building your self-esteem

—so you can live a more enjoyable, satisfying life.

Use this workbook in the way that works best for you.

You may want to use it over many months or longer. You may want to do the activities in a different order than they are given here—or keep coming back to them as things change.

Improving self-esteem takes time and effort. But the rewards are worth it!

CONTENT

WHAT IS SELF-ESTEEM?

It's how you feel about yourself—about your worth as a person and your ability to meet life's challenges.

A person may have many different feelings about him or herself, depending on:

The different roles he or she plays in life

For example, a person may have different feelings about his or her worth and abilities:

- At work—some people are confident at work and do not question their future there, while others may feel insecure and often worry if they will keep their job.
- At home—some people feel competent and secure in their home life, while others feel they cannot manage their relationships or responsibilities as well as they "should."
- At school—some people may enjoy the academic and/or social challenges at school, while others lack confidence in their abilities.
- At social events—some people may feel comfortable around lots of people, while others have trouble starting conversations.

The same person who feels confident in one setting may feel insecure in another.

His or her varied personal qualities

For example, a person may have different feelings about his or her:

- Appearance—some people are confident in how they look, while others focus on what they see as "flaws" in their appearance.
- Intelligence—some people are confident in their knowledge, while others feel self-conscious about how much they know or how much education they've had.
- Romantic appeal—some people may see themselves as attractive, while others may feel no one would be interested in them.

Again, the same people who feel confident in one area may feel less so in another. For example, someone may feel he or she is smart, but not attractive.

Your self-esteem is made up of these many different views.

The more positive views you have, the higher your self-esteem. Many people are used to focusing so much on what they don't like about themselves that they forget they have many positive qualities. This workbook will help you take a closer look at all of your positive qualities— and learn to celebrate them!

It is difficult to make a man miserable while he feels worthy of himself...

Abraham Lincoln

HAVING HIGH SELF-ESTEEM HELPS YOU GET THE MOST OUT OF LIFE.
It can help you:

Meet challenges

When you believe in yourself, you are more likely to:

- add new challenges as you meet old ones
- take risks and develop your abilities
- try new things

Value yourself

To value yourself means to know that you matter, despite any mistakes you make or any weaknesses you have. Learning to value yourself involves looking for the things that make you you. You have unique qualities that make you special. Knowing what these are can help make you feel important—because you are!

Have better relationships

When you feel comfortable in your own skin, you're more likely to:

- feel comfortable around other people
- be more eager to meet new people—and develop closer relationships

Sometimes when people don't feel good about themselves, they allow other people to put them down or use them unfairly. People who value themselves are more likely to stand up for their rights so people don't take advantage of them.

Be flexible

Sometimes change can be scary. Feeling confident about yourself can make it easier to accept new ideas and ways of doing things.

Having high self-esteem does not mean having an ego that's too big.

It means being able to be honest with yourself about:

- your strengths and weaknesses
- changes you can— and want to—make
- what things you cannot change—or can accept as they are—so you can work on more important changes

Thinking about these can help you start raising your self-esteem to a healthy level.

I'm not afraid of storms, for I'm learning how to sail my ship.

Louisa May Alcott, Little Women

HAVING LOW SELF-ESTEEM MAKES LIFE LESS SATISFYING.
Low self-esteem can lead to:

Lack of confidence

People with low self-esteem often have little faith in their abilities. They tend to think that if they failed in the past, they are doomed to fail again. This can affect how they perform in school, at work and in other aspects of life.

Without confidence, people are less likely to take any risks or challenge themselves to try new things or meet new people.

Not reaching your full potential

People with low self-esteem may find themselves doing less than they are really able to do. For example, they may:

- not make an effort because they expect to fail
- have low expectations of themselves

Unhealthy relationships

People who feel bad about themselves tend to find it hard to develop close relationships. The result may be a lonely and unsatisfying personal life. People who feel bad about themselves are also less likely to stand up for themselves when others don't treat them fairly. This can lead to:

- poor work situations (others may take advantage of the person)
- poor personal relationships (family members or a spouse may not treat the person with respect if the person does not stand up for him—or herself

Pushing yourself too hard

Worrying about not being good enough can make people feel like they need to be perfect.

A distorted view of yourself and others

When people see themselves as failures, they don't give themselves credit for their accomplishments. They tend to think most people are "better" than they are. When people feel this way, they also tend to feel they don't deserve to be happy.

When people with low self-esteem compare themselves to others, they tend to focus on all the things the other person can do rather than their own unique abilities.

A man cannot be comfortable without his own approval.

Mark Twain

LOW SELF-ESTEEM OFTEN EXISTS TOGETHER WITH OTHER PROBLEMS.
These include:

Depression

Depression is a long-lasting unhappiness characterized by many symptoms, including feelings of worthlessness or hopelessness.

People who are depressed may avoid:

- work
- other people
- activities that used to be of interest

(See page 126 for symptoms of depression and when to seek help.)

Anxiety

People with an anxiety disorder and low self-esteem may feel worry, fear or panic. They may be afraid of making changes or trying new things. Anxiety disorders can include:

- panic attacks
- phobias (intense, irrational fears)
- obsessive-compulsive disorders

Trouble managing anger

The person may feel angry at him- or herself for not being "good enough." He or she may also feel angry at others—and feel worse about him- or herself because of it.

Problems with alcohol or other drug use

The person may turn to alcohol or other drugs to try to dull the painful feelings that are part of having low self-esteem. Having a problem with alcohol or other drugs may make a person feel worse about him—or herself.

Eating disorders

These include:

- anorexia nervosa
- bulimia nervosa

People with eating disorders often have negative feelings about their self-image or feel a lack of control. These feelings are also related to low self-esteem.

Getting help can improve your sense of self-worth.

If you have any of these problems or any other concerns, talk with your health-care provider. (See page 126 for other sources of help, too.) Talk about how your self-esteem and the problem may be affecting each other—and about treatments that can help. Use this space for questions and notes:

_____

_____

_____

_____

_____

_____

_____

_____

_____

_____

_____

_____

_____

_____

A higher self-esteem is worth working for

ASSESSING YOUR SELF-ESTEEM IS THE FIRST STEP IN CHANGING IT.

Think about how you view yourself.
These questions can help you get started. Write yes or no on the line after each question.

1. Do you feel easily hurt by criticism? _____
2. Are you very shy or too aggressive? _____
3. Do you hide how you feel from other people? _____
4. Are you afraid to have close relationships? _____
5. Do you try to blame your mistakes on other people? _____
6. Do you avoid trying positive new activities? _____
7. Do you wish you could change how you look? _____
8. Do you avoid sharing your personal successes with others? _____
9. Do you feel glad when other people fail? _____
10. Do you look for excuses not to change? _____

1. Do you accept polite, helpful criticism? _____
2. Do you feel comfortable meeting new people? _____
3. Do you share your feelings openly and honestly with others? _____
4. Do you value your close relationships? _____
5. Can you laugh at your mistakes, as well as learn from them? _____
6. Do you seek out and enjoy new challenges? _____
7. Are you happy with the way you look? _____
8. Do you give yourself credit for your achievements? _____
9. Do you feel happy for others when they succeed? _____
10. Do you accept changes in yourself as they occur? _____

If you answered most of these questions yes, your self-esteem could probably use improvement.

If you answered most of these questions yes, you probably have a healthy opinion of yourself.

Think about possible sources of your feelings.

A person's self-esteem is first formed in childhood. People who have low self-esteem often see relationships and events in terms of past experiences. For example, a person may not feel his or her opinions matter if, as a child, he or she:

- was criticized often for what he or she said
- often did not receive attention when he or she spoke

Thinking about possible sources of your feelings can help you start separating past experiences from events and relationships in your life now.

Fill in the worksheet on the next page.

See how your answers change when you view yourself in different roles, such as a parent or friend. Why do you think your self-esteem changes in different situations?

SELF-ESTEEM CHECKLIST

Put a check in the box next to each statement that best describes how you view yourself when it comes to different areas in your life. Does your view of yourself differ by area?

I Am	As a Parent			As An Employee			As a Friend			As a Partner In a Relationship		
	Agree	Neutral	Disagree	Agree	Neutral	Disagree	Agree	Neutral	Disagree	Agree	Neutral	Disagree
Smart	☐	☐	☐	☐	☐	☐	☐	☐	☐	☐	☐	☐
Able to Accomplish Things	☐	☐	☐	☐	☐	☐	☐	☐	☐	☐	☐	☐
Likable	☐	☐	☐	☐	☐	☐	☐	☐	☐	☐	☐	☐
Able to Ask For What I Want/Need	☐	☐	☐	☐	☐	☐	☐	☐	☐	☐	☐	☐
A Person With Strong Morals	☐	☐	☐	☐	☐	☐	☐	☐	☐	☐	☐	☐
Deserving of Respect From Others	☐	☐	☐	☐	☐	☐	☐	☐	☐	☐	☐	☐

Statements you marked as "disagree" or "neutral" show where higher self-esteem could help. Use your answers to think about what you want to try improving first.

POSSIBLE SOURCES OF LOW SELF-ESTEEM
Think about areas of your life where you feel you have low self-esteem, and what the possible sources might be. You can fill out this worksheet over time, as things occur to you.

Feelings of low self-esteem

Examples:

I feel like a failure if I do not do everything just right.

I avoid situations where I have to meet people—If I feel
like they would rather be talking to someone else.

_____

_____

_____

_____

_____

_____

_____

_____

_____

_____

_____

_____

_____

_____

_____

_____

_____

_____

_____

Possible source(s)

Examples:

When I was a child, my mistakes always got more
notice than what I did right. I feel like I
have to be perfect to have others' approval.
As a child, other kids called me fat a lot. I feel like I
should have a perfect body for other people to want
to be with me.

_____

_____

_____

_____

_____

_____

_____

_____

_____

_____

_____

_____

_____

_____

_____

_____

_____

_____

_____

SELF-ESTEEM JOURNAL

Keep a journal to track your self-esteem.

This can:

- help you see how you tend to view yourself in certain situations and roles
- help you keep noticing and improving negative self-views
- help you maintain positive self-views

Use this journal to keep track of times when you are feeling low self-esteem and times when you are feeling good about yourself.

In the Notes sections, include information that may help you see patterns. For example, do you often feel better or worse about yourself after a specific activity? Write down where you were, what was happening or being said, who was there, etc.

Try using this journal for a week or two to start with. Keep using it for as long as you find it helpful.

Date _____

How I felt _____

Notes _____

_____

_____

Date _____

How I felt _____

Notes _____

_____

_____

Date _____

How I felt _____

Notes _____

_____

_____

Date _____

How I felt _____

Notes _____

_____

_____

YOU CAN CHANGE HOW YOU FEEL ABOUT YOURSELF.

It's not easy and it won't happen right away. But breaking the process into parts can help you take control. 2 key steps are to:

1. Identify negative views you have about yourself.

For example, people with low self-esteem often believe that they are "stupid" or "ugly." They may:

• see these beliefs as true in all situations and in everyone's eyes

• let the beliefs affect what they do and how they act toward others

Negative views can be very subtle. You may not even recognize them as negative. For example, some people naturally put themselves down because they don't want others to think they think too highly of themselves. But after a while, they may start to believe those put-downs.

The truth is, people are usually drawn to those who feel good about themselves and have a positive outlook. Remember, there is a difference between feeling good about yourself and being arrogant. It's OK to have pride in your accomplishments!

2. Identify your positive self-views.

Examples include seeing yourself as being kind and reliable. When you have low self-esteem:

• It may be hard to accept or express positive views about yourself. But remember, there is nothing wrong with feeling good about the things you do!

• It may help to involve family and friends who can help you see and accept these views. Ask them to tell you the things they like about you. Be sure to have them give you specific things they like and why. For example, they may say they enjoy your company because you are a good listener and have good ideas.

Be sure to write down what your friends and family tell you. Save what you write and reread it from time to time to remind you how special people think you are—and why.

Being aware of your self-views can help you see a truer picture of yourself.

For example:

• It can help you see how your negative self-views affect your life. When you can see how each specific view affects how you feel, you can start working on changing each one.

• It can help you focus on your positive self-views and how you can use these to improve your overall view of yourself. For example, let's say one positive view you have is "I like the way I help others." You could make a list of all the ways you've helped. That can help you see how much you've made a change in other people's lives. That's something to feel good about!

No one can make you feel inferior without your consent.

Eleanor Roosevelt

THINK ABOUT YOUR NEGATIVE AND POSITIVE SELF-VIEWS.

Use this page to list them.

You may discover some of these views as you keep your journal. Add others as they occur to you.

Each time you write down a negative self-view ask yourself:

- Is this really true?
- Why do I think this?

Then review your list of positive self-views. Ask yourself:

- Which of these views am I most proud of?
- How can I apply these qualities on a regular basis to help change my negative self-views?

Negative self-views

Examples:

"No one could like me."
"I'm never good enough at anything I do."

_____
_____
_____
_____
_____
_____
_____
_____

Positive self-views

Examples:

"I am caring and respectful."
"I am a hard worker."

_____
_____
_____
_____
_____
_____
_____
_____

CHANGING ALSO INVOLVES KNOWING YOUR STRENGTHS AND WEAKNESSES.

Everyone has skills and talents.

For example, a person may manage time well, cook well or be good at fixing cars. But if you have low self-esteem, you:

- may not see your own strengths—or not see them as anything special
- may need others to help you see your strengths and accept their value

When you're thinking about possible strengths, remember that it is OK to take pride in what you can do well! Think about:

- general things you are good at, such as being kind to others and being generous
- specific things you are good at, such as being able to play an instrument, having a knack for remembering specific details or statistics, or being able to cook a certain meal well

Be proud of ALL of your strengths, both big and small.

Everyone has weaknesses, too.

For example, a person may not be good at using computers or at talking with people he or she does not know well. Thinking about your weaknesses can help you decide:

- which ones you want to try changing
- which ones you cannot change or can accept as OK

Most people have things about themselves that they can't change. For example, someone may not like his or her voice or height. But often there are things we don't like that we can change. For example, if a person wants to improve:

- computer skills, he or she could ask a friend to help or take a class
- social skills, he or she could take steps to slowly meet more people and participate in social activities. (Professional help is also available to improve these skills)

Your self-views, strengths and weaknesses can all affect each other.

For example:

- Someone who views him or herself as "stupid" may see losing a word game as "proof." The person may not think about the ways he or she is smart (for example, understanding how cars work).
- Someone who views him- or herself as not likable may avoid meeting people. This keeps him or her from having chances to exercise important social skills, even though he or she may have the qualities that make a very good friend.

The purpose of life is undoubtedly to know oneself.

Mohandas Gandhi

STRENGTHS AND WEAKNESSES

Start thinking about what your strengths and weaknesses are.

Write them down and add others as they occur to you. What you write here can also help you fill out the worksheet on page 113.

When you're thinking about your strengths:

- try to list as many as you can— even things you think are "small"
- consider your daily routine to help you come up with strengths you take for granted. (For example, you may be a good driver, great at making breakfast or friendly to your co-workers)

When you're thinking about your weaknesses, think about ways you might use your strengths to improve them. For example, "The next time I lose my patience with someone, I will try to use my strong listening skills to get the full story before I pass judgment."

Strengths

Examples:

"I am a good listener."
"I know a lot about current events."

_____

_____

_____

_____

_____

_____

_____

_____

_____

_____

Weaknesses

Examples:

"Sometimes I lose my patience too quickly."
"I put off tasks I don't look forward to. I miss some work deadlines because of it. "

_____

_____

_____

_____

_____

_____

SILENCE YOUR INNER CRITIC.
Start changing your negative views by using positive self-talk.

Be aware of your inner negative voice.

Everyone has one. In people with low self-esteem, this voice can be very harsh. It is the voice that:

- criticizes and judges you— for example, "I'm so dumb, I'll never get that job."
- blames you for things— for example, "I didn't prepare enough for that job interview. I blew it!"
- tells you that you are not good enough—for example, "I didn't answer the questions well. I'll never get that job!"
- makes your weaknesses seem worse than they are, for example, "My computer skills are so bad that no one will ever hire me!"
- compares you negatively to others—for example, "The other applicants are probably way more qualified than I am."

Start replacing negative talk with positive, realistic messages.

To do this, put a stop to the negative thought and replace it with a positive one. For example:

- "Saying that I'm too stupid for this job is a way to avoid applying, so I won't have to face a possible rejection. I can't get a new job if I don't try."
- "That interview was challenging, but I know I did my best. If I don't get the job, the interview was good practice for my next try."
- "My computer skills aren't the best—but they aren't the worst, either. If they aren't good enough for a job I want, I can take steps to improve them."
- "This job probably had a lot of applicants. There may be some who are more qualified than I am, but I know I met the requirements on the application and did my best to present my skills."

For some people, their negative voice has been talking to them for a long time!

Replacing it with a positive, encouraging voice takes practice.

Remember, the first step in silencing your negative voice is to start noticing all of the negative thoughts you have about yourself. Then, start working on ways to replace each one with a statement that is more accurate— and positive. If there truly is something about yourself that you aren't happy about, think of positive ways you can change it.

I believe that it is harder still to be just toward oneself than toward others.

Andre Gide

PRACTICE POSITIVE SELF-TALK.

Look at what you wrote on the earlier worksheets (pages 104-107, 109 and 111) to help you start on this key step. Write down your most common examples of negative self-talk. Add others as you notice them. Next to each one, write a positive, realistic statement to say instead. Practice using the positive statements when you hear yourself saying the negative ones.

Negative self-talk

Examples:

"I hate how my chin looks. I'm so ugly."

"I'm too boring. If I go to that party, no one will want to talk to me anyway."

_____

_____

_____

_____

_____

_____

_____

_____

_____

_____

_____

_____

_____

_____

_____

_____

_____

_____

_____

Positive self-talk to replace it with

Examples:

"I do have a big chin. But I'm not ugly just because I don't fit some perfect ideal. And I have nice eyes and hair."

"I am quiet and not great at small talk. But I'm not boring. People seem interested in me when I join the lunch conversations at work."

_____

_____

_____

_____

_____

_____

_____

_____

_____

_____

_____

_____

_____

_____

_____

_____

_____

_____

_____

COMMUNICATING ASSERTIVELY

Expressing wants and needs can be hard when you have feelings of low self-esteem—but with practice, you can communicate with confidence.

Understand what assertive communication is.

Being assertive means expressing your feelings in a way that doesn't blame others—or yourself. It also means you express yourself in a clear, firm way, rather than agreeing with what someone else says just to avoid conflict.

Leaning to communicate assertively can help you:

- build better friendships— they're good for your self-esteem
- avoid or settle conflicts with relatives, friends and co-workers—unresolved conflicts can make you feel bad about yourself and contribute to low self-esteem
- learn about people and their feelings—assertive communication involves listening as well as speaking

Use "I" statements.

These can help you avoid sounding like you are blaming or criticizing. The other person may be more open to what you have to say. For example:

- Don't say, "You're such a jerk for making fun of the way I talk."
- Say, "I feel hurt when you make fun of the way I talk."

State what you feel, think and want.

For example, say, "I know you may just think of it as joking. But I feel put down when I talk about something and your only response is to make fun of how I say it. It makes me think what I have to say doesn't matter to you. I'd really like it if you could respond to the point I'm making instead."

Ask the person for a response.

For example, say, "I think we could have some good talks about things if you could do this. Do you think you could try it?"

Use body language that helps show you mean what you say.

Possible ways to do this include:

- making eye contact
- standing in a confident pose (not wringing your hands, for example).

Use a confident tone of voice, too. But be careful not to look or sound like you're attacking the other person.

> **Many things are lost for want of asking.**
>
> *George Herbert*

PRACTICE ASSERTIVE COMMUNICATION.

How can you be assertive in your daily conversations?

Think of some things you want to ask for and the people you want to ask. Write what you could say in the space provided. You may want to practice asking in front of a mirror so you can check your body language.

Don't forget to listen.

Listening is more than just hearing. It is a skill you have to practice, just like speaking. Active listening means:

- looking at the person
- not interrupting
- paying attention—not thinking about what you want to say in reply

When the person is finished, summarize what you've heard in your own words to show you've listened and understood.

What I want (and from whom)

Example: Help from family members with keeping the house neat

Possible statement

Example: I feel discouraged when I find things lying around after cleaning up. I'd really like a neat house and this makes me think that what I want doesn't matter. Can we come up with a way for you to help more with picking up?

What I want (and from whom):

_____

_____

_____

Possible statement:

_____

_____

_____

What I want (and from whom):

_____

_____

_____

Possible statement:

_____

_____

_____

KEEP IMPROVING YOUR SKILLS AND KNOWLEDGE.

Accomplishing things—even the effort itself—can help you feel better about yourself. Ask yourself:

What skills and knowledge do I already have?

Think about all the roles you play, and what it takes to do these. Possible examples include:

- doing certain kinds of math, if you regularly do food shopping on a budget
- working with your hands, if you have a hobby or a job that requires it
- organizing people to get tasks done, if this is part of your home or work routine

Remember, you probably have many more skills than you realize! If you have trouble coming up with skills, think about all the things you do each day, at home and at work. Make a list of all of your daily responsibilities and what skills are required to carry them out. For example:

- Do you help family members get ready for work and school? Then you have good organizational skills!
- Do you pay bills? Then you have math skills!

What new skills and knowledge would I like to develop?

Think about things you may have wanted to try, but never have. Perhaps you keep telling yourself you wouldn't be good at them. Remind yourself that things you enjoy are worth doing, even if you are not as good at them as you think you should be. For example, perhaps you've thought about:

- learning to dance
- joining a summer softball league
- being involved in community theater
- volunteering for a community organization

In addition to new things, think of some skills you already have that you'd like to improve. For example, if you are skilled at cooking a certain meal, maybe you'd like to learn new cooking techniques so that you can expand on what you can make for yourself and others.

How will these skills help me feel better about myself and improve my life?

When thinking about things you'd like to try, learn or improve, think also about how they might improve your daily life. For example:

- learning to play an instrument may help you relax after a busy day, or help you meet new people if you perform or practice with a group
- volunteering can help you feel good about yourself as well as help you meet other people and make a difference in your community

Few (are) too young, and none too old, to make the attempt to learn.

Booker T. Washington

MAKE A PLAN.

Think about specific skills or interests you would like to improve and develop.

Write them in the space provided. Include any areas you want to learn more about, too.

For each one, think about small steps you could take to carry these out. Write the steps down. Be sure to make each step something that is not too overwhelming. Like any big job or goal, you are more likely to succeed if you plan it out into reasonable steps that make sense for you.

Celebrate your success at every step!

Skill/knowledge/interest

Example: Join a summer softball league next season.

Steps

Example: 1. Ask Pat to join with me. 2. Go watch some games together this season and practice ahead of time. 3. Ask the coach or players about the league.

Skill/knowledge/interest:

_____

_____

_____

_____

Steps:

_____

_____

_____

_____

Skill/knowledge/interest:

_____

_____

_____

_____

Steps:

_____

_____

_____

_____

DO GOOD THINGS FOR YOURSELF.

It's important to meet your emotional needs and other needs. Like other steps you take to improve your self-esteem, this can take practice.

It can be easy to think that only others deserve good things.

When you have low self-esteem, you may think that:

- you don't deserve good things or haven't done anything worth rewarding yourself for
- you should devote your time to others' needs

Keep reminding yourself that you would want others you care about to have good things—and that you deserve them just like they do.

Being good to yourself can help change how you feel.

Over time, you'll start feeling like being good to yourself is more natural and acceptable.

Think about things you may enjoy doing.

For example, you may enjoy:

- relaxing in a hot bath after a busy day
- spending an evening out with friends
- putting chores on hold to take a walk on a beautiful day
- having a good talk with a family member or close friend
- shopping for a new outfit, music CD, etc.

Plan to try one or two enjoyable activities every week or two.

Think about what makes you happy.

In addition to activities like the ones described above, think also about the general things that make you happy and how you can expose yourself to these things more often. Even something as simple as listening to music more often can make a difference.

Take good care of yourself.

It's easy to overlook doing the things that make us feel good in body and mind. But healthy daily habits can improve how we feel inside and out. For example:

- Eat well. A healthy, balanced diet can improve your overall health and make you feel good about yourself. Visit www.ChooseMyPlate.gov for details on a diet that's right for you.
- Stay active. Regular physical activity can give you more energy and help you stay physically fit. (Talk to a healthcare provider before starting an exercise program.)
- Get plenty of sleep. Being well rested can help you have more energy throughout the day.
- Practice good personal hygiene. Keeping up your appearance shows you care about yourself.

> **It is a happy talent to know how to play.**
>
> *Ralph Waldo Emerson*

WHAT GOOD THINGS CAN YOU DO FOR YOURSELF?
Make a plan!

Follow these steps:

- In the left-hand column, write as many things that you enjoy as you can think of (include things that don't cost a lot).
- Number each activity in order of importance to you.
- In the right-hand column, make a plan for doing each of your 3-5 top activities.

- Write about it! Once you've carried out your plan, write about the activity and how it made you feel. You can write in a journal or notebook. Keep your entries to remind you of your experience—and to inspire you to do it again!

I enjoy...

Example: Turning on the music and singing along

I enjoy...

Example: Going to the movies with my best friend

I enjoy...

_____

_____

_____

_____

_____

_____

_____

_____

_____

_____

_____

_____

_____

I plan to...

Example: Take 10 minutes to listen to music when I get home from work

I plan to...

Example: Schedule a "date" with my friend to see a movie once a month

I plan to...

_____

_____

_____

_____

_____

_____

_____

_____

_____

_____

_____

_____

_____

BUILD A CIRCLE OF SUPPORT.

Support from others is vital to having high self-esteem.
Here are some ways to build a support network:

Work to improve existing relationships.

People with low self-esteem often give a lot without asking for anything in return. They also judge themselves by others' standards. It's important that others:

- show love and acceptance toward you
- give you credit for what you do
- respect you

One way to help improve relationships is to be assertive (review pages 114-115). When you are assertive, you help keep yourself from being taken advantage of.

Being assertive can also help you feel better about yourself. For example, sharing your true feelings rather than agreeing with someone to avoid an argument can help you feel strong and sure of yourself. People are more likely to respect you when you stand up for what you believe in, even if they don't agree with you.

Try making some new friends.

Think about whether you might benefit from having a wider circle of support. You might try:

- meeting others with similar interests—for example, by taking a class or through a community or religious organization
- joining or starting a support group that focuses on self-growth. For information, try asking your health-care provider or checking your local newspaper or phone book

Avoid people who don't respect you.

You don't need to be friends with everyone. Avoid people who don't listen to you or who take advantage of you. You deserve friends who are willing to give you the same respect you show to them.

Ask others to help you improve your self-esteem.

Think of friends, family members and others from different areas of your life whom you feel could be helpful. Ask them to encourage and support your efforts. For example:

- Share your list of good things you'd like to do for yourself, and ask them to participate with you (if any of the activities involve others).
- Talk about skills you'd like to improve and ask them to help you track your progress and offer encouragement.
- Ask them to help you recognize times when you put yourself down or don't act assertively.

Asking for help is not a sign of weakness. It shows you care enough about yourself to want to make a change for the better!

I felt it shelter to speak to you.

Emily Dickinson

BE A SOURCE OF SUPPORT, TOO.

Be positive toward others.

Having negative feelings about yourself can lead to having these same feelings about others.

Try to:

- Avoid criticizing, judging or blaming other people.
- Understand others' feelings and views.
- Be a good listener. Pay attention without judging while others talk. You don't have to agree with the person, but it's important to respect other people's points of view.
- Offer encouragement and support to others. Point out their strengths and positive qualities.
- Be accepting of flaws and mistakes.
- Forgive others for past hurts. Focus on the present and future.

Being positive toward others can help you feel more positive about yourself, too.

Help others improve their self-esteem.

If you know someone who may benefit from what you've learned about self-esteem, share your knowledge.

Talk about ways you plan to improve your self-esteem and whether those steps might help the person. Discuss how you might help each other and take these steps together.

Along with the tips above, you can also help the person by:

- showing an interest in the person (by asking questions about him or her, for example)
- expressing your belief in the person's ability to achieve goals and make changes
- talking with—and listening to— the person to show you care

Helping others feels good!

There are other ways to help others—and help yourself! When you take the time to help others, it shows you value yourself. You have something to give!

Think about ways you might be able to help others in your life. For example, consider:

- spending time with someone who lives alone, such as an older relative or friend— you could share a meal, read to the person, or simply be there to talk
- volunteering your time at a place that could benefit from the help of people with different skills—for example, a hospital, nursing home or soup kitchen
- offering to help someone in need, such as someone who needs transportation somewhere or help with housework

MAP OUT YOUR CIRCLE OF SUPPORT.

Write your name in the small circle. Outside the big circle, write the names of people who could give you support. For each person, draw a line to your name and write how he or she could help. You may also want to write names and phone numbers on the inside front cover.

Example:

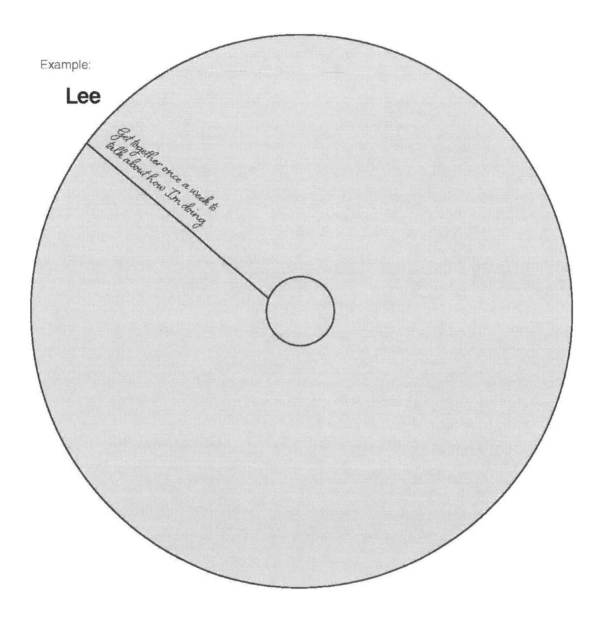

Lee

Get together once a week to talk about how I'm doing

You may also want to make a map showing the support you can give others. Or you can include the information in this map, using a different color.

START SETTING SOME REALISTIC GOALS.

Set goals for the next few days, weeks or months.

These are called short-term goals. Meeting these goals can help you feel more confident about setting and meeting longer-term goals. Here are some examples.

- "For the next 3 days, I'll call 1 community organization a day to ask about volunteering."
- "For the next week, I'll look into clubs or classes offered in my community that I might enjoy."
- "For the next month, I'll write down every time I notice myself thinking I'm stupid. I'll write something helpful to say instead."

When making goals, look over the lists you made earlier of your strengths and weaknesses and the things you enjoy. Try to choose goals that will help you improve the areas you want to work on or do things you enjoy.

Set some longer term goals, too.

Starting to think about these can help you decide on shorter term goals to start with and to keep setting more along the way. For example, the short term goals listed to the left may be steps toward a larger goal. Here is how the next step might look for each example:

- "I'll attend the next volunteer training at an organization whose work interests me."
- "I'll choose a group or class to sign up for and make a commitment to try it for at least 1 month."
- "I'll be able to stop telling myself I'm stupid by 4 months from now."

To help you stay motivated:

- Keep goals realistic. Make them specific. For example, say "I want to do 2 fun things each week," instead of "I want to have more fun." Think about what you will need (money, time, etc.) to meet the goal.
- Aim to make just 1-2 changes at a time.
- Celebrate your achievements. For example, go out with friends after reaching a certain goal.
- Avoid judging yourself if you fail to reach a goal. Instead, focus on what you achieved along the way and what you might want to try doing differently.

To climb steep hills requires slow pace at first.

William Shakespeare, Henry the Eighth

MY GOALS FOR THE NEXT FEW DAYS, WEEKS OR MONTHS

Set 1-2 short-term goals. Remember to follow the tips on page 123. In the Notes section, write down information such as how your progress is going, changes you may want to make in the goal, when you achieved it and what goal to set next.

Goal	Time frame/needs for meeting it	Notes
Examples:	Examples:	Examples:
For 1 week, start 1 conversation a day with a co-worker during lunch.	1 week for ½ hour each day-I'll try to sit with people at lunch rather than by myself	The first few days, the person seemed rushed. I did not take it personally. Today, I had a nice talk with the person about our recent vacations
For 1 week, say something positive about myself every morning.	1 week for 5 minutes each morning remind myself of the positive thing throughout the day.	I was able to find something to say every day. I felt better about facing the day.

MY LONGER TERM GOALS

Start thinking now about what some of these might be.
Keep them in mind as you set shorter-term goals.

Goal	Time frame/needs for meeting it	Notes
Examples: Talk more with co-workers during lunch.	Examples: 3 months	Examples: Good progress in the last 2 months. I still get nervous with someone I don't know well. May need to continue shorter-term goals a little longer
Stop putting myself down and focus on the positive.	2 months	Doing well, but sometimes I still blame myself when things go wrong, even if it wasn't my fault. I need to keep working on this.

CONSIDER SEEKING PROFESSIONAL HELP.

This may help you have more success more quickly.

You may be able to do a lot on your own and with the support of family and friends. Review pages 120-121, and go over your support circle on page 122.

You may also find it helpful to talk with:

- your health-care provider
- a therapist, counselor or other mental health professional
- a religious or spiritual leader

If you are not sure where to find help, start by contacting your health-care provider or local hospital. Use this space for notes:

_____

_____

_____

_____

_____

Remember—asking for help is not a sign of weakness. It means you care enough about yourself to improve your overall wellness. And that's a sign of improved self-esteem!

Know when professional help may be needed.

Possible signs include:

- having low self-confidence for a prolonged period of time

- having frequent mood changes

- feeling no improvement after making your own efforts

You may find that you can do some things on your own but need help doing other things. If you have any questions or concerns about your efforts, talk with your health-care provider.

It can be no dishonor to learn from others when they speak good sense.

Sophocles, Antigone

Be alert for signs of serious problems, such as depression.

Signs of depression include:

- persistent sadness or irritability
- inability to enjoy activities that were once enjoyable, such as work, hobbies or sex
- a sense of hopelessness or guilt
- anxiety or restlessness
- trouble concentrating or remembering things
- trouble sleeping, or sleeping too much
- unexplained headaches, backaches or stomachaches
- eating too much or too little
- low energy
- thoughts of death or suicide (see below)

Most people have some of these symptoms from time to time, but if symptoms occur nearly every day for 2 weeks or longer, may be a sign of depression. Talk with your health-care provider if you think you may be depressed.

If you or someone you know has thoughts of suicide, seek help immediately by calling 9-1-1 or your local medical emergency number.

ADD HIGH SELF-ESTEEM TO YOUR OTHER GOOD QUALITIES!
Start taking steps day by day:

Keep focusing on your strengths.

Accept your weaknesses, too. Set goals to improve the ones you want to change, if it's possible to change them.

Work to make your relationships more satisfying.

Keep practicing assertive communication skills and being positive toward others.

Take pride in your accomplishments and efforts.

Give yourself credit for the things that you do well and work hard at.

Keep learning about self-esteem and how to improve it.

For more information:

- Ask your health-care provider or your local health clinic or hospital.
- Check at your local library or bookstore. Ask for help finding books or other materials.

Imagine all that a higher self-esteem can do for you. Enjoy your efforts and results—enjoy life!

COMMUNITY REENTRY
TOOLS FOR SUCCESS

REENTRY
ESSENTIALS, INC.

Life Skills Series
Basic Skills for Lifelong Success

Please read:

Talk to a professional! This workbook is not a substitute for the advice of a qualified expert.

REENTRY
ESSENTIALS, INC.

Reentry Essentials, Inc.
2609 East 14 Street, Suite 1018
Brooklyn, NY 11235-3915
P: 347.973.0004
E: info@ReentryEssentials.org
I: www.ReentryEssentials.org

This workbook belongs to:

_____

You may find it helpful to keep important names and phone numbers handy.

Write them below.

Parole officer (or social services counselor, if not on parole)

Name_____

Phone_____

Address_____

Case manager or pre-release staff

Name_____

Phone_____

Address_____

Health-care provider

Name_____

Phone_____

Address_____

Other

Name_____

Phone_____

Address_____

Conditions of parole
Remember to contact your parole officer as soon as you're released

_____

_____

_____

_____

_____

_____

_____

_____

_____

_____

YOU'VE BEEN DREAMING OF THE DAY WHEN YOU'LL RETURN TO SOCIETY.

But once on the outside, you'll need a plan to succeed. This workbook can help you build your future—starting right now.

This workbook can help you:

- Figure out what kind of work you might like to do.
- Get a job.
- Find a place to live.
- Find transportation.
- Manage your money.
- Live a safe and healthy life.
- Find the many services ready to assist you on the outside!

There's a lot you can do now—before your release.

And it's important that you do as much as you can. The head start it gives you can make a big difference when your release date finally arrives.

This workbook is yours to keep.

CONTENT

START WITH PROPER ID

You'll need them for job searches, housing and benefits, for example. It may take many weeks to get them. So check off the items below that you need and start working on them today! Ask your case manager or a pre-release staff member to help you.

☐ **Birth certificate**

Write to the bureau of vital statistics where you were born. Ask your case manager or a pre-release staff member to help you find out this information.

- The office name and address to write to:

  _____

  _____

- The fee for the certificate and how you can pay it:

  _____

  _____

- The information or documents you need to include:

  _____

  _____

This information is also usually available on state Web sites.

☐ **Social Security card**

To replace a lost card, you'll need to fill out an application form. The form lists the documents you'll need to submit. To get the form:

- Call 1-800-772-1213 or 1-800-325-0778 (TTY).
- Visit www.ssa.gov or go to your local Social Security office or Social Security Card Center, once you're out.

In most cases, you can mail back the completed form—follow instructions on the form. To get a new (first–time) card, you'll need to apply in person once you're out. There is no fee for a new or replacement card.

Sample request for a birth certificate

See instructions from your state, county or city for the exact information you need to supply—it may vary.

Address
City, State and ZIP
Date

Bureau of Vital Statistics
Address
City, State and ZIP

Dear Sir or Madam:

Please send me a certified copy of the long form of my birth certificate.

My name: John Michael Doe

Sex: Male

Date of birth: November 22, 1978

Place of birth: Good Samaritan Hospital,

                  Anytown, State

Father's name: James Lee Doe

Mother's maiden name: Susan Ann Smith

I have enclosed a check for the fee and a stamped, self-addressed envelope. Thank you.

Sincerely,
John Michael Doe

☐ **Military discharge papers**
If you're a veteran, a copy of your DD214 ("Report of Separation") can be a useful ID. It may also help you get veterans benefits. You can get your DD214:

- at www.archives.gov/veterans
- by submitting Standard Form 180 ("Request Pertaining to Military Records"), available from:

  o National Personnel Records Center
  1 Archives Drive
  St. Louis, MO 63138

- 1-314-801-0800

☐ **Driver's license and record**
Consider contacting your state department of motor vehicles now for a copy of your driver's license record. This can give you a head start on resolving any fines or other problems with your license. Once you're out of prison, you can request a license. Call or write to:

_____

_____

_____

_____

_____

☐ **Photo ID**
To get a photo ID (instead of a driver's license), call or write to:

_____

_____

_____

☐ **Green card (alien registration card)**
If you're not a US citizen, you'll need this card to work. If you've lost yours, apply for a replacement through the U.S. Citizenship and Immigration Services:

- www.uscis.gov
- 1-800-375-5283 or 1-800-767-1833 (TTY)

☐ **High school diploma, General Educational Development (GED) certificate or High School Equivalence Degree (HSED)**

Call or write to the school or agency that awarded it to you:

_____

_____

_____

You should also request a transcript.

☐ **College diploma or vocational school certificate**

Call or write to the college or school that awarded it to you:

_____

_____

_____

You should also request a transcript.

☐ **Occupational or professional license**

Call or write to the school, organization or other agency that awarded it to you:

_____

_____

_____

☐ **Your criminal record**
It's a good idea to review your record. Make sure it doesn't include errors. Call or write to:

_____

_____

_____

Also, find out if certain parts can be expunged or sealed so they don't count against you in job searches.

WHAT KIND OF JOB WILL YOU LOOK FOR?

Try to find a job that's a good fit for your interests and your strengths.

What did you do for enjoyment before your conviction?

Write the things you liked to do below. Here are a few examples some people might give:

- working on cars
- building things
- cooking special meals

What do you do for enjoyment now?

Write what you like to do below. Here are a few examples some people might give:

- reading
- playing basketball
- tutoring other inmates
- doing arts and crafts

What are your strengths?

Write your strengths below. Here are a few examples some people might give. A person might describe him or herself as:

- a team player
- a leader
- a good listener
- good with numbers
- organized
- reliable

You may want a counselor, friend or someone else who knows you well to add to your list of strengths. You probably have strengths you don't realize you have!

What jobs have you held outside of your institution, and when?
Include part-time, summer and volunteer work on your list. Think about what the work involved. Write down at least one skill important to each job.
(If you have a job counselor, he or she can help you think of more.)

Employer	Dates Employed	Title/Description	Skill(s) Used
Ace Hardware Store	Summer, 2010	Stock Clerk	Attention to Detail

What trades or skills have you used or learned while incarcerated?
Even if you haven't been paid for your work, the experience is still valuable!

Job Title	Skill(s) Used or Learned
Clerical Worker	Word processing 50 wpm; other computer skills.

WHAT ELSE HAVE YOU ACHIEVED DURING YOUR TIME INCARCERATED?
Make note of those things here.

My achievements

Check off any of these examples that apply to you. Add any others.

☐ got high school or college diploma
☐ got certificate of completion from chemical dependency class
☐ took parenting class
☐ finished counseling program
☐ led spirituality study group
☐ took basic skills course, such as math or writing (Note the subjects):

- _____
- _____
- _____
- _____
- _____
- _____
- _____
- _____
- _____
- _____

Can't think of anything to include?

Then start putting your time to good use now! Write down the educational, self-help or vocational programs your institution offers. Talk to your case manager or a pre-release staff member about which ones might be good for you.

Program	What it offers	Right for me?
		☐ Yes ☐ Maybe ☐ No
		☐ Yes ☐ Maybe ☐ No
		☐ Yes ☐ Maybe ☐ No
		☐ Yes ☐ Maybe ☐ No
		☐ Yes ☐ Maybe ☐ No
		☐ Yes ☐ Maybe ☐ No

Also, ask how you can continue your education when you get out. For example, could you attend a vocational-technical school or local college?

PUTTING IT ALL TOGETHER

Knowing your interests, skills and strengths can help you see what types of work might be right for you.

You can learn about different types of work by talking to:

- other inmates
- counselors
- supervisors
- case managers or pre-release staff
- teachers
- correctional officers
- correctional facility volunteers
- family and friends

You can also learn more by reading about work in:

- books about careers
- articles in newspapers and magazines
- the Occupational Outlook Handbook (OOH). If your facility has a library, ask the librarian if the OOH is available. You can also find it online at www.bls.gov/ooh

You may also want to try O*NET Online, another career resource service, at www.onetonline.org.

Looking at the yellow pages in a phone book can also give you a sense of the range of jobs.

Write down some jobs you think you can succeed in:

1._____

_____

2._____

_____

3._____

_____

4._____

_____

5._____

_____

Keep in mind you may have to start at the bottom and work your way up.

Certain jobs may be barred

Returning citizens may be barred from some types of work. Talk to your case manager or pre-release staff member about whether your conviction might keep you from any of the jobs you're interested in.

Once you're out, remember that your local public library may offer free Internet access for your research.

FINDING JOB LEADS
Here are some places to look:

Programs at correctional facilities

Some facilities have pre-release programs or parole employment units that help inmates find jobs. Take advantage of your program!

Reentry programs in the community

Your community may offer programs to help returning citizens reenter society through job assistance and other services.

The Internet

For example:

- Many companies post job openings on their Web sites.
- Several Web sites are devoted to helping job seekers and employers connect. To find them, try doing an Internet search on a phrase such as "job search."

Temporary agencies

"Temp" agencies hire out workers to other companies, usually for a short time.

- The workers are employed by the temporary agency, not by the companies using their skills.
- Being a "temp" is one way to learn about different kinds of jobs.
- Sometimes companies offer permanent jobs to "temps" who do good work.
- Look in the yellow pages under "Employment Agencies."

Classified ads

The "help wanted" section of the Sunday newspaper usually has the most ads for jobs.

State employment service office

- Each state has offices that try to match workers to employers. Ask your case manager or a pre-release staff member for the address and phone number of your nearest office. Ask if there's a particular person you should speak to. Write this information on page 139.
- These offices can also tell you about any federal programs that provide free job training.

Other national, state and community agencies

These can also help with employment and other needs. (Some may serve only returning citizens.) Federal job search and training services can be found through Career One Stop at:

- 1-877-US2-JOBS (1-877-872-5627).
- 1-877-889-5627 (TTY).
- www.careeronestop.org.

Use the worksheet on page 140 to keep track of the job leads you learn about.

JOB LEADS WORKSHEET
Use this worksheet to keep track of the contact information for job possibilities.

Agency/Program	Address/Phone	Website	Contact Person	Services Offered

APPLYING FOR A JOB

Create a résumé —a summary of your experience and education. Its purpose is to get you an interview.

A résumé should include these basics:

- a heading with your name and contact information
- a profile or summary that briefly explains who you are and what you have to offer
- summaries of your education or training, work experience and any special skills

If you worked or took classes while incarcerated, you may be able to include that information. Ask your case manager, prerelease staff member or job readiness program about it.

Learn about different résumé styles.

The main types include:

- chronological (which focuses on work history)
- functional (which focuses on skills)
- combination (which lists a mix of skills and specific job accomplishments)

Each has advantages and disadvantages. Library books, job readiness programs and other sources can help you decide which style is best for you. Online resources such as www.careeronestop.org can also help.

A functional or combination style may be recommended.

These styles can help draw the focus to your skills rather than your work history. They are often used by people who:

- are returning to the workforce after an absence
- are changing careers

The example below shows a functional style résumé.

Create a list of references

—people who employers can contact to learn about your skills or capabilities. For example, ask:

- past employers or instructors
- a chaplain or counselor

Have them write letters of recommendation for you, too. Bring copies of the letters and your reference list (with contact information) to interviews.

JOHN M. DOE   16 East Street Kingston, MN 00000
(333) 555-5555 / jmdoe@anyprovider.net

PROFILE
Automotive parts salesperson with 5 years of experience in a fast–paced environment. Proficient in English and Spanish.

SKILLS AND ACCOMPLISHMENTS
  Sales
  Consistently exceeded monthly sales goals.
  Achieved salesperson-of-the-month status 4 months straight.

  Software
  Skilled in use of inventory-management software.

  Warehousing
  Operated forklift.
  Created organization system to improve efficiency.

WORK HISTORY
  Bloomfield Correctional Facility, Bloomfield, Minnesota (2013-2016)
  RD's Auto Supplies, Alexandria, Minnesota (2009-2013)
  4-A Auto Supplies, Ashland, Minnesota (2007-2009)

EDUCATION
  Anytown High School, Anytown, Minnesota Graduated June 2007

Some tips for your résumé:

- Don't include unnecessary personal information, such as race and religion. You also don't have to note that you're in prison. But if the subject comes up—in an interview, for example—be truthful. (See page 142.)
- Stress what you have to offer. (See pages 134-136.) But be honest. Don't exaggerate or give false information. Employers usually check the information.
- Use keywords and phrases instead of complete sentences. Limit your résumé to 1-2 pages.
- Start with action verbs (such as "supervised," "organized," "planned," "developed" and "created") whenever possible. Don't use the pronoun "I."
- Check phone directories, the Internet, and the library for employer addresses or other information you can't remember.

Be sure to check your spelling and grammar! Ask a friend or your case manager or pre-release staff member to review your letter and résumé.

Use a cover letter such as this one to introduce your résumé and request an interview.

Keep it short and focused on the positive. Ask a relative or friend if replies can be sent to his or her address starting about a week before you get out. (If you are submitting a résumé online or via e-mail, you can use your e-mail address in place of a mailing address.)

[Your address]
[City, State and ZIP]
[Date]

[Name of contact-or "Personnel Dept." or "Human Resources" if you don't have a name]
[Name of company]
[Address]
[City, State and ZIP]

Dear [Name of contact, or "Sir or Madam"]:

I am writing in response to your classified ad for an automotive parts salesperson, which appeared in The Daily Chronicle on February 14.

[Add "As the enclosed résumé indicates," here if including a résumé] I have several years of experience selling automotive parts. I would like to put my experience and strong sales skills to work for you.

I will be available for an interview after [name a day soon after your release]. I will receive mail at the address above until [name a day about 1 week before your release]. After that, you may reach me at [your "outside" address].

Thank you for your consideration. I look forward to hearing from you soon.

Sincerely,
[Your name, signed]
[Your name, typed or printed]

[Add "Enclosure" here if including a résumé]

HAVE YOU EVER BEEN CONVICTED OF A CRIME?

You'll likely face this or a similar question on an application form or during an interview. You need to answer honestly. But you can also put a positive "spin" on your time incarcerated.

On an application

First, answer the yes/no question honestly. Then tackle explaining your crime. You have a few options. In the space provided, you can write:

- A brief explanation of your crime.
- "See attached," then attach an explanation you've written ahead of time.
- "Will discuss during an interview," and leave it at that.

In an explanation, admit you made a mistake—take responsibility. Don't be secretive, make excuses or blame others. Also, point out how you used the time in your institution to improve yourself. For example, did you learn job skills, get a diploma or have other achievements? (See your list on page 136.)

Lying on an application can get you fired.

Employers often verify the information you provide—they may even do a background check.

During an interview

Follow the same basic ideas as for an application. Write down and practice what you plan to say if you're asked about your conviction. Reviewing your criminal record ahead of time can also help you be prepared. (See page 133)

_____

_____

_____

_____

_____

_____

_____

_____

_____

You can also mention tax credits and bonding.

- The Work Opportunity Tax Credit program reduces the federal tax on employers who hire ex-offenders meeting certain eligibility requirements. Find out more at www.doleta.gov.
- The Federal Bonding Program protects employers who hire ex-offenders from loss of money or property. You can learn more at www.bonds4jobs.com.

Your state employment service office or department of corrections may also be able to tell you more.

Employers are willing to hire returning citizens.
Be patient and keep at it.

PREPARING FOR AN INTERVIEW

Along with questions about your conviction, also plan answers to questions like these. Be honest! As you gain experience in interviewing, you can change or expand your answers based on what you've learned.

What kind of training have you had?

_____

_____

Do you prefer to work as part of a team or alone?

_____

_____

What are your 3 greatest strengths?

_____

_____

What are your 3 greatest weaknesses?

_____

_____

How do you work under pressure?

_____

_____

What do you see yourself doing 5 years from now?

_____

_____

Why should I hire you?

_____

_____

THE DAY OF THE INTERVIEW

Be neat and clean.

Make sure you:

- Take a bath or shower.
- Use deodorant or antiperspirant.
- Brush your teeth.
- Arrange your hair in a neat, clean style that will fit the work setting.
- Avoid wearing strong—smelling aftershave, perfume or hairspray.

Dress with care.

- Business clothes are generally safest. But you may not need to wear a suit to interview for a "hands-on" job, such as one in auto repair or building maintenance, for example.
- Whatever you wear should be neat, clean and ironed.
- Consider wearing clothes that hide any tattoos you may have.

Bring your documents.

These include your:

- Social Security card or green card
- birth certificate
- driver's license or another photo ID
- copies (not the originals!) of school transcripts, your letters of recommendation and other important documents

Make the right impression.

- Be on time (or a little early).
- Do not smoke or chew gum.
- Be polite to the secretary or receptionist. (He or she may be asked for an opinion of you.)
- Shake hands with the interviewer. Make eye contact, and smile.
- Avoid using slang or prison "lingo."
- Talk about what you can do for the company—not how much you need a job. If you are not offered a job right then, ask when you may call or write to follow up.
- Thank the interviewer when you leave.

Write a brief thank-you note to your interviewer after the interview.

Mention again your skills, strengths and interest in working for the company. For example:

Dear [Name of interviewer):

Thank you for the opportunity to discuss the automotive parts sales position.

I enjoyed meeting you and was impressed by your organization. I'm confident that my strong sales skills and automotive experience would be an asset to you and that I would fit in well. It would be a privilege to join your team.

Again, thank you. I appreciate your time and consideration and look forward to your decision.

Sincerely,
[Your name, signed)
[Your name, typed or printed]

See page 141 for an example of how to address and format your note.

Keep at it! If you don't get the job, try not to let it get you down.
Think of your experience as good practice for your next interview—which will go even better!

KEEP TRACK OF YOUR CONTACTS.
Use this form to record your progress.

Company				
Person Contacted/ Address/ Phone Number				
Date I Sent Letter or Completed Application				
Date of Follow Up Letter or Phone Call				
Response				
Date/Time of Interview				
Date I Sent Thank-You Note				
Notes				

UNDERSTANDING YOUR PAYCHECK

When your planning pays off, you'll be hired and get a paycheck. But:

You probably won't see your paycheck right away.

- Most workers get paid for their work a week after the pay period ends. If your pay period ends on a Friday, for example, you might be paid the following Friday.
- Some workers are paid every 2 weeks or once a month.
- Many companies offer "direct deposit" as a service to workers. If you choose this service, your pay is automatically deposited into your bank account.

Your paycheck may not be as big as you expected.

- Your "gross pay" is what you earn each pay period. But the check will be made out for your "net pay."
- Your net pay is what is left after "deductions"— money taken out for taxes and other expenses.
- Taxes include federal, state, Medicare, Social Security (FICA), and any county or city taxes.

Here is an example of a paycheck.
Your paycheck may look different.

HOURS AND EARNINGS			TAXES AND DEDUCTIONS	
HOURS/UNITS	CURRENT EARNINGS		DESCRIPTION	CURRENT AMOUNT
40.00	360.00		SOC SEC	22.32
			MEDICARE	5.22
			FED TAX	30.00
			STATE TAX	13.66
			TOTAL	71.20
			DEDUCTIONS	
TOTAL	40.00	360.00	Health insurance	20.00
			Dental insurance	2.00
			Total	22.00

	GROSS	TAXABLE	LESS TAXEs	LESS DEDUCTIONS	EQ NET
CURRENT	360.00	360.00	71.20	22.00	266.80

BANK NAME
STATE, ZIP CODE
DATE 06/07/18

PAY two hundred sixty–six and 80/100 .... $286.80 DOLLARS

TO THE
ORDER OF

JOHN DOE
STREET
CITY, STATE   SIGNATURE
ZIP CODE

_____

MANY JOBS ALSO OFFER BENEFITS
beyond a paycheck

Some examples of benefits are:

- health insurance
- paid vacations and holidays
- paid sick leave—usually limited to a certain number of days a year
- life insurance
- retirement benefits

Sometimes employees and employers share the costs of benefits.

For example, it's common for employees to pay for part of their insurance and the company to pay the rest. When this happens, the employee's cost is deducted from the gross pay.

Some benefits may not start right away.

They may not begin until you've been on the job for a certain length of time.

A job with benefits may not pay as much as one with no benefits.

But, the benefits may be more helpful to you than a larger paycheck.

For example, paying your own medical bills can be expensive. In the long run, you might be better off with a job that pays less but offers health insurance.

Which benefits are important to you?

List them here. Then rank them in order of how important they are to you.

Benefit	Rank
_____	#_____
_____	#_____
_____	#_____
_____	#_____
_____	#_____
_____	#_____
_____	#_____
_____	#_____
_____	#_____
_____	#_____
_____	#_____
_____	#_____
_____	#_____
_____	#_____

If you have to choose between job offers, it can help to compare the benefits offered by each company, and how important they are to you.

KEYS TO SUCCESS AT YOUR NEW JOB
It's important to meet expectations and get along with others.

Most employers will expect you to:

- show up on time
- limit your breaks and lunch period to the time allowed
- stay through your shift
- call your supervisor if you'll be late or won't be in (because of illness, for example)
- be dependable
- get along with others
- do the work assigned
- ask questions when you don't understand what you are supposed to do (it's better than doing it wrong)
- tell the truth
- not drink alcohol or use other drugs on the job (some jobs also do not allow smoking or other tobacco use)
- have a positive attitude

Some tips for getting along with your boss and other co-workers:

Pull your share of the load.

Teamwork is very important.

Don't blame others for your mistakes.

Taking responsibility will earn you their respect.

Say "Please" and "Thank you."

Treat others as you'd like to be treated. Don't gossip about co-workers.

Don't use foul language.

Words that may have been acceptable while incarcerated may not be acceptable in the workplace.

Know how to state your point of view.

When you're upset with someone:

- Don't use put-downs or call names. ("You idiot!")
- Don't focus on the other person's mistakes. Starting sentences with "you" can sound like blaming. ("If you mess up again, we'll never finish this on time!")
- Instead, use "I-messages" to quietly talk about how you feel, and why. ("I don't like turning work in late. I don't want to look bad. Let's try to wrap this up.")

Be sure you understand what all your job duties are. Ask how your performance will be reviewed, too. Going beyond what's expected can help you move up!

FINDING TRANSPORTATION

You may not have a car or license. Unless you have family or friends willing to drive you, you may need to take a bus, train or subway, or join a carpool.

Where you choose to live or work may depend on:

- whether the job or housing is close to bus, train or subway stops
- how long it will take you to get back and forth
- how much it will cost. Bus, train and subway fares can add up and cut into your pay
- Write or call transportation companies and ask them to send you:
- route maps, if allowed by your institution (you may have to send the companies a fee first)
- schedules
- information about fares

Get a street map

of the area, if allowed by your institution.

Use the route and street maps

to find out if jobs and housing you are considering are close to public transportation.

Use the schedules

to see if the days and times will work for you. Figure out how long it will take you to get from one place to another.

Think carefully before buying a car

—there are hidden costs. Besides the car itself, you'll need to pay for:

- sales tax (in most states)
- insurance
- license and registration
- yearly inspection fees
- gas
- oil changes, routine maintenance, tires and other replacement parts
- possible parking fees

Get the names, addresses, and phone numbers of your local bus, train or subway companies.

Some job assistance programs and service agencies may also offer transportation help. Write the contact information here. Ask your case manager, pre-release staff member or librarian for help, if you need it.

Name/ Phone

_____

_____

Name/ Phone

_____

_____

Name/ Phone

_____

_____

Name/ Phone

_____

_____

Name/ Phone

_____

_____

FINDING A PLACE TO LIVE

Try to find a supportive friend or relative who will take you in while you look for housing and a job. If there's no one you can stay with, here are some other possibilities.

Renting

You may want to rent a room— or an entire apartment. If you decide to rent, be sure you understand all the fees and rules. For example:

- Is it furnished or unfurnished?
- What is the rent and when must it be paid?
- Is there a lease, or will you rent on a month–by–month basis? If there is a lease, how long is it for? If you move out before it is up, will you be charged a penalty?
- Are utilities (such as heat and hot water) included in the rent? If not, what's their average monthly cost? (Ask the apartment manager or current tenant for an estimate. You can also call the utility and ask for average monthly costs.)
- Is there a security deposit? (This is a fee you pay before you move in. If the apartment is in good shape when you move out, you should get the deposit back. If there's been damage, the cost will be deducted from your deposit.)
- Are there any special features, such as a laundry room?

Transitional housing

Some areas may have transitional housing (also called "halfway houses"). People can live there for several months or more.

- This can give a person time to save enough money for permanent housing.
- Some transitional housing is for people in recovery from alcohol or other drug problems. Residents may receive a variety of services from counseling to job search help—in addition to food and shelter.

Ask your case manager or a pre-release staff member what's available in your area and how to apply. You should begin applying before your release.

Overnight shelters

These are available in many communities for short-term stays. There is no charge.

In some areas, it's legal to deny housing to certain ex-offenders.

To help avoid this, it can help to supply your parole officer's contact information, as well as a list of references.

Choose your location carefully.

Think hard before deciding to return to your old neighborhood. Are there people there who may try to pull you back into crime?

HOUSING WORKSHEET

Ask your case manager or a pre-release staff member to help you fill in this worksheet.

Make note of housing leads here.

Type of Housing	Address	Phone	Contact Name	Notes

Estimate the total cost of any housing you're considering here.

(Use "other" for any extra expenses you may learn about when talking with the housing manager.)

Expenses	Address _____ _____	Address _____ _____	Address _____ _____	Address _____ _____
Rent				
Security Deposit				
Heat/Hot Water				
Electricity/Gas				
Parking				
Garbage Removal				
Other				
Other				
Total Cost				

MANAGING YOUR MONEY WELL
is the first step toward reaching many goals.

Budgeting

Keep track of every dollar that comes in and goes out— especially in the first few months after release. The budget worksheet on page 24 can help you avoid overspending.

Checking and savings accounts

Before opening a new account, compare banks. For example, banks may charge:

- a monthly fee
- a fee for each check you write
- ATM (automated teller machine) or debit card fees
- an overdraft fee each time you write a check or use your ATM or debit card for more than you have in your account
- a fee for falling below a minimum balance

Use the worksheet on page 158 to list sources of financial assistance.

ATM and debit cards

These give you access to the money you have in the bank.

- Know what it costs to use your card. For example, there may be a fee each time you use it or if you use another bank's ATM.
- You can use a debit card where credit cards are accepted. But a debit card draws money from your checking account— it isn't loaned money.

Be sure to record every check and ATM or debit card transaction. And keep your register balanced. Overdraft fees can be steep!

About credit

Interest charges and fees can add up quickly.

- Use credit cards only for emergencies and purchases that are large and necessary or that can only be made with a credit card.
- Be careful. Late payments and accounts turned over for collection go on your credit report. They can affect job and housing opportunities for years.
- Check your credit report for errors. You can get a free copy from each credit reporting company once a year at www.annualcreditreport.com.

My savings goals

In 6 months, I want to have enough money saved to:

_____

In 1 year, I want to have enough money saved to:

_____

In 5 years, I want to have enough money saved to:

_____

Aim to save up for at least 3 months' worth of expenses in an emergency fund, too.

CREATE A MONTHLY BUDGET.

Your income should equal or exceed your expenses. If it's less, you'll need to cut expenses, find more work—or both. Note that you should treat savings like an expense!

	Month: _____	Month: _____	Month: _____	Month: _____
Income				
Wages and Tips (after taxes)				
Other: _____				
Total Income				
Expenses				
Rent				
Utilities				
Telephone				
Groceries				
Child Care				
Clothing				
Laundry				
Transportation				
Health Care or Insurance				
Dental Care or Insurance				
Savings				
Eating out				
Entertainment				
Cable				
Gifts				
Court–Ordered Restitution				
Other: _____				
Other: _____				
Other: _____				
Total Expenses:				
Income - Expenses =				

TAKE CARE OF YOUR HEALTH
once you're out. Here are some basics:

Find health-care providers.

It's best to choose a doctor and a dentist before you need them.

- Ask your case manager or a pre-release staff member if you can get Medicaid or other medical assistance. If you're a veteran, you may also qualify for benefits.
- There may be free or low cost clinics in your area.
- Your local health department is also a great resource.
- If your job offers health insurance, you may be given a list of health-care providers to choose from.

See pages 158-159. You can write down the names of doctors, dentists, clinics and other resources there.

If you don't have health insurance, go online to www.healthcare.gov to see if you may qualify for a low or no-cost plan.

Eat for good health.

No single meal will make or break your health. But consistently making healthier choices can help you maintain a healthy weight and lower your risk for chronic diseases

- Make a variety of nutrient dense choices from each food group in the right amounts for your calorie needs. Choose items that fit your culture, tastes and budget.
- Vary your choices from each food group over the week.
- Make small shifts to healthier choices. For example, switch to fat-free or low-fat dairy products. Choose seafood, lean meats, lean poultry, nuts, seeds and soy products over high-fat meats.
- Fill half of your plate with fruits and vegetables.
- Make at least half of your grains whole grains.
- Limit saturated fat, added sugars and sodium. (Avoiding processed foods helps.)
- Use vegetable oils (like canola and olive) in place of solid fats (like butter, shortening, lard and coconut oil).
- Handle food safely to help avoid illness.

Get enough physical activity.

Find a healthy balance between the calories you eat and those you burn. Brisk walking or bicycling are just 2 of the activities you could enjoy. Be sure to talk with your health-care provider before starting an exercise program.

• Get at least 150 minutes of moderate—or 75 minutes of vigorous—physical activity each week.

• For greater health benefits, get at least 300 minutes of moderate—or 150 minutes of vigorous—physical activity each week.

• Try to spread your activity throughout the week, getting at least 10 minutes at a time.

• In addition, do muscle strengthening exercises at least 2 days each week. Learn more at www.ChooseMyPlate.gov.

NOTE: These guidelines are for adults and for children age 2 and older. Ask a healthcare provider about nutrition for younger children.

Wash your hands often.

This helps prevent colds, flu and other illnesses. For example, wash:

- any time hands are visibly dirty
- after coughing, sneezing or blowing your nose
- after using the bathroom
- before and after any contact with someone who is sick

Wash well with soap and water. Scrub all surfaces of hands for 20 seconds. Use a hand sanitizer (that's at least 60% alcohol) if soap and water aren't available and hands aren't visibly dirty.

Keep clean.

This will help with your health. (Looking and smelling good will also help with job searches.)

- Brush your teeth at least twice a day. Floss daily.
- Shower or take a bath every day. Use deodorant or antiperspirant.
- Wash your hair often.
- Keep your home clean, too. Be sure to dust and to disinfect bathrooms and kitchens.

If you need a place to shower or wash clothes, try the resources added on pages 151 and 158.

Consider abstinence.

Not having sex is the only 100% safe way to prevent pregnancy and to avoid getting STDs through sex.

Use male latex condoms if you decide to have sex.

Condoms don't make sex 100% safe. But they can help lower the risk of HIV and other STDs.

Be sure to use a new latex condom properly for each act of vaginal, anal or oral sex.

Remember, you can get STDs (including HIV) from anal and oral sex, too.

- Read the condom package. Make sure it says the condom helps protect against STDs. Check the expiration date.
- Put the condom on as soon as the penis is hard and before any vaginal, anal or oral contact.
- Use a water-based or silicone—based lubricant for vaginal and anal sex.
- Do not use any oils, petroleum jelly or lotions that have oil. Do not use nonoxynol-9 spermicide either.

Also, some STDs can be caused by contact with infected areas not covered by a condom.

Condoms also help prevent pregnancy. If you're a woman, your healthcare provider or clinic can tell you about other forms of birth control.

AVOIDING HARMFUL HABITS

Programs in your institution may have helped you deal with alcohol or other drug problems. Once you're out, follow through on any treatment programs you started there.

Limit alcohol—or don't drink at all.

For some, moderate drinking may help reduce the risk of heart disease. But for others, it may increase health risks. People who should not drink at all include people recovering from alcoholism and women who are pregnant or trying to get pregnant. Ask your health–care provider what's best for you. Moderate drinking means no more than:

- 2 drinks per day for men
- 1 drink per day for women

If you're 65 or older, ask your health-care provider if a lower limit is right for you. In general, one drink is 12 oz. beer, 5 oz. wine, or 1½ oz. liquor.

Breastfeeding women should not drink without their healthcare provider's permission. An occasional single drink may be OK but wait at least 2 hours after the drink before breastfeeding.

Remember to give yourself time to adjust once you're released.

Do not use other drugs.

Drugs can put your health as well as your job at risk—some companies test employees for drug use. If you didn't have treatment in your institution (or even if you did), get treatment if you find yourself wanting to use drugs. Contact SAMHSA's National Helpline:

- 1-800-662-HELP (1-800-662-4357)
- 1-800-487-4889 (TDD)
- http://findtreatment.samhsa.gov

On page 159, make note of the names and numbers you're given.

Do not use tobacco products, either.

They can lead to serious health problems. If you smoke or use other tobacco products, ask your health-care provider about ways to quit.

Find healthy ways to reduce stress.

For example, you could try:

- deep breathing— slowly breathing in, holding your breath a few seconds, then slowly breathing out
- visualization—closing your eyes and imagining yourself in a peaceful place
- listening to relaxing music

Taking part in exercise programs, support groups, arts and crafts and other healthy activities are other ways to reduce stress– and make new friends.

What other healthy ways do you like to de-stress?

_____

_____

_____

_____

_____

_____

_____

_____

_____

_____

_____

REDISCOVERING RELATIONSHIPS

When you're doing time, time doesn't stand still. While you're inside, you change.

Outside, family and friends change, too.

For example:

- A partner may learn to do things around the house—such as budgeting or car repair—that you did before you went to your institution.
- Children may get used to living without their mom or dad.
- Children grow up.

Be patient. It will take time for everyone to really know each other again and settle into a new life.

Counseling and support groups can help.

Getting back together can be exciting—but also stressful. A counselor can help you and your loved ones adjust to new roles. In support groups, people who have been in situations like yours may give encouragement and helpful tips. (See page 159.)

Some of your old friends may not have changed.

If people you used to spend time with were into drugs, violence or stealing, they may still be at it. Don't be pulled back into that lifestyle!

Plan for how you'll deal with pressure.

Use this space to write down things you could do or say if old friends pressure you to follow their ways. Ask your counselor, a case manager or a pre-release staff member for ideas.

For example: If I did that, I'd be breaking the terms of my parole. No way am I going back to prison!

If they do or say:

_____

I can do or say:

_____

If they do or say:

_____

I can do or say:

_____

If they do or say:

_____

I can do or say:

_____

THERE ARE MANY PEOPLE WAITING TO HELP YOU!

It's not a sign of weakness to turn to them—everyone needs support now and then. Ask your case manager or a pre-release staff member about agencies or programs that can help you. Or check the phone book's Government and Community Services section. Write the information here. (Make note of housing assistance on page 151.) Remember even if an agency or program says they can't help directly, ask if they know who can.

	Name	Address/Phone	Website
Social Services			
Reentry Programs			
Food Assistance			
Free or Low Cost Clothing			
Free or Low–Cost Health Care and Dental Care			
Mental Health Care			

	Name	Address/Phone	Website
Support Groups			
Substance Abuse Treatment Programs			
Legal Assistance			
Places of Worship			
Other Resources			

Congratulations! By completing this workbook, you've taken important steps toward the day of your release. Be proud of your effort. Soon, you'll begin a new life. Take this workbook with you—and remember, you can make it on the outside!

HOW TO MANAGE STRESS

REENTRY
ESSENTIALS, INC.

Life Skills Series
Basic Skills for Lifelong Success

This workbook belongs to:

_____

You may find it helpful to keep important names and phone numbers handy.

Write them below.

Health-care provider

Name_____

Phone_____

Therapist or counselor

Name_____

Phone_____

An emergency contacts

Name_____

Phone_____

Other important numbers

_____

_____

_____

_____

_____

_____

_____

_____

_____

_____

_____

_____

_____

_____

_____

_____

_____

Reentry Essentials, Inc.
2609 East 14 Street, Suite 1018
Brooklyn, NY 11235-3915
P: 347.973.0004
E: info@ReentryEssentials.org
I: www.ReentryEssentials.org

FEELING STRESSED?

If so, this workbook can help you understand stress—what causes it and how you can manage it.

Friends and family members
can be a wonderful source of support. Share your thoughts and feelings with them. Brainstorm together for ways to reduce stress.

Some stress will always be a part of your life.
You can learn to manage it better, become more productive and enjoy the challenges life throws your way.

CONTENT

WHAT IS STRESS?

Stress is sometimes referred to as the "pressure" or "tension" you feel when faced with a situation that's new, unpleasant or threatening.

Stress is a fact of life.

It affects everyone. Some stress is actually helpful because it can spur you to meet life's challenges. Without some stress, life would be boring.

Stress can be an automatic reaction to a demand or danger.

Your muscles tense and your heart rate and breathing speed up. A rush of adrenaline gives you the strength and energy needed to deal with danger or run away. This reaction is often called the "fight-or-flight" response.

Too much stress can cause problems.

It can affect your mental and physical health and damage relationships with friends and family.

STRESS CAN TAKE ITS TOLL ON YOU.
Unless you take steps to reduce or control stress, tension can build up inside.

Over time, stress can harm your health, possibly contributing to:

- allergies
- muscle tension, often in the form of a stiff neck or sore back
- upset stomach or heartburn
- sore throats, sinus infections, colds and flu
- migraine or tension headaches
- sleep disorders
- menstrual irregularity
- high blood pressure
- angina
- heart disease and heart attacks
- stroke (brain attack)

If you already have any of the conditions listed above, don't just assume stress is to blame. Talk to your health-care provider.

Poor health can lead to more stress, making your problems even worse.

For example:

- living with chronic pain, such as pain caused by a back problem, may make you feel frustrated and alone
- missing important events due to colds and flu may cause anxiety

If you have an untreated health problem, see your health-care provider right away. Once a problem has been diagnosed, be sure to follow your health-care provider's directions for treating it. A positive attitude and improved health will help you handle stress.

WHAT ARE YOUR "WARNING SIGNALS"?

You'll be better able to manage stress if you recognize the symptoms. Check the symptoms you frequently feel when you're stressed. Add any symptoms you've experienced repeatedly that aren't listed. Please note that some of the symptoms listed below also have causes other than stress. See your health-care provider if symptoms are severe or persistent.

You'll be better able to manage stress if you recognize the symptoms. Check the symptoms you frequently feel when you're stressed. Add any symptoms you've experienced repeatedly that aren't listed. Please note that some of the symptoms listed below also have causes other than stress. See your health-care provider if symptoms are severe or persistent.

Physical symptoms:

☐ a change in appetite

☐ back pain

☐ high blood pressure

☐ breathlessness

☐ chest pain

☐ clammy hands

☐ a cold

☐ constipation or diarrhea

☐ fatigue

☐ headaches

☐ racing heartbeat

☐ jaw clenching and/ or grinding of teeth

☐ muscle tension

☐ rashes

☐ restlessness

☐ sleeping problems

☐ stomachaches

Other physical symptoms:

_____

_____

_____

_____

_____

_____

_____

_____

_____

_____

_____

_____

_____

_____

_____

_____

_____

_____

Emotional symptoms:

- ☐ anger
- ☐ anxiety
- ☐ denial of a problem
- ☐ depression
- ☐ forgetfulness
- ☐ difficulty making decisions
- ☐ feeling powerless
- ☐ feeling rejected
- ☐ feeling unhappy for no reason
- ☐ being easily upset
- ☐ worrying frequently
- ☐ feeling worthless.

Behavioral symptoms:

- ☐ arguing with friends or partner
- ☐ avoiding tasks and responsibilities
- ☐ crying easily
- ☐ decreased job performance
- ☐ difficulty concentrating
- ☐ increasing use of alcohol, tobacco or other drugs
- ☐ neglecting appearance
- ☐ overeating or underrating
- ☐ snapping at people withdrawing from family and friends

Notes:

_____
_____
_____
_____
_____
_____
_____
_____
_____
_____
_____
_____
_____
_____
_____
_____
_____
_____
_____
_____
_____
_____
_____
_____
_____
_____
_____
_____
_____
_____

Other emotional symptoms:

_____
_____
_____
_____
_____
_____
_____
_____
_____
_____
_____
_____
_____
_____

Other behavioral symptoms:

_____
_____
_____
_____
_____
_____
_____
_____
_____
_____
_____
_____
_____
_____

WHAT'S CAUSING ALL THAT STRESS?

Some people don't know—they're too busy and too stressed to stop and think about why they feel that way. But by recognizing the sources of stress, called stressors, you may be able to make changes and reduce stress.

Everyone's stressors are different.

What's stressful for one person may not bother someone else at all. For example, you may feel stressed by caring for an aging parent, but a sibling may enjoy it.

Not all stressors are bad.

For example, a sudden financial gain can also create stress.

Read the following lists of potential stressors. Check the ones that are stressful for you. Feel free to add other stressors to the list. (You may want to consider making your biggest stressors part of your stress management plan. See pages 29 and 30.)

Financial stressors:

- ☐ alimony
- ☐ bankruptcy
- ☐ child support
- ☐ growing debts
- ☐ sudden financial gain
- ☐ fixed income
- ☐ reduced income due to retirement
- ☐ taxes
- ☐ _____

Daily hassles:

- ☐ car trouble
- ☐ child care
- ☐ household chores
- ☐ forgetting or misplacing something
- ☐ oversleeping
- ☐ traffic jams
- ☐ waiting in lines
- ☐ _____

Environmental stressors:

- ☐ crime
- ☐ noise
- ☐ overcrowding
- ☐ pollution
- ☐ traffic
- ☐ weather
- ☐ _____

Health-related stressors:

- ☐ arthritis
- ☐ poor eyesight
- ☐ poor hearing
- ☐ headaches
- ☐ illness, injury or disease
- ☐ trouble with medicines
- ☐ loss of mobility
- ☐ being overweight
- ☐ chronic pain
- ☐ sleep disorders
- ☐ _____

Family-related stressors:

- ☐ arguments with partner or children
- ☐ a child moving out or returning home
- ☐ poor communication between
- ☐ family members
- ☐ the death of a family member or partner
- ☐ divorce or separation
- ☐ alcohol or other drug problems (self or other
- ☐ helping an older relative
- ☐ serious illness, injury or surgery
- ☐ problems with in-laws or other relatives
- ☐ marriage
- ☐ moving
- ☐ parenting challenges
- ☐ pregnancy or adoption
- ☐ sexual problems with partner
- ☐ being single or alone
- ☐ _____

Work-related stressors:

- ☐ a business move or merger; downsizing
- ☐ a long commute
- ☐ being fired or laid off
- ☐ a noisy or unpleasant work environment
- ☐ few opportunistic advancement
- ☐ little recognition or a lack of feedback
- ☐ new responsibilities
- ☐ retirement
- ☐ starting a new job or getting a promotion
- ☐ a lack of training
- ☐ trouble with a boss or co-workers
- ☐ too much wore
- ☐ _____

KEEPING A JOURNAL
can help you manage stress.

Keeping a journal has many benefits.

It can be:

- a tool to help you see what causes you stress and how it affects you
- an outlet for emotion and frustration
- a decision-making tool, allowing you to explore pros and cons of possible choices
- a helpful way to confront problems or make a change in your life
- a fun activity, because you don't have to follow any rules
- a way to gain insights, because you may discover solutions to a problem or find ways to change stressful situations

Try it out.

Each day this week, write about something that made you feel stressed—or that made you feel good. If you need help getting started, try answering some of these questions:

- How did you respond to a stressful situation today?
- Did you laugh today? At what?
- Are you facing any big decisions? Explain them.
- Are you feeling anxious or frustrated? Why?

Today's date is _____

_____

_____

_____

_____

_____

_____

_____

_____

_____

_____

_____

_____

_____

_____

Today's date is _____

_____

_____

_____

_____

_____

_____

_____

_____

_____

_____

_____

_____

_____

_____

Today's date is _____

_____

_____

_____

_____

_____

_____

_____

_____

_____

_____

_____

_____

_____

_____

Today's date is _____

_____

_____

_____

_____

_____

_____

_____

_____

_____

_____

_____

_____

Today's date is _____

_____

_____

_____

_____

_____

_____

_____

_____

_____

_____

_____

_____

_____

Today's date is _____

_____

_____

_____

_____

_____

_____

_____

_____

_____

_____

_____

_____

Today's date is _____

_____

_____

_____

_____

_____

_____

_____

_____

_____

_____

_____

_____

YOU CAN STOP CONTRIBUTING TO YOUR STRESS.

Some people have certain personality traits that help them overcome stress—optimism, a tendency to take action and a sense of humor. You can develop these traits—and stop adding to your stress.

Accept what you cannot change. Be optimistic.

Many people worry about things they have no control over. To manage stress, you need to learn to accept things you cannot change and be optimistic about the outcome. For example, imagine your company has just purchased machines you don't know how to use. Worrying about it will only increase your stress. Instead, think about getting the training you need to use them.

When you can't change a situation, be optimistic.

Try thinking:

- "I'll laugh about this someday."
- "Maybe some good will come of this."
- "What can I learn from this?"

By focusing on something positive, you can discover solutions to problems and feel less stress.

Exercise control over what you can change.

Rather than feel stressed by something you can control, take action! Change the situation.

For example, if your job is causing you too much stress, consider finding another one.

Cope with stress through humor. Be playful.

Laughter not only makes you feel good, it can also help you relax. Look for the silly and absurd activities going on around you, and learn to laugh at them. By taking things a little less seriously and adding laughter to your life, you can better control stress.

HOW DO YOU RESPOND TO STRESSORS?

Look back at the lists of stressors on pages 168 and 169. List the 3 stressors that bother you the most.

1_____   2_____   3_____

Describe a situation you recently experienced involving each of these 3 stressors. How did you react? How could you react to a similar situation in the future so you would feel less stress?

Situation	Initial reaction	Possible change
Bills were piling up, and I didn't have enough money to pay them all.	Felt overwhelmed and stressed. Was convinced I'd never get out of debt.	Explain the problem to my creditors, and ask for more time to pay. Set a budget, and stick to it.

1._____

_____

_____

_____

2._____

_____

_____

_____

3._____

_____

_____

_____

When confronted with a stressor in the future, stop for a moment and think about how to react. Can you control this stressor? Think about how to react to it in a positive way that can give you more control!

ARE YOU HEARING NEGATIVE SELF-TALK?

Whether you're conscious of it or not, you probably talk to yourself silently every day. This mental conversation is called self-talk.

Negative self-talk "loops"

Unfortunately, we often criticize ourselves during these mental conversations, turning a minor fault or problem into a big one. These "loops" replay themselves in our heads, reinforcing negative (and incorrect) beliefs. They can also add to our stress—it's our self-talk that helps determine how we will respond to any situation.

Recording a new loop

Every time you hear a negative message play in your mind, erase it and record a new, positive one in its place.

For example, instead of saying, I'll never be any good at making speeches," try saying, I'll just keep practicing and do my best. No one expects me to be perfect."

Or, instead of saying, "I know I'll probably be fired and never find another job" when you're stuck in traffic and late for work, try saying, "This happens to everyone. I'll get there as soon as I can."

By learning to identify, challenge and change negative messages, you can reduce stress.

POSITIVE THINKING CAN HELP.

Using the space below, write down several stressful situations you've recently faced. Did you hear a negative message? What positive message could you "play" when you face the situation again?

Situation	Negative message	Positive message
1._____	1._____	1._____
2._____	2._____	2._____
3._____	3._____	3._____
4._____	4._____	4._____

The next time you face a potentially stressful situation, stop and listen to the loop playing in your head. Does it have a negative message? Try to change the message to a positive one. Over time, your mind will automatically play the new, positive messages, making it easier for you to manage stress.

TIPS FOR REDUCING STRESS

These tips can be adapted to a variety of situations— college life, parenthood, volunteer activities, the workplace, and so forth.

Get up on time

So you aren't rushed.

Designate a time and place to do your work

—and leave it there. For example, a college student could study at the library and leave work in a locker.

Understand what's expected

Before starting a project. It might not be as overwhelming as it seems.

Minimize interruptions,

Especially if you need to concentrate. Close the door or don't answer the phone.

Get help

When needed, or delegate less important chores and tasks. For example, ask children to set the table or help with housework. By doing so, you'll be better able to focus on your priorities.

Get organized

So you can find things quickly. Remind yourself of your accomplishments rather than concentrating only on what hasn't been done. Doing so will help motivate you.

Alternate mental and physical tasks,

if possible, to save energy and reduce fatigue.

Look positively at change, instead of fearing it.

While change may bring challenges, it may also bring many benefits you don't expect. For example, moving to a new town may be scary, but you'll make new friends.

Look back on a crisis

As a learning opportunity. This will help you respond better to similar problems in the future.

LEARN TO BETTER MANAGE YOUR TIME.

Poor use of time, not a lack of time, may be contributing to your stress level. Here are some tips for handling almost any situation.

Plan ahead

by determining when a task must be finished and how much time it will take. Overestimate how long it will take to finish jobs, such as a term paper or a report for work, especially if you haven't done them before.

Break big jobs down

Into small chunks. They will seem more manageable, and you'll feel a sense of accomplishment as you finish each part.

Determine priorities

And spend your time on the most important activities. For example, spending time with your family may be more important than keeping your home spotless.

Look for ways to be more efficient.

Such as cooking several meals at once and refrigerating them for the week ahead.

Take breaks periodically

You'll work more efficiently when you return to a project.

Group similar tasks

Do them at the same time. For example, make all of your phone calls at once or pay all of your bills at the same time.

Schedule work

Based on your energy level. Work on more difficult tasks when you generally have the most energy for example, first thing in the morning or after lunch.

MAKE TIME FOR FREE TIME.

Poor use of time, not a lack of time, may be contributing to your stress level. Here are some tips for handling almost any situation.

Include yourself in your schedule.

Don't think of free time as what's left over after you've done everything else. Along with scheduling your work responsibilities and family commitments, plan time to exercise, read, rake a bubble bath or do anything else you find relaxing. Making time for things you enjoy will help you "recharge your batteries."

Learn to say no.

Saying no to another volunteer activity, an optional presentation at work or even a social event can give you more free time or more time to devote to other responsibilities.

Don't feel guilty when you say no. It's not always easy, but with practice, you can learn.

HOW ARE YOU SPENDING YOUR TIME?

Writing down your activities for a week or even a month is one of the best ways to see where you're wasting time. It can also help you see where you can schedule free time and how to become more efficient month is one of the best ways to see where you're wasting time. It can also help you see where you can schedule free time and how to become more efficient.

Using the chart below, or one like it, note how you spend your time. Note time spent at work, shopping, talking on the phone, commuting, watching TV or making dinner.

Day	Activity	Time Spent
_____	_____	_____
_____	_____	_____
_____	_____	_____
_____	_____	_____
_____	_____	_____
_____	_____	_____
_____	_____	_____
_____	_____	_____
_____	_____	_____
_____	_____	_____
_____	_____	_____
_____	_____	_____
_____	_____	_____
_____	_____	_____
_____	_____	_____
_____	_____	_____

Review your chart, and answer the following questions:

- Are there tasks that could have been delegated?
- Could you have done anything more efficiently?
- Are you getting enough time for your favorite activities?

Try changing your schedule so that it is more realistic, gives you free time and reduces stress.

TAKE A LOOK AT YOUR LIFESTYLE.

In addition to changing your reaction to stressors, consider:

Seeing your healthcare provider

Have regular checkups. Talk to your health-care provider about stress and how it affects you.

Talking it over

Talking with a friend or family member can help you son out your feelings and get a new perspective on problems.

Getting plenty of sleep

Most adults need 7-9 hours of sleep each night. Often, people under stress give up sleep to finish more work. Others can't sleep because they're thinking about their stress. If you have trouble sleeping:

- Exercise during the day.
- Don't drink alcohol or caffeinated beverages in the evening. They can keep you awake.
- Take a warm bath before going to bed.
- Go to bed at the same time every night.
- Write about your worries in a journal, or mentally set them aside. Plan to think about them another time.

Getting enough physical activity

The key is to find a health balance between the calories you eat and those you bum.

- Get at least 150 minutes of moderate—or 75 minutes of vigorous physical activity each week.
- For greater health benefits, get at least 300 minutes of moderate—or 150 minutes of vigorous physical activity each week.
- Try to spread your activity throughout the week, getting at least 10 minutes at a time.
- In addition, do muscle strengthening exercises at least 2 days each week.

Be sure to consult your healthcare provider before starting or changing an exercise program.

Exercise levels

- Moderate activity is any activity that increases your heart and breathing rates—but still allows you to carry on a conversation without difficulty.
- Vigorous activity is any activity that increases your heart and breathing rates to the point that conversation is difficult or broken.

Taking a break

A relaxing activity can revitalize you and boost your spirits. Afterward, you'll have more emotional strength to face challenges.

Avoiding stress

Too many major changes at once can lead to tension. Deal with a few stressful events before working on others.

Taking up a new hobby

Hobbies can take your mind off your problems, help you relax and increase your self-esteem.

Listening to music

Quiet, soothing music, alone or with the relaxation techniques on pages 186 and 187, may help you relax.

"Treating" yourself

Find something to look forward to, such as eating lunch outside or going for a short walk.

Watching what you eat

An unhealthy diet can lead to problems that may add to your stress. The tips on the next page will give you a good start to creating a healthy diet.

List any other stress-reducing techniques you think of:

_____

_____

_____

Which stress-reducing techniques do you think will work best for you? Write them below.

_____

_____

_____

Not every technique will work for everyone. Try different techniques to see which ones work best for you. Remember—changing behavior takes time, so stick with it!

GOOD NUTRITION MAKES GOOD SENSE.

Your body needs extra energy when you're under stress.
Pay special attention to what you eat—and what you don't eat.

Don't skip breakfast.

Your body needs energy after 8-12 hours without food. Skipping breakfast can make you feel tired and cause headaches.

Eat for good health.

No single meal will make or break your health. But consistently making healthier choices can help you maintain a healthy weight and lower your risk for chronic diseases.

- Make a variety of nutrient dense choices from each food group in the right amounts for your calorie needs.
- Vary your choices from each food group over the week.
- Make small shifts to healthier choices. For example, switch to fat-free or low-fat dairy products. Choose seafood, lean meats, lean poultry, nuts, seeds and soy products over, high-fat meats.

Cut back on caffeine.

Caffeine, which is found in coffee, tea, soft drinks and chocolate, is a stimulant. It can worsen the impact of stress on your body. Ask your healthcare provider if there is caffeine in the medicines you cake.

Stick to a regular meal schedule.

Skipping meals or eating at irregular times can lower your energy level.

Don't overeat.

Many people tum to food when they are under stress. However, overeating can lead to weight gain and other stressful health problems.

Your body needs extra energy when you're under stress. Pay special attention to what you eat and what you don't eat

For more information on nutrition, or to tailor a diet to meet your needs, talk to a dietitian, nutritionist or your health-care provider.

You can also visit www.ChooseMyPlate.gov.

TRY RELAXING YOUR BODY AND MIND.

The relaxation techniques on pages 186-187 will not only help you manage stress, but they can also improve your concentration, productivity and overall well-being. To get started:

Find a quiet, relaxing place.

Where you will be alone for 10-20 minutes, to do these exercises. The techniques work best if there are no distractions.

Practice once or twice a day,

at whatever time works best for you. (Some people practice before breakfast to ease into the day, while others practice after work to unwind.)

Stick with the technique that works best

For you. Not every technique will work for every person.

Keep trying

Don't worry if you don't notice a major change immediately. You may need to practice for a few weeks before you begin to feel the benefits. Remember, you should see your healthcare provider if symptoms of stress are severe or persist.

CONSIDER ONE OR MORE OF THESE RELAXATION TECHNIQUES:

Progressive muscle relaxation

This technique can help you relax the major muscle groups in your body. And, it's easy to do.

1. Wear loose, comfortable clothing. Sit in a favorite chair or lie down.
2. Begin with your facial muscles. Frown hard for 5-10 seconds and then relax all your muscles.
3. Work other facial muscles by scrunching your face up or knitting your eyebrows for
4. 5-10 seconds. Release. You should feel a noticeable difference between the tense and relaxed muscles.
5. Move on to your jaw. Then, move on to other muscle groups—shoulders, arms, chest and legs-until you've tensed and relaxed your whole body.

Visualization

This technique uses your imagination, a great resource when it comes to reducing stress.

1. Sit or lie down in a comfortable position.
2. Imagine a pleasant, peaceful scene, such as a lush forest or a sandy beach. Picture yourself in this setting.
3. Focus on the scene for a set amount of time, then gradually return to your other activities.

Meditation

This is the process of focusing on a single word or object to clear your mind. As a result, you feel calm and refreshed.

1. Wear loose, comfortable clothing. Sit or lie in a relaxing position.
2. Close your eyes and concentrate on a calming thought, word or object.
3. You may find that other thoughts pop into your mind. Don't worry—this is normal. Try not to dwell on them. Just keep focusing on your image or sound.
4. If you're having trouble, try repeating a word or sound over and over. (Some people find it helpful to play soothing music while meditating.)
5. Gradually, you'll begin to feel more and more relaxed.

Deep breathing

One of the easiest ways to relieve tension is with deep breathing.

1. Lie on your back with a pillow under your head. Bend your knees (or put a pillow under them) to relax your stomach.
2. Put one hand on your stomach, just below your rib cage.
3. Slowly breathe in through your nose. Your stomach should feel like it's rising.
4. Exhale slowly through your mouth, emptying your lungs completely and letting your stomach fall.
5. Repeat several times until you feel calm and relaxed. Practice daily.

Once you are able to do this easily, you can practice this technique almost anywhere, at any time.

Notes

Use the space below to keep track of how these techniques work for you and any areas you want to improve on.

_____
_____
_____
_____
_____
_____
_____
_____
_____
_____
_____
_____
_____
_____
_____
_____
_____
_____
_____
_____
_____
_____
_____

ALCOHOL AND OTHER DRUGS WON'T HELP.

Using alcohol, tobacco and other drugs can actually cause problems that may lead to even more stress.

Alcohol

Alcohol is a depressant and slows down the central nervous system.

- Alcohol may make some stressed—out people feel even worse.
- Heavy use can even lead to depression.

Limit alcohol—or don't drink at all. (People who should not drink at all include women who are pregnant or trying to get pregnant and people recovering from alcoholism.) Ask your health-care provider what's best for you. Also talk to him or her if you think you may have a problem with alcohol use.

Other drugs

Never use illegal drugs. If you do, get help to stop.

Tobacco

This contains nicotine, which is addictive. At first, it acts as a stimulant, but later it works as a depressant and tranquilizer. Smoking can cause lung cancer, heart disease and many other conditions. If you smoke or use other forms of tobacco, get help to quit. Your health-care provider can be a great resource for information on quitting.

If you take any medication for symptoms of stress, be sure to follow your health-care provider's advice exactly.

ASKING FOR HELP IS NOT A SIGN OF WEAKNESS.

It shows you are strong enough to admit you need help.
Getting professional help is smart!

If stress and its effects start to get out of hand, consider contacting:

Your health-care provider

He or she may suggest changes in your diet and activities, or prescribe medication. He or she may refer you to a therapist or counselor.

Your local hospital

Many hospitals offer stress management courses and sponsor support groups. Mental health centers These provide a variety of services, such as emergency help and outpatient treatment.

Employee Assistance Programs (EAPs)

Many employers offer these programs. An EAP can provide employees with referral or counseling for issues like drug and alcohol abuse, relationship problems or job stress.

State and local mental health associations

These organizations are good sources of information and advice on stress. If cost is a problem, they may be able to help you find care based on ability to pay.

Other professionals

Clergy, social workers, counselors and therapists, psychiatrists, psychologists or nurses can provide information on stress and help solve problems.

By working through the exercises in this workbook, you'll be able to target areas where these professionals can help.

DEVELOPING A STRESS MANAGEMENT PLAN

Now that you have greater insight into what causes your stress, how you respond to stressors and how you use your time, you can start developing a plan to bring stress under control. Follow these steps:

1. Set a goal and a time frame

Your goal should address both a specific behavior and your reaction. For example, over the next month, your goal could be to meditate whenever you feel stressed.

You may want to set more than one goal. That's OK, however, don't try to meet too many at one time—you could add to your stress.

2. Get support

Tell family, friends or co-workers about your goals. They can offer you encouragement.

3. Track your progress

Consider keeping a daily log as you move toward your goal. Seeing improvement over time can keep you from feeling discouraged.

4. Reward yourself

Treat yourself when you reach a goal or get halfway there. For example, go to a movie or enjoy a special meal.

Keep in mind that stress will not disappear just by reading this workbook. Relieving stress takes time. It's also an ever-changing process—stress-reducing techniques may work better for you than others. When your stress change, change your strategy for dealing with them, if necessary.

Commit to change.

Congratulations! Now that you've reached this point, you've probably uncovered some ideas to help you reduce stress. Pick the ones that will help you reach your goals, and make a plan to start practicing them. Don't forget to include a target date for reaching your goals. Good luck!

Goal	Plan of action	Target date
_____	_____	_____
_____	_____	_____
_____	_____	_____
_____	_____	_____
_____	_____	_____
_____	_____	_____
_____	_____	_____
_____	_____	_____
_____	_____	_____
_____	_____	_____
_____	_____	_____
_____	_____	_____
_____	_____	_____

My supporters: _____

Method of tracking progress: _____

Reward for meeting my goal(s): _____

_____

_____

Date _____ Your signature _____

MANAGING ANGER AND CONFLICT

REENTRY
ESSENTIALS, INC.

Life Skills Series
Basic Skills for Lifelong Success

Please read:

Talk to your health-care provider! This workbook is not a substitute for the advice of a qualified health-care provider.

Reentry Essentials, Inc.
2609 East 14 Street, Suite 1018
Brooklyn, NY 11235-3915
P: 347.973.0004
E: info@ReentryEssentials.org
I: www.ReentryEssentials.org

This workbook belongs to:

_____

You may find it helpful to keep important names and phone numbers handy.

Write them below.

Primary health-care provider

Name_____

Phone_____

Other health-care providers

Name_____

Phone_____

Health plan

Plan Name_____

ID Number_____

Phone _____

Counselor

Name_____

Phone_____

An emergency contact

Name_____

Phone_____

Other important numbers

_____

_____

_____

_____

_____

_____

_____

_____

_____

THIS WORKBOOK IS ABOUT CONFLICT AND THE WAY IT MAKES YOU FEEL.

You'll learn about what conflict is, where it comes from and ways to resolve it.

Anger is a normal emotion.

Conflict can be a source of anger—people often have conflicts with each other. But learning to deal with angry feelings is your responsibility.

This workbook will help you focus on ways to resolve conflict without letting anger take control.

CONTENT

Conflict is a disagreement between 2 or more people.

It can occur when people:

- see things in different ways— for example, a parent and child may disagree on what a clean room should look like
- want different outcomes— for example, one member of a couple may want to get married while the other wants to keep dating
- have different ideas about how something should be done— for example, coworkers may disagree on how to divide up a group project among several people

Sometimes, a conflict happens because the people believe they have different goals or ideas, when really they have the same goal. That's why communication is key to solving conflicts in a healthy way.

Conflict often occurs because of misunderstandings.

These may involve:

- broken friendships and changing relationships—for example, friends may develop new interests and appear to grow apart, causing conflicts
- different perceptions about a person's race, sex, culture, class or religion
- dealings with difficult people— these could be co-workers, classmates, customers, relatives, neighbors, etc.
- jealousy over appearance, achievements or money— jealousy because a co-worker got a promotion, for example
- gossip and rumors

Conflict is normal.

Everyone faces conflict in his or her life. It's a natural part of relationships. Conflict can occur anywhere about anything. You could experience conflict with friends, family members or people at work. You may also experience conflict with a stranger (for example, if you feel you weren't given good service at a restaurant). Any part of your life can be affected.

It's how you deal with conflict that's important.

WHY DOES CONFLICT MAKE PEOPLE ANGRY?

Conflict can bring out many feelings that may lead to anger.
Conflict can make you feel:

Stressed

You may feel anxious and irritable because of work, family, health or money problems. Addressing these problems in a healthy way can help reduce your stress.

Frustrated

This can happen when things aren't in your control or if things don't work out the way you would like. Learning to let go of what you can't control— and focus on the things you can—can reduce frustration.

Afraid

Threats of violence and physical, verbal or emotional abuse can lead to fear. Or, you may be afraid that the relationship will fall apart because of the conflict.

Annoyed

Minor irritations and daily hassles can leave you feeling upset.

Disappointed

If something you expected doesn't happen, or if you don't get something you want, you may get angry. Learning to communicate clearly about what you want and expect can help prevent disappointment.

Resentful

If you've been hurt, rejected or offended, you may react with anger. Communicating your feelings and expectations positively can help make you feel empowered in a conflict situation.

Have you ever felt this way?

Write about a time you felt stressed, frustrated, afraid, annoyed, disappointed or resentful. What caused the feeling? What did you do about it?

_____

_____

_____

_____

_____

_____

_____

_____

_____

_____

Anger is a natural emotion. But to resolve conflict, you need to learn to deal with anger in a positive way.

CONFLICT CAN BE A GOOD THING
—If people work together to find a solution.
Resolving conflict can help:

Strengthen relationships

When people learn to work out their differences, they can overcome difficulties and make their relationships stronger.

Achieve personal growth

Unresolved conflict can prevent people from growing and changing. Learning to resolve conflict helps people overcome those barriers and grow personally and professionally.

Encourage greater understanding

For example, when 2 people have different backgrounds, they may look at the same situation in different ways. Resolving conflict can help them understand how the other person looks at things, and it can help them resolve or prevent future conflicts.

Foster good feelings

Resolving conflict can help:

- reduce stress
- make situations feel more positive
- increase self-esteem
- reduce anger

Have you had a good experience with conflict?

Write about a time when dealing with a conflict led to a positive outcome in your life.

What was the conflict about?

_____

_____

How did you work things out?

_____

_____

What was the positive outcome?

_____

_____

Learning to resolve conflict is in your best interest!

HOW TO YOU DEAL WITH CONFLICT?

Think about conflicts you've had in the past and how you dealt with them.

When faced with conflict, I've felt:

- ☐ angry
- ☐ hurt
- ☐ frustrated
- ☐ afraid
- ☐ powerless
- ☐ annoyed
- ☐ disappointed
- ☐ resentful
- ☐ upset
- ☐ overwhelmed
- ☐ other _____
- ☐ other _____

If I had a conflict with someone, I:

- ☐ avoided him or her
- ☐ yelled
- ☐ lost my temper
- ☐ pretended there was no problem
- ☐ talked about it
- ☐ criticized him or her
- ☐ resorted to violence
- ☐ thought of solutions
- ☐ other _____
- ☐ other _____

What could you have done differently?

Think of a conflict you've had recently that you wish you had handled better.

Describe the conflict:

_____

_____

_____

How did you deal with it?

_____

_____

_____

How do you think you could have handled it better? (If you're not sure, leave this blank for now and read on!)

_____

_____

_____

_____

_____

_____

_____

_____

UNRESOLVED CONFLICT CAN LEAD TO VIOLENCE.

It's common for people to feel angry during conflict. But if anger is not kept under control, it can be dangerous. Anger can lead to:

Verbal attacks

These may include:

- criticizing
- insulting
- threatening
- yelling

None of these are healthy ways to deal with anger— or solve conflicts.

Physical violence

For example, uncontrolled anger can lead to:

- hitting, slapping, shoving or kicking
- throwing or breaking things

Violence hurts everyone involved— and it never solves problems.

Abuse

Anger can cause people to lash out at others, even if the conflict has nothing to do with them. This abuse could be:

- Physical—hitting, kicking, etc.
- verbal— criticizing, insulting, threatening or yelling
- sexual—unwanted sexual contact, including rape

If you or someone you know is abusing or being abused, seek help right away.

Crime

Anger can also result in destruction of property, murder and other violent crimes.

Consequences of violence

Violence never has a happy ending. When uncontrolled anger leads to violence, it can result in:

- injury— to you, the victim or even a bystander
- hurt feelings, which can make it harder to mend the relationship
- prison time, if the victim presses charges
- death, if the violence gets out of control

Violence doesn't resolve conflict— it only makes things worse.

ALCOHOL AND OTHER DRUGS CAN ALSO MAKE CONFLICT WORSE.

Some people turn to alcohol or other drugs to help them deal with problems.

What alcohol and other drugs won't do:

- help you solve problems
- make you feel better about things when the effects wear off
- make angry feelings go away

What alcohol and other drugs will do:

- impair your judgment
- make it more difficult to think of solutions to conflict
- increase the risk of violence
- put you at risk for addiction

Alcohol or other drugs may increase your anger.

Alcohol or other drug use may mask angry feelings for a short time. But those feelings don't go away! The only way to deal with anger is to learn to manage it. Substance use can intensify angry feelings. Many cases of violence are related to the use of alcohol and other drugs.

Does substance use affect how you deal with conflict?

- ☐ I turn to alcohol or other drugs when I'm under stress.
- ☐ I use alcohol or other drugs to avoid dealing with problems.
- ☐ I sometimes get upset, angry or violent after using alcohol or other drugs

If you checked any of these statements, alcohol and/or other drugs may be affecting how you deal with conflict.

If you have a problem· with alcohol or other drugs:

- Contact the Center for Substance Abuse Treatment's Referral service at:
  1-800-662-HELP
  (1-800-662-4357)
  1-800-487-4889 TDD)
  www.findtreatment.samhsa.gov.

• Look in the phone book for numbers of local support groups.

Alcohol and other drugs are no excuse for losing control of your anger.

RELATIONSHIPS CAN BE A SOURCE OF CONFLICT.

People in any type of relationship can have a misunderstanding or disagreement.

Family

Conflict can occur with a spouse, child, brother or sister, parent, grandparent or other family member. What are sources of conflict you've experienced with your family?

☐   finances

☐   school performance

☐   choice of friends

☐   lack of privacy

☐   household responsibilities

☐   other _____

☐   other _____

☐   other _____

Think of the last time you had a conflict at home. How did it affect your family life?

_____

_____

_____

_____

_____

_____

Friends

Even the closest of friends can experience conflict. Think about friendships you've had. What sources of conflict did you experience?

☐   disagreement about what to do

☐   pressure to use alcohol or other drugs

☐   dislike of person's other friends

☐   less time to see each other because of a new boyfriend or girlfriend

☐   other _____

☐   other _____

☐   other _____

Think of the last time you had a conflict with a friend. How did it affect your friendship?

_____

_____

_____

_____

_____

_____

You can also have conflicts with people you don't know that well.

CONFLICT CAN OCCUR AT WORK.
Professional relationships can also be a source of conflict.

Your supervisor

Think of jobs that you have had or that you have now. What sources of conflict have you had with your supervisor?

☐ work performance

☐ working conditions

☐ tardiness

☐ lack of recognition

☐ lack of promotion

☐ unrealistic goals

☐ disagreement over salary or performance reviews

☐ lack of communication

☐ other _____

☐ other _____

Other workers

Think about the people you've worked with. What are some sources of conflict you've had with them?

☐ questions about a person's competence

☐ one person promoted over the other

☐ different salaries

☐ a person not being productive for a group project

☐ one person taking credit for a group project

☐ conflicting personalities, communication styles or work preferences

☐ other _____

☐ other _____

Think of the last time you had a conflict at work. How did it affect your job?

_____

_____

_____

_____

_____

_____

_____

_____

_____

_____

_____

_____

_____

_____

_____

_____

_____

_____

_____

_____

OTHER SOURCES OF STRESS CAN PLAY A ROLE IN CONFLICT.

All of us experience stress. But stress can build up and add to any angry feelings during conflict.

Check off any sources of stress that you've experienced:

Health and emotional problems

☐ a chronic illness

☐ chronic pain

☐ depression

☐ anxiety

☐ problems with a loved

☐ one's health

☐ worry about treatment

☐ loss of a loved one (grief)

☐ other _____

☐ other _____

Daily hassles

☐ traffic

☐ long/difficult commute

☐ rude people

☐ long lines

☐ other _____

☐ other _____

☐ other _____

Money problems

☐ mounting bills

☐ a large financial loss or gain

☐ medical costs

☐ a job loss

☐ a new loan or mortgage

☐ credit card debt

☐ legal fees

☐ bankruptcy

☐ other _____

☐ other _____

Other problems

☐ moving

☐ changing jobs or schools

☐ separation or divorce

☐ a child having trouble at school

☐ other _____

☐ other _____

SOMETIMES, THE CONFLICT YOU'RE FACING IS NOT THE SOURCE OF ANGER.

You may find yourself in a conflict with someone right now. But it may be other factors or conflicts that make you feel angry.

Past events

You may still carry angry feelings toward someone because of a conflict in the past that was left unresolved. These feelings can surface when a new conflict occurs with that person.

Feelings and doubts

For example, you may feel that a person doesn't trust you. But instead of asking the person about it, you may start an argument over something else. Or you may be jealous if a friend starts spending time with another person, and wonder if the friend likes the other person better. You may start arguing with your friend because of these doubts— whether they're true or not.

Associations

Someone may look or act like another person with whom you didn't get along. When you interact with this new person, you may think about things that went wrong with the other person. This can lead you to dislike the new person—even if you don't know him or her.

When you feel angry during a conflict, think about these other factors.

Ask yourself if there is something else besides the current conflict that may be making you feel angry. If there are other factors, they need to be addressed before any conflict can be resolved.

What are the sources of anger in your life?

Do you have angry feelings about someone or something in your past? Is it affecting the way you deal with conflict now? Write about it here.

_____

_____

_____

_____

_____

_____

_____

_____

_____

_____

_____

_____

_____

_____

_____

_____

_____

_____

_____

It's important to sort out your feelings when faced with conflict

WHAT IS THE SOURCE OF YOUR CONFLICT?

Think of a conflict you're having with someone now.
Try to sort out your feelings by answering these questions.

What is your relationship with this person?

_____

_____

_____

_____

Describe the conflict with this person and how it started. Be as specific as you can.

_____

_____

_____

_____

_____

_____

_____

_____

_____

_____

_____

_____

_____

_____

_____

_____

_____

_____

_____

How does the conflict make you feel?

☐ angry

☐ annoyed

☐ hurt

☐ disappointed

☐ frustrated

☐ resentful

☐ afraid

☐ upset

☐ powerless

☐ overwhelmed

☐ other _____

☐ other _____

☐ other _____

How have you been treating this person since the conflict began?

☐ avoiding him or her

☐ talking about it

☐ yelling

☐ criticizing him or her

☐ losing my temper

☐ getting violent

☐ pretending there is no problem

☐ thinking of solutions together

☐ other _____

☐ other _____

☐ other _____

Other factors

Did this person do something in the past that you're still angry about?

☐ Yes   ☐ No

If yes, what was it?

_____

_____

_____

Are there any feelings or doubts you have about this person that could be making you angry?

☐ Yes   ☐ No

If yes, what was it?

_____

_____

_____

Does this person remind you of someone you don't like?

☐ Yes   ☐ No

If yes, what was it?

_____

_____

_____

How has your relationship with this person been affected by the conflict?

_____

_____

_____

_____

_____

_____

_____

_____

_____

_____

_____

_____

_____

_____

_____

_____

_____

_____

_____

_____

_____

_____

_____

_____

_____

_____

_____

_____

Now learn some effective ways to deal with conflict—without letting anger take control.

LEARN TO RELAX.

When you're feeling tense and stressed, you're likely to get angry when faced with conflict. This means you are less likely to be able to work out a solution.

Some good ways to reduce stress include:

Regular physical activity

Exercise is a great way to work off stress and relax. It also keeps you healthy! Get at least 150 minutes of moderate— or 75 minutes of vigorous— physical activity each week. In addition, do muscle-strengthening exercises on 2 days.

Check the activities you might enjoy:

☐ walking

☐ running

☐ swimming

☐ golf

☐ tennis

☐ basketball

☐ other _____

☐ other _____

Be sure to consult your healthcare provider before starting an exercise program.

Hobbies

These can be a productive outlet for tension and energy. Check the hobbies you enjoy or would like to try:

☐ reading

☐ collecting (stamps, antiques, etc.)

☐ cooking

☐ arts and crafts (painting, ceramics, drawing, knitting, etc.)

☐ playing a musical instrument

☐ other _____

☐ other _____

Progressive muscle relaxation

You tense and then relax muscle groups one at a time from head to toe until you feel relaxed. Here's how:

1. Get comfortable. Wear loose clothing. Sit in a comfortable chair or lie down.
2. Tense the muscles in your face for 5-10 seconds. Then relax them for about 20 seconds.
3. Tense the muscles in the back of your neck for 5-10 seconds. Then relax them for about 20 seconds. Notice the difference in how your muscles feel when relaxed.
4. Move down to your shoulders. Tense and relax the muscles the same way you did in step 3.
5. Repeat the same steps with the other muscle groups in your body— arms, chest, hands, stomach, lower back, buttocks, thighs, calves and feet— one at a time.

Deep-breathing exercises

These can help you calm down when you feel yourself getting angry. Follow these steps:

1. Sit comfortably or lie on your back.
2. Breathe in slowly and deeply through your nose for a count of 5.
3. Hold your breath for 3-5 seconds.
4. Breathe out slowly through your mouth for a count of 5, pushing out all the air.
5. Repeat until you feel calm and relaxed.

Other relaxation techniques

These include:

- visualization— you imagine a pleasant, peaceful scene and focus on it for a set amount of time
- guided imagery— you are guided through a series of exercises in which you visualize peaceful scenes

What helps you relax?

You may have something special you like to do to relax, such as taking a long walk, calling a friend or writing in a journal. Describe what you do to relax here.

_____

_____

_____

_____

_____

_____

_____

_____

_____

_____

_____

_____

_____

_____

_____

_____

_____

_____

_____

PREPARE YOURSELF FOR CONFLICT.

You can't always predict what kind of conflict you'll have to face.
But you can learn to handle it better.

Build your communication skills.

It's easier to resolve conflict when everyone involved can explain his or her thoughts and feelings. Anyone can improve his or her communication skills. See page 214 to learn how to improve your communication skills.

Be ready to discuss the problem.

- Be willing to talk about what the problem is and what can be done about it. Don't avoid the person. This does nothing to solve the problem and may make it worse.
- Don't attack or criticize the other person. Also, avoid name-calling.
- Try to keep the conversation focused on the problem at hand. Don't bring up unrelated problems from the past.
- Don't drag others into it, such as friends, family members or co-workers. It's up to you and the other person to try to work out the problem.

Develop an anger management plan.

- Use the chart on page 212 for your anger management plan.
- Begin by setting 1 or 2 goals for your behavior and actions. For example, over the next month, your goal could be to exercise 3 times a week.
- Talk to family, friends and co-workers about your goals. Ask if they'll support you and if you can call them when you're having trouble with angry feelings.
- Track your progress. Keep a daily log or journal. Write down the times you get angry and how you handle it.
- Reward yourself. When you reach a goal, treat yourself to a movie or something fun!

IF YOU FEEL YOURSELF GETTING ANGRY
If a conflict gets heated, don't let anger take control!

Get away.

Walk away from the person. Don't go back until you've calmed down. Staying may only make your angry feelings stronger, and things could get violent.

Work off your angry feelings.

- Exercise.
- Spend time with your hobby.
- Use a relaxation method (such as deep-breathing exercises, progressive muscle relaxation or visualization).
- Talk with someone. This could be a close friend, healthcare provider or counselor.

Don't think about the conflict with the person during this time. Give yourself a chance to calm down. Then go back and try to solve the problem.

Approach the person and try to work it out.

Ask the person if the two of you can agree to have a calm discussion about the conflict. If the person does not agree, don't pursue it. He or she may also be angry and may need time to cool down. Ask the person again another time.

Consider mediation.

A mediator is a third person who tries to help people work out a solution to their conflict. A mediator:

- listens to both sides
- finds out what each person wants out of the situation
- makes sure only 1 person speaks at a time
- helps both sides agree on a way to settle the problem

A mediator doesn't take sides! He or she is a neutral party who is there to help 2 sides reach an agreement. A mediator doesn't make decisions, but he or she can help other people resolve their differences. (To find a mediator, check your local phone book.)

When you're dealing with conflict, try to keep anger out of the process.

MY ANGER MANAGEMENT PLAN

Goal	Action Plan	Target Date	Reward

People I can call on if I need help:

_____

_____

_____

_____

_____

_____

_____

DON'T GET PERSONAL.

Remember the other person is not the problem—the conflict is.

Don't abuse the other person.

This includes:

- hitting, kicking or slapping
- yelling
- criticizing, blaming or accusing
- insulting or name-calling
- threatening

Be prepared to talk.

If you're faced with a conflict:

- Discuss what the problem is and how you can work together to fix it.
- Focus on the problem that is causing the conflict— not other things that might be bothering you.

Don't bring up past conflicts.

If you've had conflicts with this person before, now is not the time to discuss them. If these conflicts were resolved, don't bring them up. If there is an unresolved conflict that you would like to talk about, bring it up in another conversation. Deal with one conflict at a time.

Has this happened to you?

Write about a conflict you had where you or the other person "got personal" in a way described to the left.

What was the situation?

_____

_____

_____

How did the conflict "get personal"?

_____

_____

_____

How did it make you feel?

_____

_____

_____

What was the outcome?

_____

_____

_____

Getting personal gets in the way of resolving conflict. Don't make the person the focus— even if you don't like him or her.

GOOD COMMUNICATION HELPS PREVENT MISUNDERSTANDINGS.

Improving your communication skills can help resolve—and prevent—conflict.

Listen to what the other person is saying.

- Give the person your full attention when he or she is talking.
- Focus on what he or she is saying— not on your next response.
- Keep your eyes on the person as he or she speaks, so he or she knows you care about what's said.
- Don't judge or criticize.
- Don't interrupt.

Pay attention to body language.

Posture and facial expressions say a lot about how a person feels. For example, a scowling face probably means the person is unhappy.

Make sure you understand.

Repeat what the person told you in your own words. This can:

- help you understand what was said
- give the other person a chance to correct any misunderstanding
- let the other person know you are paying attention

Ask questions if you don't understand what he or she said.

Consider the other person's point of view.

Try to look at the conflict through his or her eyes. Ask yourself:

- Is this person under any kind of pressure?
- Could he or she be having a bad day?
- How does this conflict affect him or her?

Be specific.

Now state the problem as you understand it. Be as specific as possible. For example, "You're always doing this!" is too general. A better way to state a problem would be: "I don't like it when you don't call and let me know you're running late."

Use 'I' statements.

These are statements that help you focus on your needs, wants and feelings— without blaming the other person. For example: "I feel angry when things are left on the floor because it makes a mess. Next time, I would like you to put them away."

How would you describe your conflict?

Think of the conflict from page 206. Use an "I" statement to explain it:

"I feel _____

when _____

_____."

"Next time, I would like _____

_____

_____."

Watch your body language.

- Your body sends messages when you're angry.
- Keep your arms uncrossed. Take your hands off your hips.
- Don't point or wag your finger at the person.
- Speak in a calm voice.

Practice rephrasing the following statements into specific "I'" statements.

"You're always tracking mud into the house'"

"I" statement: _____

_____

"You're never ready to leave on time! Why can't you be more organized?"

"I" statement: _____

_____

You're always on my back. Leave me alone!

"I" statement: _____

_____

"You didn't finish the report on time. Now I'm behind with my work because of you."

"I" statement: _____

_____

You can improve your communication skills with practice.

BE ASSERTIVE.

When you're faced with a conflict, it's important to tell the other person
What you want. People often react to conflict by being:

Aggressive

People who act aggressively:

- are only concerned about what they want
- often give in to their anger
- don't really care about what the other person wants or how he or she feels
- may not even let the other person talk
- may demand, threaten or use force to get what they want Aggressive people don't mind fighting.

Passive

People who act passively don't like to deal with conflict. They:

- often don't express their feelings or tell anyone what they want
- give in to what the other person wants
- try to withdraw from the conflict or try to ignore it completely
- might say that they don't care about the conflict— but they do

Some people act in "passive-aggressive" ways. They may react passively. Then they give the "silent treatment" or act in ways that indirectly go against what the other person wants.

Assertive

People who act assertively express their feelings and are able to say what they want. But they also want a solution that's good for the other person, too. They stand up for their rights but recognize that the other person also has rights. They are willing to listen to another point of view.

What style do you use?

Think about your own communication style. Do you tend to be aggressive, passive or assertive? Write it here:

_____

_____

_____

_____

_____

_____

_____

_____

_____

_____

_____

_____

_____

_____

When you are assertive, you stand a better chance of working out the best possible solution— for both of you!

PRACTICE BEING ASSERTIVE.

Not sure if you know how to be assertive during a conflict? Practice here first.

Here's an example.

Ray's roommate keeps leaving his things on the floor and doesn't put them away. Here are 3 ways Ray could talk to his roommate about it:

Aggressive

"Stop throwing your stuff all over the floor! If you do it again, I'm throwing it away!"

Passive

"I was thinking maybe if it's not a problem, you could put that stuff away, if you think of it."

Assertive

"I don't like it when there's stuff on the floor. Could you please pick it up and put it away? I'd appreciate that."

Which approach do you think would work best?

What could you say?

Think about the conflict you wrote down on page 206. What would you like the person to do about the problem? Write down 3 ways of saying it:

Aggressive: _____

_____

_____

_____

Passive: _____

_____

_____

_____

Assertive: _____

_____

_____

_____

The assertive approach should be the one that explains how you feel without blaming the other person.

WORKING ON A SOLUTION
You can work out a solution to your problem if you follow these steps.

1. Stay calm.

When you're angry or upset, you're not able to focus on solutions. Remember, if you feel yourself losing your temper and think your anger might get out of control, walk away. Come back to work on the conflict once you've calmed down.

2. Agree on what the problem is.

Before you think about solutions, take turns describing the problem. Use the communication skills on page 214. Repeat this process until both of you feel you have defined the problem.

For example, one person was angry because he tripped over his roommate's stuff, which was all over the floor. His roommate told him he needs to watch his step. After talking about it, both decided that the actual problem was that the roommate was leaving his stuff on the floor.

3. Brainstorm.

Think of ways to solve the problem. The solution has to be one that works for both of you. If it only works for one side, then nothing is resolved, and the conflict will probably come up again. Think of as many different ideas as you can. For now, don't worry about if they would actually work.

For example, Ray doesn't like the way his roommate throws his stuff on the floor. He comes up with 3 possible solutions to the problem:

1. Asking the roommate to move out.
2. Telling him he can't keep his stuff in the apartment.
3. Asking him to keep his stuff in the closet.

4. Weigh the pros and cons.

After you've come up with several different solutions, think about the good points (pros) and bad points (cons) of each one.

For example, here are some pros and cons of Ray's 3 possible solutions:

1. *Pro:* His roommate won't be able to leave stuff on the floor.
   Con: He can't afford the apartment by himself.
2. *Pro:* The stuff will be out of the apartment, and not on the floor.
   Con: His roommate might need that stuff.
3. *Pro:* The stuff could be off the floor.
   Con: His roommate might forget to use the closet sometimes.

Solutions 1 and 2 probably wouldn't work. But the third solution might. Think of as many pros and cons to each solution as you can.

The solution with the most pros and the least cons generally has the best chance of working. Remember— stay positive!

WHAT ARE POSSIBLE SOLUTIONS TO YOUR CONFLICT?
Think again of the conflict you wrote down on page 206.

The problem	**Three possible solutions**	**Pros and cons**

The problem

Work with the other person to define what the problem is in your conflict. Write down what you both come up with:

_____

_____

_____

_____

_____

_____

_____

_____

_____

_____

_____

Three possible solutions

Now, try to think of solutions to the problem and write them down:

_____

_____

_____

_____

_____

_____

_____

_____

_____

_____

Pros and cons

Weigh the pros and cons for each solution and write them down. (Use a separate sheet of paper if you need more room.)

1. Pro: _____

    _____

    Con:_____

    _____

2. Pro: _____

    _____

    Con:_____

    _____

3. Pro: _____

    _____

    Con:_____

    _____

Which solution has the most pros and the fewest cons?

CHOOSE A SOLUTION AND TRY IT.
Remember the solution needs to be the best one for both of you.

Agree to try it.

Discuss the solutions with the other person. When you agree on one that sounds good for both sides, agree to try it out. Be specific about what you each expect to happen. For example, Ray's roommate can agree to put his stuff in the closet each day when he comes home.

Give it time to work.

Solutions may not work right away. Many times, people need to learn a new habit or new way of doing things. This takes time. The person's roommate may not put his stuff in the closet one day. This doesn't mean he's ignoring the solution that was agreed on. He might be busy and forget.

Talk to the other person and agree on a specific amount of time you'll give the solution to work. Also agree not to argue about the problem during that time.

If it doesn't work, try something else!

The solution you agree on won't always work. Wait until the time you agreed on is up. If either side feels that the solution is not working, talk about the problem again. Try to find another solution. Don't give up!

What solution might work best for you?

Look back on page 219. Which solution do you think might work best for your conflict?

_____

_____

_____

_____

Talk to the other person and compare the solutions you each came up with. Tell the person what solution you think would work best and why. Don't get upset if the person doesn't agree with you. Keep talking until you find a solution you can both accept.

How is your solution working?

Use this space to write down how you feel the solution you agreed on is working overtime.

_____

_____

_____

_____

_____

_____

_____

_____

_____

_____

_____

_____

_____

_____

_____

_____

DEALING WITH SOMEONE ELSE'S ANGER
Here's what you can do:

Keep calm.

Don't respond to the person's anger with anger of your own. This will only make things worse and could lead to violence. Try to stay calm.

Don't take it personally.

The person may yell at you, criticize you or call you names. Remember, people say many things they don't mean when they're angry. Try to understand why the person is angry. It may have nothing to do with you at all.

Listen.

Let the person express his or her feelings. He or she may just need to "blow off steam." Pay attention and don't interrupt.

Try to focus on the problem.

If the person seems to have a conflict with you, think about what the problem could be. Suggest that you both agree to discuss it at another time when you are both calm.

Think of your own safety.

If you don't feel safe, get help. Leave yourself an escape path and run away if you feel the person is going to attack you.

If the person has a weapon, don't waste any time. Go for safety as soon as possible. Don't confront the person or try to restrain him or her. Get away at the first opportunity and call the police or sheriff.

Remember, safety first.

Things can quickly escalate to violence when a person is:

- speaking to you in an aggressive way (yelling, insulting, name-calling)
- using intimidating body language (standing very close, raising hands or fists)
- threatening you with physical violence
- refusing to calm down when you try to defuse the situation

Trust your instincts. If you feel threatened or unsafe, get away as fast as you can.

SOURCES OF HELP

If you're having problems dealing with conflict or controlling your anger, there are many people who can help.

Your health-care provider

He or she can suggest relaxation techniques. Your health-care provider may also prescribe medications for health conditions related to your anger.

Mental health professionals and mental health centers

They may offer help with conflict resolution and anger management through outpatient treatment, support groups and other services.

Counselors, family therapists or social workers

They can help you learn ways to deal with conflict, manage anger, control stress and solve problems.

Mediators

They can help you resolve conflict—if both you and the other person decide to try mediation. Check your local phone book.

Hotlines

Hotlines may provide emergency counseling to help you control angry feelings or behavior. Check your local phone book.

Employee Assistance Programs (EAPs)

These may offer referrals or counseling to help employees deal with issues like alcohol or other drug problems, job stress and relationship problems.

Religious leaders

They may offer advice and reassurance— or just listen if you need someone to talk to.

CONFLICT CAN BE A GOOD THING
—if you learn to manage anger and solve conflicts in a healthy way!
When you are faced with a conflict, remember to:

Manage your anger.

When you feel yourself getting angry, take steps to calm down. Follow the management plan you created on page 212.

Define the problem.

Think about what you're really upset about— and what your goal is.

Communicate.

Take the time to talk with the other person in a calm, respectful way. Work together to solve the problem.

You can learn to manage conflict and anger in a positive way!

MANAGING CREDIT WISELY

REENTRY
ESSENTIALS, INC.

Life Skills Series
Basic Skills for Lifelong Success

Please read:

Talk to a professional! This workbook is not a substitute for the advice of a qualified expert.

Reentry Essentials, Inc.
2609 East 14 Street, Suite 1018
Brooklyn, NY 11235-3915
P: 347.973.0004
E: info@ReentryEssentials.org
I: www.ReentryEssentials.org

This workbook belongs to:

_____

You may find it helpful to keep important names and phone numbers handy.

Write them below.

Bank/credit union

Name _____

Phone _____

Website _____

Credit card companies

Name _____

Phone _____

Website _____

Name _____

Phone _____

Website _____

Mortgage lender

Name _____

Phone _____

Website _____

Credit/debt counselor

Name _____

Phone _____

Other important numbers

_____

_____

_____

_____

_____

_____

USED WISELY, CREDIT CAN BE A HELPFUL TOOL.

Credit comes in different forms.

These include:

- credit cards
- auto and personal loans
- home mortgages

Credit allows you to borrow money, with the promise to repay the loan over time or at a later date.

Credit isn't free money. In addition to paying back what you borrowed, you will likely have to pay interest and fees.

Managing credit is a skill.

The keys are to:

- understand credit
- know when to use credit and when not to use it
- manage debt the right way
- get help if you need it

Having good credit can help you reach your goals.

Having credit problems can hurt your chances of getting the things you want most.

This workbook can help you take control of credit.

CONTENT

HAVING CREDIT HAS ADVANTAGES.

Credit can help if you are:

Planning to buy a home

For many people, buying a home is an important long-term goal. A mortgage loan lets you pay for a home over a long period of time. This can help you enjoy the benefits of owning a home sooner than if you had to save for the whole home price. For example, you can:

- avoid paying rent
- build equity (ownership) in your home as you make regular payments
- deduct interest payments from your taxes

Making large purchases

Paying with a loan or credit card can make sense when you plan to purchase large items that will be useful for a long period of time. These items can include:

- a vehicle
- a major appliance

Paying for an education

Education can be a smart investment in a person's future. You may choose to borrow money to pay educational expenses for:

- your child
- your spouse
- yourself

Starting or investing in a business

Borrowing money to make a business investment, or to start a business, can help you or your spouse reach your financial goals.

Facing an emergency

Credit can help you pay for events you don't plan for, such as:

- fixing a vehicle
- replacing an appliance

Traveling

If you travel, a credit card can offer convenience and security. For example, you can:

- avoid carrying a lot of cash
- pay for items and services at businesses that don't accept checks
- keep track of purchases you've made
- get the best exchange rate when traveling out of the country

Shopping online or by phone

Paying with a credit card can be faster and easier than paying by check.

MISUSING CREDIT CAN COST YOU.

Credit is not a tool for living beyond your financial means. Misusing credit can lead to:

Overspending

Credit is not meant to pay for everyday expenses. You may end up spending more than you make if you use credit for:

- clothing and household goods
- car payments
- groceries
- eating out and entertainment

If you don't pay your entire credit card balance each month, you will have to pay interest charges, which could be very high.

Budget trouble

Having to make regular payments on credit cards and loans may mean you have less money to:

- pay necessary monthly expenses, such as utility bills and insurance premiums
- build your savings

Debt problems

Misusing credit can lead to debt that is difficult or impossible to control. For example:

- If you get behind on payments, you may have to pay penalty fees and higher interest charges. This can make it even harder to pay off what you owe.
- You may have to choose between making payments for regular expenses or for debt.
- You may find it hard to get more credit from reputable sources.

Problems like these can lower your credit score. (See pages 243-245 for information on credit scores.)

Difficulty reaching your goals

A credit problem can get you off track from reaching long-term goals, such as:

- an emergency fund
- home ownership
- a secure retirement

Stress

For example, you may:

- worry about how to provide for your family
- fear that you will lose your home or vehicle
- be forced to deal with creditors asking you to pay your bills

Stress can lead to physical illness and emotional problems.

Strained family relationships

You and your spouse may disagree about how to best handle money matters.

Career problems

For example:

- Stress about money matters can make it hard to focus on your job.
- Some employers look at credit reports before making job offers or promoting employees.

CREDIT IS ONE TOOL—BUT NOT THE ONLY ONE— THAT CAN HELP YOU REACH YOUR GOALS.

Think about your goals and how you plan to reach them. Consider:

Short-term vs. long-term goals

- A short-term goal may be something you want or need within a year or so.
- A long-term goal may be something you plan for many years down the road.

Wants vs. needs

Decide whether something is a necessity or a luxury. This may help you decide whether it is a priority—and what is the best method to pay for it.

Avoid buying something because it feels good at the moment. You may regret it later.

Your financial options

Think about how much your goal will cost. Then, consider your options for getting there. For example, you could consider:

- saving to reach your goal
- paying with a credit card
- taking out a loan

Use this worksheet to help organize your goals—and plan the best way to reach them.

Goal: _____

Short-term or long-term? _____

Want or need? _____

Pay with savings, credit or a loan? Note a positive and negative of each: _____

_____

Goal: _____

Short-term or long-term? _____

Want or need? _____

Pay with savings, credit or a loan? Note a positive and negative of each: _____

_____

GIVE YOURSELF CREDIT.

Building a good credit history can help you make sure credit is available when you need it. Having good credit can also help you get lower interest rates on loans.

Open checking and savings accounts.

This helps show that you can manage money responsibly. In addition, some banks and credit unions make better loan offers to their account holders. Here are some tips:

- Shop around at different banks and credit unions. Ask about account options and the benefits of each. Be sure you understand what the fees are, whether you must keep a minimum balance and other requirements.
- Add to your accounts on a regular basis. Consider having money automatically deposited to your accounts each time you get paid.
- Keep careful track of your checking account. Record all deposits and withdrawals as they happen. Balance your checkbook each month by comparing your statement to your register. Understand that "bouncing" a check can hurt your credit record! (You may also want to use your bank's online banking services.)

Consider applying for a store card.

If you have no credit history, this type of card may be easier to get than a bank-issued credit card. You can use the card to make small purchases that you pay for in full right away. Once you have a history of making payments on time, you may be approved for a bank credit card.

Keep in mind that many store cards:

- carry higher interest rates than bank-issued cards
- start off with a low interest rate that quickly changes to a much higher rate
- offer coupons and other discounts to try to get you to use your card more often

That's why it's so important to charge only what you can afford to pay for in full each month.

Learn about secured credit cards.

Secured credit cards may help you build a credit history in a short time. Here's how they work:

- You deposit a certain amount of your own money in an account. This is your credit line.
- You get a credit card and can buy things up to the amount in your account.

Consider getting someone to cosign.

If you have no credit history, you may be able to get a credit card or loan by asking a friend or relative to cosign for it. Beware that if you make late payments, this will hurt both of your credit scores.

See pages 243-245 to learn about credit scores— and how to improve a poor credit record.

CHOOSING A CREDIT CARD

Plan how to use the card.

- It's best to pay off the balance in full each month. If this is your plan, look for a card with a long grace period (the length of time you are given to pay in full before being charged interest) and a low, or preferably no, annual fee.
- If you know you will carry a balance, look for a card with a low-interest rate.

Consider "perks" carefully.

Many credit card companies offer rewards to get people to sign up for and use credit cards. For example, some cards offer:

- cash back on purchases
- points that can be used for goods or services
- discounts at certain businesses

These offers may seem like a good deal. But consider the possible downside. The offers may also come with higher interest rates and annual fees. Avoid these if you think you may carry a balance from month to month.

Shop around.

Read the offers you get carefully so you understand all fees, rates and payment terms. (Companies must post standard credit card pricing and terms online, too.) Be aware that some credit card companies may try to lure you with offers, such as:

- a low introductory rate
- the chance to transfer balances from other credit cards

It's important to ask questions before choosing a card. The list of questions on this page can help you compare offers.

Don't assume that "pre-approval" means a better deal.

You may get many credit card offers. Being pre-approved simply means that you may have met certain credit standards. It doesn't automatically mean you'll get a lower interest rate or no annual fee.

Ask these questions.

When comparing credit card offers, get answers to the following questions:

- Is there an annual fee? If so, how much is it and when is it billed?
- What is the grace period before interest is charged?
- What is the grace period for making a payment?
- Do you offer an introductory interest rate? What is it and how long does it last? What will the rate be when this period ends? (See page 236 for more information about how finance charges may be calculated.)
- Is the interest rate fixed or variable? Will it go up if I pay late? How will I find out about rate changes?
- Are there any other situations in which the rate can go up?
- Is there a late payment fee?
- What other fees do you charge (for example, fees for balance transfers, cash advances, going over the credit limit or closing an account)?

OTHER TYPES OF CARDS

Some cards may look like regular credit cards, but there are important differences.

Travel and entertainment cards

These are sometimes called charge cards. Here's how they work:

- When you first use them, they work like a credit card. Instead of paying with cash or a check, you can use the card.
- When the statement arrives, you must pay the entire balance by the due date.
- If you don't pay on time, you may face very high interest rates and your card may be canceled.
- Unlike credit cards that may offer no annual fee, these cards usually have high annual fees (which may be called membership or service charges).

Debit cards

A debit card is not a credit card. It may be issued by a bank or credit union and is linked to a checking account. When you use the card to buy something, the amount is taken out of your account right away. A debit card may be a good option if you:

- want the convenience of a credit card but want to avoid paying a bill at the end of each month
- don't want to carry cash with you

Many businesses accept debit cards in addition to cash, credit cards and checks.

To manage debit cards wisely:

- Subtract the amount of each transaction from your checkbook register.
- Compare your statement with your receipts to make sure there were no mistakes. Report any unauthorized transactions or errors immediately. (You may be able to check your account online or by phone. Ask your bank or credit union for more information.)
- To avoid paying fees, use an automated teller machine (ATM) that is owned by your financial institution or is part of its network.
- Consider an overdraft protection plan if you're worried about overdrawing your account. This is a line of credit that allows you to use more money than what's in your account—but you have to pay the bank interest on that amount.

MANAGING CREDIT CARDS

Responsible credit card use can help you avoid debt—and keep your budget in check.

Limit credit card use.

Don't charge items you can't afford. Only charge items and services that you can pay for in full when the credit card bill comes. Carrying a balance can cost you a lot in interest charges. (See page 237 for more information.) It may help to set a monthly limit for charge purchases.

Be wary of sales and discounts.

Shopping for bargains makes sense. But if you charge items that you can't afford, the amount you save may be less than the finance charges you must pay.

Write down all of your charges.

This can help you:

- track spending and know when you're reaching your limit
- avoid being surprised by a large credit card bill
- spot any incorrect or false charges on your bill

You can use the chart on the next page to keep track. (You may also be able to track charges online.)

Pay with cash, when possible

Paying in cash can

make it easier to:

- avoid buying things you don't really need
- stay within your budget

Limit yourself to one card, if possible.

Making charges to multiple cards can make it harder to:

- keep track of how much you're charging
- stay within your budget, since you'll have to make payments on each account

Also, avoid using your entire credit limit. Just because it's there doesn't mean you can afford it.

Avoid cash advances.

Cash advances from credit card companies may allow you to get cash from an automated teller machine (ATM) or write a check on your credit card account. They may seem like an easy way to get cash quickly. However, these transactions can cost you in the long run. Cash advances may be subject to:

- a higher interest rate than the rate you are charged to buy things
- interest charged beginning on the day you take the advance (in other words, there is no grace period)
- a fee, sometimes a percentage of the amount you take in cash

Compare your receipts with your monthly statement.

If you spot an error, be sure you know:

- how long you have to report the mistake
- the process for fighting a charge

Pay your bill on time.

Mail your payment 7-10 days before the due date to be sure it arrives in time. This can help you:

- avoid interest rate increases (late payments can trigger rates of 20-30% and higher!)
- avoid late payment fees
- raise your credit rating or keep it high

You may also be able to pay your bill online.

Pay the entire balance, if possible.

If you pay the entire balance within the grace period, you can avoid paying any finance charges.

Report address changes in advance.

Even if you don't receive a bill, you are still responsible for making payments on time.

Help prevent credit card fraud

- Don't give your credit card information in response to an e-mail or a telephone call unless you asked the business to contact you.
- When shopping online, only buy from trusted Web sites that use security features. If you see "https://" in your browser's address bar, the site is secure.
- Don't loan your card to anyone.
- Keep your copy of every receipt.

Credit Card Purchase Record

Write down the month and the charge limit you have set for yourself. Also, list when the payment is due. Keep track of all credit card purchases and total them up at the end of the month.

Month: _____ Monthly charge limit: _____ Payment due date: _____

Date	Description of Items/Services	Amount
	Total amount:	

UNDERSTAND CREDIT CARD INTEREST CHARGES.

In general, the interest charge on your credit card is your unpaid balance multiplied by your interest rate. But creditors may use any of the following methods to calculate your balance:

Average daily balance

This is the most common method used by credit card companies. To calculate a balance, the creditor:

1. Takes each day's beginning balance and then subtracts payments (credits) made to your account on that day.
2. Adds up all the daily balances for the billing period (for example, 1 month.)
3. Divides the total by the number of days in the billing period.

Some creditors include new charges (purchases and/or cash advances) in your daily balance. Others do not.

Previous balance method

This method uses the balance owed from the last billing period. It does not subtract payments or credits or add in new charges. This is typically the most expensive method.

Adjusted balance method

This method is usually the best for credit consumers. This method:

1. Takes the balance on your account from the last billing period.
2. Subtracts payments or credits made during the billing period.

The amount left over is your balance.

Calculating your monthly interest charges

Once you know how your balance is calculated, you can figure your monthly interest charges based on your annual percentage rate (APR). Find the APR listed on your statement. Then:

1. Divide your APR by 12 months. This gives you a monthly percentage rate.

   For example, suppose you have an APR of 18%: 18% + 12 months = 1.5%

2. Multiply your balance by this monthly interest rate. The result is your interest charge.

   On a balance of $500, your interest charge would be: $500 X .015 = $7.50

3. Add the interest charge to your balance to determine your new balance.

   So, your new balance would be: $500 + $7.50 = $507.50

CARRYING A BALANCE CAN REALLY COST YOU.

Credit card companies usually require that you make a minimum payment each billing period. If you pay only this amount:

You will pay a lot in interest charges.

Remember that your interest is charged according to your balance. Each billing period, the interest is charged on your new balance (the original amount plus interest).

It can take years to pay off your balance.

With only a small reduction in your balance and the added interest charges each billing period, your balance may go down very little—even if you don't make any more charges to the account.

Here's an example:

You get a new credit card with the following terms:

- 18% APR (1.5% per month)
- minimum payment = 2.5% of total balance
- balances calculated using the adjusted balance method

You decide you want to purchase an HDTV with your card. After shopping around, you find the TV you want. Better yet, it's on sale for $1,000. This is $100 off the regular price. You believe you've found a great deal.

When your credit card statement arrives, you see that the minimum payment is only $25 (remember, that's just 2.5% of your balance). Instead of paying the entire bill, you decide just to pay the minimum amount to spread out the cost of the TV. Each month, you continue to pay only the minimum amount due. (Keep in mind that the minimum payment due will go down each month.)

Do you think this plan is a good one?

Take a look at the numbers. If you make only the minimum payment each month:

- It will take 153 months—or nearly 13 years—to pay for your TV.
- You will pay $1,115.41 in interest. That makes the total cost of the TV $2,115.41.

Your $100 savings is not worth it with this plan.

What happens if you decide to pay more?

Suppose you look over your budget and decide you can pay $50 each month instead of just the minimum. If you make this adjustment:

- It will take 24 months to pay for your TV.
- You will pay $197.83 in interest, making the total cost of the TV $1,197.83.

Paying more than the minimum amount due would save you $917.58 in interest.

The lesson: if you can't pay the entire balance, always pay more than the minimum amount due.

LOANS CAN HELP YOU FINANCE LARGE PURCHASES.
Before applying for a loan:

Think about what it's for.

For example, you may consider borrowing to:

- combine high-interest debt into a loan with a lower interest rate
- pay for an education
- buy a home or vehicle

Learn about different types of loans.

For example:

- Installment loans require you to make regular monthly payments—usually with interest—for a certain length of time. Mortgage and vehicle loans are often installment loans.
- Single payment loans require you to pay the full amount plus interest on a future date.
- Combination loans may require you to make regular payments followed by one large payment at the end of your repayment period.

Understand secured and unsecured loans.

- An unsecured loan lets you borrow without having to provide any collateral (something of value that acts as security if you fail to pay). An education loan is one example.
- A secured loan means that you have some collateral, such as equity in your home or the vehicle you purchased, to offer as security. These loans typically have lower rates than unsecured loans.

Compare sources of loans and terms being offered.

Be sure you understand:

- interest rates
- fees, prepayment penalties and other costs

Look for a reputable lender that will offer you reasonable rates and low fees.

Consider how a loan will fit into your budget.

Be sure you know:

- what your monthly payment will be, including interest charges
- how long it will take to pay off the loan

Can you afford to add the debt payment to your budget?

Be prepared.

The lender may ask for a number of documents, including:

- an application
- several recent pay statements
- a list of your credit card debt
- tax records from the last year or two

Don't make any untrue statements.

See pages 240-242 for details about mortgage and vehicle loans.

AVOIDING PROBLEM LOANS

Predatory lenders target consumers by advertising easy-to-get short-term loans. But the loan terms may be very expensive and financially risky—and are sometimes illegal. To protect yourself, avoid:

Payday loans

These are short-term cash loans that are based on:

- a personal check that is held for deposit in the future
- electronic access to the borrower's bank account to repay the loan

Payday loans typically have very high interest rates, high fees and short terms before payment is due. If you are unable to pay back the loan, you will face more fees. These loans may be offered by pawn shops, check cashers or loan stores.

Vehicle title loans

These are short-term loans that typically charge very high interest. With this type of loan, your vehicle serves as collateral. If you are unable to repay the loan, the loan company may take your vehicle or sell it to cover the amount of your loan.

Tax refund anticipation loans

These are loans based on expected tax refunds. Instead of having to wait for the refund in the mail, a person can borrow the expected amount. However, the loan usually carries very high-interest charges and fees. Plus, you have to repay the whole loan plus interest if all or some of your refund is withheld to pay an old debt.

Rent-to-own

Rent-to-own arrangements for items such as furniture, appliances and electronics can end up costing you much more than the item itself costs. This is true even if you do not intend to purchase the item.

Advance-fee loans

These loan scams often target people who have credit problems. The loan offer may guarantee that you will get a loan before you have applied. You may also be required to pay a fee ahead of time. This type of loan could put your personal information in the hands of identity thieves. Some of these loans are illegal.

If you are thinking about a short-term, high-interest cash loan, think again.

Lenders may try to convince you that this is a quick and easy way to get the cash you need. But their practices can be deceptive— and are sometimes illegal. Before taking a risk with this type of loan:

- Decide if you really need the money right away.
- If you do, contact one of the sources on page 254 for advice.

ABOUT MORTGAGE LOANS

If you are thinking of buying a home, here are some issues to consider:

Renting vs. buying

This is a very big decision that may be based on your long-term goals, current financial situation, lifestyle and other factors. For example:

- Owning a home can be a good investment that increases in value over time.
- Renting may make sense if home prices are very high or your finances are limited.

Your budget

Buying a home may be the biggest financial decision you make. Take a close look at your budget to see if you can afford the monthly expense of a mortgage. If so, how much can you afford? Remember to consider the additional costs of home-ownership, such as taxes, insurance, utilities and maintenance.

Mortgage types

Mortgage lenders offer different types of loans. The two most common types are fixed-rate mortgages and adjustable-rate mortgages. Here are the basics:

- A fixed-rate mortgage offers a fixed interest rate and a regular monthly payment amount. The borrower does not have to worry about rising interest rates that may result in a higher monthly payment. Fixed-rate mortgages are typically offered for a 15-year or 30-year loan period.
- An adjustable-rate mortgage (ARM) provides a loan with an interest rate and a payment amount that may vary many times over the life of the loan. Many ARMs combine a fixed rate with a variable rate. For example, a 5/1 ARM offers a fixed interest rate for the first 5 years. After that, the rate is changed depending on rising or falling interest rates. The initial rate may be lower than the rate of a fixed-rate mortgage. However, the adjustable rate may rise higher than fixed rates.

Lenders

There are many types of mortgage lenders, including banks, credit unions, mortgage companies and Internet lenders. Before making a decision, be sure to:

- Ask friends and family members to recommend lenders.
- Check up on lenders to be sure they're reputable. (Some states regulate lenders. You can also contact the Better Business Bureau to see if there are complaints about certain lenders.)

Rates

Mortgage rates vary depending on the lender, loan amount, loan type and length of the loan. Here are some tips for comparing rates:

- Get a list of current rates from several lenders. Be sure you know whether the rate is for a fixed-rate mortgage or ARM.
- Find out the loan's APR, which takes points, fees and other charges into account.

Special loan programs

For example:

- FHA (Federal Housing Administration) mortgages are loans backed by the U.S. government. These loans may make it easier for first-time home buyers to qualify for a loan. FHA loans offer competitive rates and typically require a smaller down payment than other loans.
- VA (Department of Veterans Affairs) mortgages are also backed by the U.S. government. They are offered to veterans and their spouses. They usually do not require a down payment.

Paying discount points

A discount point is a fee paid to lower the interest rate of the loan. A point is 1% of the loan amount. Whether to pay a point or not depends on your specific situation.

Amount of down payment

If you have less than 20% of the home's sale price for a down payment, you may have to buy private mortgage insurance (PMI). PMI protects the lender in case you can't pay your mortgage. It can cost about 1% of the amount of the loan.

Fees

There are a lot of costs involved with a home purchase. These could include:

- application and appraisal fees
- recording fees
- attorney fees
- title insurance
- escrow (deposits for future tax payments)

Be sure you have a clear understanding of these costs and how they may affect your loan amount and monthly payments.

About home equity loans A home equity loan or line of credit is a type of secured loan that uses your home as collateral. The money borrowed may be used to:

- pay off high-interest credit card debt
- pay educational expenses
- purchase a vehicle or another expensive item
- make improvements on a home

Because the loan is secured, the borrower may be charged a lower interest rate than the rate charged for a personal loan. Also, the interest paid may be tax deductible.

ABOUT VEHICLE LOANS
If you need to buy a vehicle:

Know what you can afford.

Look at your budget and consider how much you can really afford to pay for a vehicle. When you consider the costs of buying a new or used vehicle, be sure to take into account:

- insurance premiums— the cost of insurance can vary greatly depending on the make and model
- fuel costs—a large car, truck or SUV will use more gas than a small or mid-sized sedan
- maintenance costs—some foreign vehicles cost more to maintain and repair than American-made models
- other costs—such as taxes and title fees

Choose the vehicle that's right for you.

Compare various makes and models to find a vehicle that will meet your needs.

Here are some tips:

- Choose the right size and type of vehicle. For example, if you have a family, you may want to choose a sedan over a pickup truck or small sports car.
- Look for models that can save you money. Think about how much gas a car may use per mile and the costs of keeping it running. A used vehicle, for example, may cost less to buy. However, it may cost more to maintain than a new one.
- Consider extras and options carefully. Avoid getting talked into buying anything you don't really need.

Shop around for the best deal.

- Use the Internet to research the true value of a vehicle before agreeing on a price.
- When you talk with vehicle sellers, avoid talking only about the monthly payment. Be sure you know the total price of the car. Then work out the financing.

Consider your payment options.

For example:

- Vehicle dealers may advertise discounted interest rates. However, not every customer will qualify for the low advertised rate.
- Banks and credit unions may offer competitive vehicle loan rates.
- If you get a good interest rate from one lender, ask if another lender will match or beat it.

Read the warranty.

Understand the terms of the warranty—how long it's good for and what it covers. If there are any options you don't want, such as an extended service contract, don't sign for them.

THE IMPORTANCE OF CREDIT REPORTS
Information on your credit report helps determine whether you will get a loan or credit—and how much it will cost you.

What is a credit report?

Three separate credit reporting agencies collect and organize information about you into a file called a credit report. Your credit report includes:

- your name and the name of your spouse (if you're married)
- your Social Security number
- your birth date
- your current and past addresses
- your current and past employers
- account information, such as loans and credit cards— and whether you have made payments on time
- bankruptcy, tax liens and other public records
- a listing of others who have asked for a copy of your report

The report also includes a credit risk score. A higher score means you are a better credit risk.

Your credit score is more than just a number.

It helps lenders decide how likely you are to make timely payments and repay a loan. They use the number to help decide:

- whether to give you credit (a loan or credit card)
- how much you may borrow or what your line of credit will be
- what interest rate you will be charged

Credit reports are used for other purposes too.

For example:

- Insurance companies may use the information to decide if they will insure your home or vehicle.
- A rental group or landlord may decide whether or not to give you a lease based on your report.
- Some employers check an applicant's credit reports before making a job offer. (They must get your written consent to get copies of your reports.)

You can get a free copy of your credit report.

The law requires each of the 3 credit reporting agencies to give you a free copy of your report once every 12 months upon your request. You should ask for a copy of your credit report:

- if you're planning to buy a home or vehicle
- if you've been denied credit and are not sure why
- once a year to check for mistakes or identity theft

Remember, you won't automatically receive your report. You have to ask for it. And your credit score is not included in the free report—you have to pay for it. See page 254 for contact information.

HOW DOES YOUR CREDIT RATE?

When you get your credit report:

Read the report carefully.

Check to be sure the information included is correct and up-to- date.

Look for:

- any misspelling of your name or other personal information
- false information about your current accounts
- information about accounts you have cancelled or no longer use
- accounts you did not set up

Errors on your report could hurt your chances of getting credit and good rates. In some cases, "errors" may alert you that someone is using your personal information to commit fraud.

(See pages 252-253 to learn more about identity theft and what you can do to protect yourself.)

Understand factors that could lower your score.

These may include:

- a short credit history
- having a lot of debt
- a lot of requests for your credit report in a short period of time
- having a lot of available credit, such as cards with no balances—even if you are not planning to use them
- your payment history— even a few late payments can work against you
- a spouse's bad credit score

Know what doesn't affect your score.

Information about your age, sex, education and race, and other personal information is not considered in your score. See page 251 to learn more about rights that can protect your ability to receive credit.

If you spot any errors on your credit report, take action. See page 245 for information about fighting something on your credit report.

WORKING TO IMPROVE YOUR CREDIT SCORE

Take steps to get back on track.

Here are a few ideas:

- Pay off your debt.
- Pay bills on time. Consider signing up for automatic bill payment to help you pay bills on time.
- Avoid applying for more credit cards.

Dispute mistakes.

To correct an error:

- Write a letter to the credit reporting agency. Point out the mistake. (See the sample dispute letter on this page.)
- Send the letter and any information that supports your claim (such as a copy of a canceled check or receipt) via certified mail.
- Wait to hear back. The agency has 30 days to investigate and notify you of the results. If they correct the error, they can notify the other agencies for you if you ask.

If the agency determines that the information is not an error, you can complain to the lender you believe made the mistake.

Be wary of organizations that claim they can "fix" your credit rating.

These organizations may charge high fees and offer no help. Their practices may even be illegal. Instead, seek out help from reputable sources, such as those listed on page 254.

Sample dispute letter

Your name

Your address

Date

Complaint department
Name of company
Address

To Whom It May Concern:

I am writing to dispute information included on my credit report. I have circled the item in dispute on the attached copy of my report.

This item is inaccurate because [explain what is inaccurate and why]. I request that this item be [deleted or corrected] on my report.

I have enclosed copies of [reference any supporting documents you have enclosed].

Thank you for your attention.

Sincerely,

Your name

Enclosures: [List the items you are sending with the letter.]

ARE CREDIT PROBLEMS AND DEBT BRINGING YOU DOWN?

Check yes or no for the following statements about your debt and use of credit.

		Yes	No
1.	I am at or near the credit limit on one or more credit card accounts	☐	☐
2.	I continue to apply for new credit cards to try to get more credit	☐	☐
3.	I often charge more than I can afford to pay in full each month	☐	☐
4.	I need to use credit cards to pay for everyday expenses, such as groceries or gas	☐	☐
5.	I can usually make only minimum payments on credit cards and loans	☐	☐
6.	I sometimes skip payment on one bill in order to pay another	☐	☐
7.	I have been charged late fees and other penalties because I can't pay what I owe	☐	☐
8.	I have been forced to use savings to pay regular monthly expenses	☐	☐
9.	Creditors have contacted me about past-due bills	☐	☐
10.	I don't know how much I owe	☐	☐
11.	I am not honest with my spouse about spending and paying off debt	☐	☐
12.	I am worried about losing my home because I can't pay my debts	☐	☐
13.	I am worried that I will never be able to pay back everything I owe	☐	☐

If you checked yes for any of these statements, you may have a serious credit and debt problem.

Use the worksheet on the next page to help get a better picture of your debt. Then see pages 248-250 for tips to get your debt under control.

EVALUATING YOUR CURRENT DEBT

Experts recommend that you keep debt payments (not including mortgage or rent) to 20% or less of your net income. This percentage is known as your "debt ratio." This worksheet can help you see where you stand.

Step 1: List credit card debt.

List the total amount you owe each month on every credit card you have. Then total the amount.

Card Name	Amount
Total	

Step 2: List monthly loan payments.

Include payments for all loans except your mortgage. Then total the amount.

Loan Type	Amount
Total	

Step 3: Calculate your total monthly debt payments.

Add the totals from Step 1 and Step 2.

Total Monthly Debt Payment	

Step 4: Determine your monthly net income.

This is your income after taxes and any other money automatically taken out of your paycheck.

Monthly Net Income	

Step 5: Calculate your debt ratio.

Divide your total monthly payments by your monthly after-tax income. The result is your debt as a percentage of income.

Total monthly debt payments + Monthly net income = Debt as a percentage of income	

If you are close to or over 20%, take steps to reduce your debt.

TAKE CONTROL OF YOUR DEBT.
You can work to reduce debt and take control of your finances.

Make a monthly budget.

This is your plan for where your money goes. Be sure to include:

- income (pay, bonuses, interest income and other income)
- savings, such as bank accounts and retirement plans
- fixed expenses (costs that are the same each month), such as rent or mortgage payments, insurance premiums and loan payments
- variable expenses (costs that may change each month), such as utilities, groceries, transportation, healthcare and entertainment

Remember, the amount going out should match the amount coming in. If there's more going out than coming in, look for ways to trim expenses. (See page 249.)

Once you have a budget, check it regularly to see if it's working.

Be smart about extra money.

Use a pay raise, bonus or any other income you weren't expecting to help pay off current debt.

Talk about money as a family.

Talk with your partner. Be sure you agree on:

- the monthly budget you've created
- the importance of reducing your debt

If possible, ask children to pitch in and find ways to save money. However, avoid making them worry about your family's finances.

Talk to your creditors.

If you have any trouble making payments, contact the creditors right away. You can tell them:

- if a payment will be late
- if you can't make a payment or can't pay the full amount
- you plan on paying what you owe

Your creditors may be able to help. But don't wait until you've already missed making payments.

Don't buy things you can't afford.

This will only make your debt problem worse. If you don't have the money to pay for something, then don't buy it.

Target high-interest debt.

Look over your credit card and loan statements to find the ones that have the highest interest rates. (In most cases, credit cards charge the highest interest rates.) Then try to pay off these debts first.

- Call the creditor and ask for a lower rate. Some creditors may be willing to give you a better rate, especially if your credit rating is good.
- Find out whether you can make payments more than once a month.
- Pay more than the minimum due whenever possible. (See page 237 for more information.)

Shop for a lower rate.

Compare credit card offers and loan options to see if you can find one with a lower rate. Then consider transferring higher interest balances. Remember:

- Don't think of the new credit line as a way to spend more.
- Some credit card companies charge balance transfer fees. Find out ahead of time what transferring a balance will cost you. Decide if the cost is worth it.
- Make sure the low-interest rate applies to balance transfers. Also, be sure the low rate is not just an introductory rate that will go up to a much higher rate in a few months.
- Once you've transferred balances, cancel credit card accounts you no longer plan to use.

Save money on everyday expenses.

Here are some tips:

- Buy generic or store brands. They're usually cheaper.
- Avoid shopping when you are hungry or bored. You may spend more.
- Don't fall for a good sale or buy something without thinking it through first.
- Pack lunches and snacks. Try not to use vending machines.
- Eat out less often.
- Rent movies instead of going to the theater.
- Look for free or inexpensive entertainment. Visit parks, libraries and museums.
- Turn off lights and appliances when you're not using them.

Keep track of how much you save. Small steps such as these can make a difference!

Cutting your expenses

Use the spaces below to write down your ideas for cutting everyday expenses to save money and reduce debt

Shopping	Entertainment	Utilities
_____	_____	_____
_____	_____	_____
_____	_____	_____
Estimated saving:_____	Estimated saving:_____	Estimated saving:_____

IF MANAGING DEBT IS A PROBLEM FOR YOU, GET HELP.
You may want to think about:

Credit counseling

Nonprofit credit counseling organizations are available to help with:

- budgeting
- debt management
- credit report and credit score issues

Credit counseling may be available at:

- a local credit union
- the cooperative extension office at a state university
- a family service center at a military base

Ask your financial institution or family and friends to suggest an organization. You can also check with the Better Business Bureau to see if there have been any complaints about the organization.

Debt consolidation

You may be able to use a home equity loan or second mortgage to combine high interest debt into one monthly payment you can afford. Talk with a credit counselor about the benefits and drawbacks.

A debt management plan

If your debt problem seems out of your control, a credit counselor may recommend that you sign up for a debt management plan. With this type of plan:

- you make a monthly deposit to the credit counseling organization
- the organization uses the money to pay your debts
- a credit counselor may be able to get you lower interest rates or fees

About bankruptcy

Bankruptcy is a legal procedure that frees a person from having to repay some debts. It is usually considered a last resort because the information stays on your credit report for 10 years. During that time, it may be difficult to:

- buy a home or get credit
- get life insurance
- get a job

If you are thinking about filing for bankruptcy, get advice from a qualified legal expert.

Questions to ask a credit counseling organization

- What services do you offer?
- What fees will I have to pay?
- Do you offer any free information?

- Is your organization accredited or certified?
- Will I receive a written contract or agreement?

UNDERSTAND YOUR RIGHTS.

There are a number of federal laws set up to help consumers make smart credit choices, get credit if they are qualified and keep a good credit rating. These include:

The Credit Card Accountability Responsibility and Disclosure (CARD) Act of 2009

This law protects credit card customers in several ways. For example:

- It requires that contract terms be clearly spelled out.
- It puts limits on how and when APRs (annual percentage rates) can be raised and requires earlier warning of changes—generally, 45 days. Customers have the right to cancel the credit card and repay the balance over time at the old rate.
- Statements must be mailed out to customers at least 21 days before the payment due date. The due date cannot change each month.
- Statements must show the payment amount needed to pay off the balance, including interest, in 36 months.
- Certain practices that led to higher costs for customers are banned. These include applying payments to balances with lower interest rates first and double-cycle billing.

The Truth in Lending Act

This law requires creditors to:

- state the interest rate as an APR
- tell you about all finance charges

You have the right to this information before making an agreement. The law makes it easier to compare interest rates and the real cost of borrowing.

The Fair Credit Billing Act

This law applies mainly to credit card companies. It requires them to record payments on the day they are received. The law also offers certain protections if you have a problem with your bill for example, if:

- your credit card is lost or stolen and charges are made to it without your permission
- you buy an item or service that is not delivered or that you do not accept upon delivery
- you find other billing problems, such as a math error or a missing payment

If you spot an error or need more information about a charge, write to your credit card company right away.

The Equal Credit Opportunity Act

This law states that you cannot be denied credit based on certain factors, including your sex, marital status, race, age and religion. It also protects you if you get public assistance or have used credit laws to protect your rights. If you are not given credit, you have the right to know the specific reasons why.

The Fair Debt Collections Practices Act

This law lists specific rules that debt collectors must follow when trying to reach you. For example, debt collectors may not:

- harass you or threaten to hurt you
- lie to you
- call you early in the morning or late at night
- call your employer, friends or relatives (except to ask where you live and work)

LEARN ABOUT IDENTITY THEFT.

Identity theft is a crime. It happens when someone uses another person's personal information to commit fraud or other crimes. It's important to know:

What information people look for

People trying to commit fraud or other crimes look for:

- your Social Security number
- credit card numbers
- checking and savings account numbers
- insurance information
- your name
- your address
- your date of birth
- your place of birth
- your mother's maiden name

Where they get personal information

They may:

- steal a purse or wallet
- steal mail, such as bank statements or credit card statements or offers
- copy credit card information when you use your credit card at a store
- steal the information from a website with poor security
- go through trash to find information on papers you have thrown away
- pretend to be a creditor or another person over the phone or in e-mails

What can happen

- Identity theft can hurt your credit rating. In turn, you may not be given a mortgage, or an educational or vehicle loan. You may also be charged higher interest on a loan.
- Fixing problems caused by identity theft can take a long time. You may feel angry, confused or stressed.

What they may do with the information they steal

Using your information, someone may:

- open a credit card account in your name
- change the billing address on your credit card and use the card to make charges on your account
- open a checking account in your name and use it to write bad checks
- set up phone service or other utilities
- get a driver's license using his or her picture and your name
- apply for a job, file a tax return or apply for government benefits

PREVENT IDENTITY THEFT.
Here are some tips:

Be careful with important information and documents.

- File your birth certificate, Social Security card, passport and other important documents in a safe place. Avoid carrying these items with you if you don't need to.
- Give out your Social Security number only when required. Don't write it on checks.
- Avoid carrying many credit cards in your wallet or purse.

Manage credit cards and bank accounts.

- Review credit card and bank statements to check for charges or deductions you did not make. Report any errors or possible fraud right away.
- Cancel credit card and bank accounts that you no longer use.
- Choose passwords and PINs (personal identification numbers) that don't include information that is easy to guess or find out.

Destroy documents.

Tear up or shred documents that include your personal information, including credit card offers and other mail offering you something.

Use the Internet and e-mail safely.

- If you enter credit card numbers or personal information online, be sure the Web site has steps in place to keep your information safe. Look for "https://" in your browser's address bar.
- Don't download any file or click a link from an e-mail unless you know and trust the sender.

Manage your mail.

- Mail letters at the post office or give them to a postal carrier.
- Get mail from your mailbox as soon as possible. Put a hold on your mail if you won't be able to pick up mail for a while.

Check your credit report.

Make sure the information on it is correct each year. (See pages 243-245 for more information.)

Take action right away if you are a victim of identity theft.

- Contact the Federal Trade Commission's Identity Theft hotline at 1-877-ID-THEFT (1-877-438-4338). You can file a complaint or ask for advice.
- Contact one of the 3 credit reporting agencies to have a fraud alert placed on your credit reports. (The agency you call is required to alert the other two.)
- Close accounts that were used or opened without your consent. Call the company. Make notes, including names and phone numbers of people you spoke with. Follow up with a letter and copies of papers that back up your claim.
- File a police report. Ask for a copy of the report to use as proof of the crime.
- Be smart when you set up new accounts. Choose new passwords and PINs.

SOURCES OF HELP AND INFORMATION

Federal Trade Commission (FTC)

To report possible fraud, file a complaint or seek advice about credit and debt issues:

- visit www.ftc.gov
- call 1-877-FTC-HELP (1-877-382-4357) or 1-866-653-4261 (TTY)

Federal Citizen Information Center (FCIC)

The FCIC offers information about many consumer issues, including credit and debt concerns and questions. Visit www.consumeraction.gov to get started.

National Foundation for Credit Counseling

To get the number of a local office that can offer low-cost or free credit and debt counseling information and services:

- visit www.nfcc.org
- call 1-800-388-2227

Your state or local government

Your state's Attorney General's office, a local consumer protection agency and other government offices may offer information and advice about lenders and credit and loan fraud. Check your phone book or visit your state's official Web site.

Better Business Bureau

You can check to see if lenders and other organizations have any complaints filed against them. Check the white pages of your phone book for the telephone number of your state's bureau, or visit www.bbb.org.

Credit reporting agencies

To order a free annual credit report from any of the 3 credit reporting agencies:

- Visit annualcreditreport.com
- Call 1-877-322-8228

This is the only source authorized by the Federal Trade Commission to provide free reports. Beware of look-alikes on the Web. You can buy a copy of your report by contacting:

- Equifax
  www.equifax.com
  1-800-685-1111
- Experian
  www.experian.com
  1-888-EXPERIAN
  (1-888-397-3742)
- TransUnion
  www.transunion.com
  1-800-916-8800

YOU CAN LEARN TO MANAGE CREDIT THE RIGHT WAY.

Be smart about credit cards.

Limit their use and pay off your entire bill on time.

Learn about loans.

Shop around to find a reputable lender with terms that fit your budget.

Take steps to build and keep a good credit rating.

Know your credit score—and understand why it matters.

Pay off debt.

Know the signs of trouble and get help if you need it.

Take control of your credit—and your future!

MANAGING FAMILY CONFLICT

REENTRY
ESSENTIALS, INC.

Life Skills Series
Basic Skills for Lifelong Success

Please read:

Talk to a professional! This workbook is not a substitute for the advice of a qualified expert.

Reentry Essentials, Inc.
2609 East 14 Street, Suite 1018
Brooklyn, NY 11235-3915
P: 347.973.0004
E: info@ReentryEssentials.org
I: www.ReentryEssentials.org

This workbook belongs to:

_____

You may find it helpful to keep important names and phone numbers handy.

Write them below.

Health-care clinic or provider

Name_____

Phone_____

Counselor

Name_____

Phone_____

Your supervisors

Name_____

Phone_____

Caregiver (for child or adult day care)

Name_____

Phone_____

Other important numbers

_____

_____

_____

_____

_____

_____

_____

_____

_____

_____

_____

_____

_____

EVERY FAMILY IS DIFFERENT.

Your family is one of a kind!

Each person in your family has interests, strengths and experiences that help make your family special.

Every family has conflicts.

Conflicts can happen because people:

- have different personalities
- need and expect different things

There's room for improvement in every family!

Conflicts can happen between anyone.

They may happen between:

- parents
- children
- parents and children
- adult brothers and sisters
- adults and aging parents

By learning to resolve conflict better, you can make your family stronger. This workbook can help.

Use this workbook in the way that works best for you.

For example.., you all may want to:

- read it on your own and then do the activities together
- read it together, doing the activities as you go

For activities sheets that you may copy, each person can just use a separate sheet of paper, if it's easier.

Or you may prefer to all work on an activity together.

CONTENT

FAMILIES COME IN ALL SHAPES AND SIZES.
They may include:

Married partners and children

These "traditional" families make up only about half of families today.

Unmarried partners and children

This arrangement is more common than ever before.

Single parents and children

About 1 in 3 families is headed by a single parent. These parents may be divorced or widowed or may have never married.

Co-parents and children

The parents:

- live apart
- share the responsibilities of raising their children

Blended families

These include:

- step families
- families with adopted children
- families with foster children

Grandparent-led families

More and more grandparents are raising their grandchildren. Their adult children may have died or are absent for other reasons.

Partners without children

They may be unable to have children or have chosen not to.

Extended families living together

In some families, parents and children share homes with:

- aunts
- uncles
- grandparents
- other relatives

Note: In the rest of this workbook, "parent" will refer to any caregiver responsible for raising a child.

WHO IS YOUR FAMILY?

Understanding how different members of your family see one another can help you resolve conflicts.

Give everyone a copy of this page.

In the box to the right, write each family member's name and the roles you think that person has in your family. (If you run out of room, use a separate piece of paper.) Family members' roles might include:

- doing most of the cooking
- handling most of the bills
- arranging holiday gatherings and other social events
- helping watch younger children
- feeding pets
- just being a young child (having time to play is important for healthy development)

Young children might enjoy drawing pictures of the family instead.

Compare your responses.

Do you all see your family the same way? If not, this may be one conflict this workbook can help you resolve! In the last section of the box, describe points of disagreement that were identified through this exercise.

Name   Role(s) in our family

_____ _____

_____ _____

_____ _____

_____ _____

_____ _____

_____ _____

_____ _____

_____ _____

_____ _____

_____ _____

_____ _____

Possible conflicts identified:

_____

_____

_____

_____

_____

_____

_____

_____

_____

YOUR FAMILY HISTORY

Knowing your history can help you see ways your family is special and give you stories to pass on to future generations. Ask older relatives to tell you about their lives—and what they know of those who came before them. Write what you learn here.

Where did our family come from? When did they come here and why?

_____

_____

_____

Where did they live in this country?

_____

_____

_____

How did they make a living?

_____

_____

_____

What were their special abilities, talents or achievements?

_____

_____

_____

_____

_____

_____

YOUR FAMILY'S STRENGTHS

Invite everyone to fill out a copy of this page.
Share your results.

What are your family's strengths?

1. Name 2 activities you enjoy doing as a family.

_____

_____

2. Name 2 good things that have happened to your family in the past.

_____

_____

3. A tradition is a regular event that has meaning to you—such as preparing a special food on holidays. What traditions do you most enjoy?

_____

_____

_____

_____

What are each person's strengths?

Write a sentence about a strength each family member has—something you find special about him or her. For example, he or she may have a great sense of humor, be very helpful or be good at organizing things. (If you run out of room, use a separate piece of paper.)

_____

_____

_____

_____

_____

_____

THERE'S NO SUCH THING AS A PERFECT FAMILY.

If people judge their families by what they see in movies or on TV, they will probably be disappointed!

Movie and TV families

often seem to have:

- lots of free time to spend together
- very tidy homes
- all the money they need
- problems that can be solved in 1 hour or less
- conflicts that are funny— and if there are any hurt feelings, they don't last long

In the world of TV, everyone's usually laughing or smiling by an episode's end.

Real-life families

may actually have:

- little free time to spend together
- trouble keeping up with housework
- financial worries
- complicated problems conflicts that aren't funny at all—and that can cause a lot of pain

In real life, conflicts take time and effort to resolve.

See for yourselves

Make a copy of this page for each family member. Then, watch a movie or TV show together. As you watch, have each person take notes about the families shown. What details seem unrealistic? When you are finished compare notes.

Name of show or movie:

_____

_____

_____

Notes:

_____

_____

_____

_____

_____

_____

_____

_____

_____

_____

_____

_____

_____

_____

_____

_____

_____

_____

_____

WHAT MAKES A FAMILY WORK?

While every family is unique, the happiest households tend to have some things in common. Their members usually:

Communicate well

Each person knows how to:

- really listen to others
- clearly express his or her thoughts and feelings—calmly, without yelling or hitting

People don't expect others to read their minds.

Respect and appreciate everyone in the family

- While adults make the final decisions, they listen to children's opinions. Even the smallest child is heard—for example, when naming a new pet.
- Sisters and brothers don't always get along. But they're encouraged to look for the good in each other, rather than focusing on what they don't like.

Have clear roles

- All family members know their responsibilities in the family. But they can also be flexible as the family's needs change.
- Adults and older children recognize how their behavior affects others in the family. They try to set good examples.

Share time together

- The family tries to relax and play together, rather than everyone always going off on his or her own.
- The family makes a point to plan special activities or outings to do together.
- When a family has 2 parents, the parents also take time to do things just with each other.

Spend time apart

Family members are allowed— and encouraged— to have friends and outside interests.

Are active in the community

- They are involved with schools, religious organizations and clubs.
- They help others in need.

You can learn ways to resolve conflict in your family. But first, consider the possible causes of the conflict.

COMMON CAUSES OF FAMILY CONFLICT
Do any of these sound familiar?

Money matters

There may be issues about:

- having too little money
- who controls the money
- how money is spent
- children's allowances

Job issues

There may be issues or worries about:

- being unemployed
- finding or keeping a job
- who will work and who will stay home
- what kind of job a person has or wants
- how much time a job takes a teen or an adult away from the family
- whether a job will mean moving

Housework

Working parents have less time for housework. Even when children help, parents may need to accept having a less-than-spotless home.

Parenting issues

Parents may have different views on how to raise or discipline a child or handle specific misbehaviors.

Unrealistic expectations

For example:

- Adults may not know what to expect of children at different ages. They may think a small child has the judgment of an adult.
- Newly blended families may expect everyone to love each other right away.

Unclear roles

Many parents today grew up in families in which roles were clear:

- Fathers worked outside the home.
- Mothers stayed home with the children.

Now, both parents may be working outside the home, but old ways of thinking can die hard. For example:

- A mother might think the father isn't doing his fair share of chores-but not ask him to do more.
- A father might think the mother should still do most of the chores—because his mother did.

Single-parent families, blended families and extended families living together may also face special concerns about family roles.

Unexpected events

Accidents, mistakes or other things going wrong (such as a car breaking down) can disrupt family life.

Health problems

Caring for a sick family member can mean that parents have less attention to give to other family members.

Alcohol or other drug use

One person's problem with substance use can affect the whole family.

Family Conflicts: A History

Complete the sentences below if they apply to you (for example, teens would only complete the first 2 sentences). Invite everyone to fill out a copy of this section and share your results.

During my childhood, conflicts sometimes arose at home over the issue(s) of:_____

_____

_____

As I got older, issues causing conflicts shifted to:_____

_____

Today, our family conflicts tend to be about:_____

_____

_____

CHILDREN MAY FACE OTHER CONFLICTS, TOO.

Children may face conflicts with brothers and sisters—or with parents—relating to:

Lack of privacy

Sharing a bedroom is a common cause.

Use of the telephone

Parents and children may accuse each other of "hogging" the phone.

Control of the TV

Children may have conflicts over which shows to watch.

Clothes

- Parents may not like the way children dress.
- Children may be upset if brothers or sisters "borrow" clothes without asking.

Competition

Children may:

- compete for adult attention or praise
- feel adults favor one child over another

Homework and housework

- Parents may be tired of reminding children to do homework and chores.
- Children may be tired of being reminded.

Growing independence

The preteen and teen years can be an emotional rollercoaster ride, as children struggle with the need to:

- define themselves and become more independent
- still have guidance from adults (even though they may not admit they need it)

Conflicts outside the home

For example, pressure from the demands of schoolwork or other activities, or conflicts with friends, may affect a child's mood and attitude at home.

A few discipline tips:

- Set clear limits.
- Explain what will happen if rules are broken. Enforce them the same way each time. (Have older children help make the rules and consequences that will apply to them.)
- Never spank or use other physical punishment. It may stop the behavior in the short run. But it also teaches that violence is an OK way to solve conflicts— and it could injure a child.

FAMILY CHANGES CAN CAUSE STRESS.
Stress leads to conflict.
Stressful changes might include:

Separation and divorce

- Children need to know that nothing they did caused the breakup—and that both parents still love them.
- Children will feel even more stress if they are ignored by the parent who does not live with them.

Co-parenting

After separation or divorce, both parents can still be involved in their children's lives. But if each home has different values and rules, it can cause:

- stress for a child
- conflict between the parents

Blending of families

After adults and children form a new family, it may be years before all the members feel close.

Caring for older relatives

If an older relative moves into the home or needs help while living nearby:

- A caregiver may feel stress from the added responsibilities.
- A child may feel stress because he or she has less attention from the caregiver.
- Everyone may feel stress if the home feels more crowded.

Moving

Leaving old friends and surroundings can be especially hard for children.

Death or serious illness

The death or serious illness of a family member may be one of the most difficult things some families must deal with. Conflict can arise over:

- differences in ways of grieving (for example, some people might become angry, while others withdraw)
- financial issues
- shifting roles and responsibilities

A disability can also lead to conflicts.

A new baby

The birth of a baby, while a joyful event, can also cause:

- conflicts over roles and responsibilities
- jealousy among the baby's siblings

WHAT'S CAUSING CONFLICT IN YOUR FAMILY?

Write down your general thoughts.

I think we have conflicts because _____

_____

Keep a conflict log.

Keep track of your conflicts for several days. See if you notice any patterns.

Sample conflict log

Date and time:	3/12 7:30 pm
Who was involved?	Bob
What was it about?	He left his empty coffee cup on the counter again!
What did I do or say?	Can't you take 2 seconds to put that in the sink?
How did I feel?	Resentful. I feel like I have to do everything.
What did the other(s) do or say?	Why the big deal about one little cup?
Was this conflict really about something else?	I feel taken for granted in a lot of ways, and not just by Bob. My boss expects me to pick up after him too. I really felt it today. Couldnt' someone take care of me for a change?

Conflict log

Date and time: _____

Who was involved _____

What was it about _____

What did I do or say? _____

How did I feel? _____

What did the other(s) do or say? _____

Was this conflict really about something else (and if so, what?) _____

_____

COMMON MISTAKES YOU DON'T HAVE TO MAKE

Many times people respond to conflicts in ways that end up making problems worse.
Before you learn effective ways to resolve a conflict, here are some samples of what not to do:

Don't drag others into family conflicts.

Keep it between you and the other person(s). Don't look for allies among friends or other family members. It's up to you and the other person(s) involved to try to work out the problem.

Don't try to avoid the other person—or the problem.

If you have a conflict with someone, you may not want to even be in the same room with him or her. Or, it may seem easiest to pretend there is no problem at all. But avoidance does nothing to resolve the matter. In fact, it can make things worse. Some people worry about conflict and keep their feelings bottled up. This can lead to increased anger and further stress.

Don't get personal.

Remember, the other person isn't the problem—the conflict is. Conflicts are seldom resolved when one person attacks another. This includes:

- yelling
- criticizing, blaming or accusing
- insulting
- threatening
- using any kind of physical force (hitting, kicking, or shoving, for example)

Some of these actions (especially physical violence) may signal an abusive situation. See page 286 for more information and sources of help.

Don't bring up past conflicts.

If you've had conflicts with this person before, now is not the time to discuss them. If these conflicts were resolved, don't bring them up. If there is unresolved conflict that you would like to talk about, bring it up at another time. Deal with one conflict at a time.

Live and learn

Everyone makes mistakes. The key is to recognize and learn from them. Do any of the responses to conflict described on this page sound familiar to you? Discuss how you have dealt with conflict on the lines below.

Way(s) I have tried to deal with conflict:

_____

_____

_____

_____

_____

_____

What happened when I responded this way:

_____

_____

_____

_____

_____

_____

_____

_____

Read on to learn about healthy ways to manage family conflicts.

FAMILY MEETINGS CAN HELP CLEAR UP CONFLICTS.

They can prevent new ones, too.
Try to meet once a week or twice a month.

Turn off the radio or TV.

Unplug your phones or let your answering machine get the call. This is special time just for your family.

Assign tasks to help meetings go smoothly.

For example, have one family member take notes and another act as moderator (lead the meeting).

Share news and plans with each other.

You can:

- Talk about work, school, your extended family or events in your community.
- Discuss family members' schedules for the week.
- Ask children what made them happy or sad this week. Praise them for their accomplishments.

Share your insights about conflicts.

Calmly share your general thoughts from page 270. (To keep your meeting from turning into a gripe session, use the communication tips on pages 274-277.)

Find solutions to conflicts.

You can use the problem-solving method on pages 284-285.

Discuss family rules and roles, as needed.

For example:

- Make new rules or review old ones. As children grow or your family changes in other ways, some rules may need to change or be dropped.
- Divide household responsibilities among family members in ways that are logical and fair. Consider rotating these from time to time.

Start family traditions.

If people didn't list many traditions they enjoy on their copies of page 263, perhaps they have ideas for things to try.

Plan other activities.

Possible examples include:

- an outing
- a video or game night
- cooking a special meal together

In today's busy families, if you don't plan time together, it may not happen.

Fill in your meeting day and time on the notice below. Copy it and post it where everyone will see it. Or ask your child to make a poster with the same message!

Family Meeting Ground Rules

We will meet every _____ at _____

We agree that: .

We will each help strengthen our family.
We will build on our strengths.
We will each have a chance to talk.
We will not interrupt others.
We will treat everyone's opinion as important.
We will listen with respect.

Use the form below to help plan each meeting—or make your own agenda on a separate sheet of paper.

Family Meeting Agenda

Share news:

_____
_____
_____
_____

Divide up or change chores:

_____
_____
_____
_____

Discuss and resolve conflicts (if any)

_____
_____
_____
_____

Discuss other topics:

_____
_____
_____
_____
_____
_____

Plan family activity/tradition(s):

_____
_____
_____
_____
_____

_____
_____

LISTEN WITH CARE

—it's one key to good communication!
Here are some tips:

Pay attention.

Don't tune out or plan what you'll say next while someone else is talking.

Show that you are listening.

Some ways to do this include:

- making frequent eye contact
- nodding now and then
- leaning forward slightly, if you're seated

Don't interrupt.

But it's OK to say things like "uh-huh" or "go on." This also shows you're listening.

Don't offer advice unless asked.

The person may have a greater need to let out feelings than being told what to do.

Hold back your reassurance.

If someone is upset, it can be tempting to say "Don't worry about it" or "It will all work out," to try to help the person feel better. But it may seem like you're making light of the person's problems or that you want to change the subject.

Be aware of body language.

- The look on a person's face and his or her body position may tell you more than the person's words. For example, if a child says "I'm fine" while clenching his or her fists, something is probably troubling him or her.
- As you listen, be aware of the message your own body language may be sending. For example, a tapping foot may suggest impatience.

Pay attention to tone of voice.

It can also tell you things that the speaker's words may not.

Listen for feelings.

Listen for clues that reveal how the person feels. Don't listen only for facts. Try to reflect the speaker's feeling or mood (excitement, sadness, seriousness) in your own tone and body language.

Check your understanding.

Sum up what the person has been saying in your own words. Include your sense of what he or she feels: "It sounds like you feel you can't trust your sister because she read your diary."

Try it!

With another family member, practice listening effectively. Take turns telling one another a story, how you feel about something or about a problem you are having. Then, review each other's listening "performance" in the following areas:

Attention/focus: _____

_____

Responses:_____

_____

Body language: _____

_____

Understanding: _____

_____

When it's your turn to speak, know how to communicate effectively.

EXPLAIN—DON'T BLAME!

When you have a conflict with someone:

Calm down first.

If you speak in the heat of anger:

• You may say things you'll regret.

• Your listeners may feel threatened or defensive— and be less able to hear the message you want to send.

Try the tips for calming down on page 282.

Choose the right time and place.

Be realistic about how much time you'll need. If you know a discussion could take an hour, don't say it will take "just a few minutes."

Accept responsibility for how you feel.

No one else can "make" you feel a certain way. A person's actions may trigger some inner emotional response, but you choose what that response is based on your:

- general attitude
- mood at the time

For example, if a teen is late for dinner, you might feel:

- calm ("we'll just start without him")
- annoyed
- very angry

Name the problem.

- State the action that is bothering you: "This is the third night in a row you've been late for dinner."
- Stick to the issue—don't add on other complaints. ("And you never pay for gas when you take my car to the mall!")
- Avoid using the words "always" or "never" when you talk about the problem— this is generalizing and can seem like an attack.

Say what you want to have happen.

Be specific. Instead of saying "Be more reliable about time," you could say "Please call when you're running late."

Use "I" statements.

These describe your feelings— not what you think of the other person. For example, you can say "I" feel upset" instead of "You are so rude!"

"I" statements tell the person how you feel without blaming him or her.

PRACTICE USING "I" STATEMENTS.

Fill in some statements below and read them out loud.
(Copy this sheet first, so others in your family can practice too.)

Example:

I feel angry
When you leave your dirty cloths all over the floor.
Next time, I would like you to use the hamper. It will save me a lot of time when I do the laundry.

I feel _____

When _____

Next time, I would like_____

_____

_____

I feel_____

When _____

Next time, I would like_____

_____

_____

I feel_____

When _____

Next time, I would like_____

_____

_____

I feel _____

When _____

Next time, I would like_____

_____

_____

I feel_____

When _____

Next time, I would like_____

_____

_____

I feel_____

When _____

Next time, I would like_____

_____

_____

KNOW HOW TO HANDLE STRESS.

When you're facing more than you can manage, stress can take a toll.
And when someone is hiding stress, it can affect the whole family.

Recognize your stress.

People don't always know when they're under stress. Common signs and symptoms of stress include:

- tight shoulder or neck muscles
- sleeplessness
- headaches
- stomachaches
- feeling tired all the time
- feeling hopeless or powerless
- getting upset over things that don't usually bother you

Keep a journal.

Each day for a couple of weeks, write about something that triggered stress. Your journal:

- can be an outlet for your tension
- can help you see patterns in what causes your stress and how you handle it
- may help you find solutions to problems—including ones that cause conflicts

You can use the space on the next page, if you want. Make copies, if needed.

Change what you can control.

- Set priorities. If you have too much to do, do only the things that are most important or can't wait.
- Ask for help from other family members.
- Say "no" now and then.

Accept what you can't control.

For example, you can't control the long lines in the grocery store. But while you wait, you may be able to:

- glance through the magazine you're going to buy
- listen to the song playing in the background
- make small talk with the shopper in front of you
- plan what you'll cook for dinner

Try to think positively.

When you're under stress, it can be easy to fall into a cycle of negative thinking. You can begin to feel better by:

- staying confident—remind yourself that you are capable of handling the situation
- putting things in perspective—consider whether the stress you're feeling is out of proportion with the situation

Be good to yourself.

Pampering yourself a little can help relieve stress. Try:

- listening to quiet music
- spending time on a hobby
- taking a warm bath
- exercising (be sure to consult your health-care clinic or provider before starting an exercise program)

Stress Journal

Day/date:_____

Stress trigger(s):_____

_____

How did you handle? _____

_____

Day/date:_____

Stress trigger(s):_____

_____

How did you handle? _____

_____

Day/date:_____

Stress trigger(s):_____

_____

How did you handle? _____

_____

Consider relaxation methods as a way to ease stress. Some methods are:

Progressive muscle relaxation

- Sit or lie down.
- Tense, then relax, muscles in the different parts of your body. Work from one part to the next—feet, calves, thighs and so on, up to the top of your head.

Visualization

Spend a few minutes imagining yourself in a peaceful place. Focus on its pleasant sights, sounds and smells.

Meditation

With eyes closed, concentrate on a single object or word (such as "one" or "peace").

Deep breathing

Breathe slowly and deeply in and out. (Your belly should rise and fall.)

UNDERSTANDING YOUR ANGER.

Anger is a natural emotion—it's not good or bad. But what you do with it can make the difference between a minor disagreement and a major conflict.

Common anger triggers

Different people get angry about different things. Check the things that trigger your anger. Add others that you are aware of. Copy this sheet for others in your family to use.

I feel angry when I:

☐ feel ignored

☐ am nagged

☐ am embarrassed or teased

☐ make mistakes

☐ am criticized

☐ have to wait for people who are late

☐ feel others aren't doing their share

☐ _____

☐ _____

☐ _____

☐ _____

☐ _____

☐ _____

☐ _____

☐ _____

☐ _____

☐ _____

☐ _____

☐ _____

☐ _____

I feel angry when faced with these situations:

☐ long lines at a store, bank or movie theater

☐ loud music

☐ yelling

☐ traffic jams

☐ toys or clothes all over the floor

☐ _____

☐ _____

☐ _____

☐ _____

☐ _____

☐ _____

☐ _____

☐ _____

☐ _____

☐ _____

☐ _____

☐ _____

☐ _____

☐ _____

How do you handle anger?

While anger can be helpful, it can also hurt you—and others.
Complete the checklist to see if you handle angry feelings in any of these ways:

	Yes	No
I keep my anger to myself	☐	☐
I yell or scream	☐	☐
I run to my room and cry	☐	☐
I break things	☐	☐
I store up my anger until I'm ready to explode	☐	☐
I say or do things I regret	☐	☐
I use alcohol or other drugs	☐	☐
I take my anger out on others	☐	☐
My anger scares people in my family	☐	☐
My anger sometimes scares me	☐	☐

If you answered yes to any question above, your anger may be hurting you and your family.
The next 2 pages have suggestions for handling anger.

HELPFUL WAYS TO HANDLE ANGER

Recognize your anger.

Your body may send you warning signs that you are getting angry. Signs may include:

- tense muscles
- clenched jaw
- fast breathing
- clumsiness (for example, bumping into things)
- upset stomach
- raised voice

Try to calm down.

Here are some ideas:

- Stop what you're doing.
- Count to 10.
- Get away from the person you are angry with. Go to another room or leave the house (if young children can be properly supervised).
- Vent your anger in a place safely away from other people—such as the shower.
- Do something physical to let off steam. For example, take a walk, shoot some hoops or pull weeds.

Let it out.

Many people were taught that it's wrong to be angry, so they try to hide it. But holding your anger in may:

- make you feel worse
- only delay—not prevent—an outburst. When your anger finally comes out, you may turn it on someone else, causing more problems (and possible conflicts)

When you're angry, talk about it with someone you trust. You may worry that the person will like you less, but he or she may feel closer to you because you opened up to him or her.

WHEN A FAMILY MEMBER IS ANGRY

Don't fuel the flame.

It's natural to want to fight anger with anger—or to completely withdraw to avoid the conflict. Neither way solves the problem.

Don't say "calm down."

That might make the person more upset. Also, don't say "You shouldn't feel that way." It's the person's right to feel however he or she feels.

Use your listening skills.

- Just listen—the person may need to let off steam at first.
- Keep your ears open for other feelings, too.
- When there's a pause, check your understanding. In your own words, repeat what the person said and give your sense of how she or he is feeling.

(See pages 274-275.)

Call for a timeout.

If you need time to calm down or think of a response, take it! Try saying "You've given me a lot to think about. I need a few minutes to sort it out." (This can also help the other person calm down.)

Stay safe.

If you feel physically unsafe, get away. (See page 286 for more information.)

Managing anger: Tips from our family

Where there's conflict, there is sometimes anger. Think about ways you and other family members have handled anger—your own and each other's. Based on your experiences, think about advice you would give another family. Write it below.

If you are angry, it's best to:_____

_____

Try not to:_____

_____

If a family member is angry, it's best to:_____

_____

Try not to:_____

_____

EVERY MEMBER OF YOUR FAMILY CAN BE A WINNER!

Anyone can use this 5-step "win-win" method to solve conflicts.
You can also use it to help make decisions at your family meetings.

1. Identify one specific issue to talk about.

For example, if a child does not put things away, talk about his or her room—not his or her messiness in general.

2. Brainstorm.

Write down as many ideas as you can think of to resolve the issue. Don't reject or comment on any idea until your list is complete.

3. Consider the pros and cons of each idea.

The pros are good points, the cons are bad points. Cross out ideas that people do not like or do not think will work.

4. Choose one solution.

Pick one that both sides can live with. For example, your child will pick up his or her room when company is coming. At other times, you are willing to live with a closed bedroom door.

4. Agree to try it.

- Put your agreement in writing—like a contract. (Include the expected consequences for breaking the agreement, if appropriate, for example, what will happen if a child does not follow a rule.) You can use the contract on the next page if you want.
- Include the length of time that you will try it.
- Set a date when you will meet again and review how the plan is working.

5. Conflicts: Not all "cons"

Many people may think of something negative when they hear the word "conflict." The fact is, conflict is a part of life—especially family life. When they are resolved in healthy, productive ways, conflicts can actually be good for families. They can:

- help children and teens learn to negotiate and compromise
- help all family members understand and respect one another

These benefits can only make a family stronger!

Our Contract

The issue:

_____
_____
_____
_____

Ideas we've considered:

_____
_____
_____
_____

Our plan:

_____
_____
_____
_____

Consequences for breaking the agreement:

_____
_____
_____
_____

We will follow our plan for this length of time:

We will meet again on: _____   Today's date: _____

Signed,

_____   _____
_____   _____
_____   _____
_____   _____
_____   _____

HELP IS OUT THERE.

Families today are often isolated from relatives or others who could offer support and advice. But when there's conflict, families do not have to struggle alone!

National organizations

- Administration for Children and Families U.S. Department of Health and Human Services www.acf.hhs.gov.

- Childhelp® National Child Abuse Hotline 1-800-4-A-CHILD® (1-800-422-4453).

- Prevent Child Abuse America 1-800-CHILDREN (1-800-244-5373) www.preventchildabuse.org.

- National Domestic Violence Hotline 1-800-799-SAFE (1-800-799-7233) (English/Spanish) 1-800-787-3224 (TTY).

State and local services

- health clinics or healthcare providers
- school counselors
- religious leaders
- social and family services
- parent groups
- hotlines (look in your phone book)
- the extension service in your state

Check the community service numbers in the front section of your phone book.

When problems are serious

Getting help is especially important in situations in which someone's (or an entire family's) health or safety is at risk. Get professional help if someone in your family:

- has a problem with alcohol or other drugs
- is physically, sexually or emotionally abusive
- is depressed or has other mental health problems. If he or she talks about suicide, this is an emergency

These problems must be addressed before your family can function in healthy ways.

Notes:_____

_____

_____

_____

_____

_____

_____

Help your family resolve conflict—and feel closer than ever!

OUR RIGHTS AND RESPONSIBILITIES

Everyone in our family has the right to:

- shelter, food and clothing
- protection from physical and emotional harm
- love and affection
- respect
- feelings—and the respectful expression of feelings
- friends and outside interests

Parents have the responsibility to:

- take care of children
- encourage children to develop their talents
- set a good example for children
- set limits and boundaries
- explain the consequences for breaking rules
- be fair with discipline

Children have the responsibility to:

- go to school when old enough, and do the best they can
- find their talents and develop them
- take part in making family rules
- accept consequences for breaking rules
- cooperate with others in the family
- help with caring for the home

Each one of us helps make our family special. Let's make our family strong!

PARENTING AND ANGER MANAGEMENT

REENTRY
ESSENTIALS, INC.

Life Skills Series
Basic Skills for Lifelong Success

Please read:

Talk to your health-care provider! This workbook is not a substitute for the advice of a qualified health-care provider.

REENTRY
ESSENTIALS, INC.

Reentry Essentials, Inc.
2609 East 14 Street, Suite 1018
Brooklyn, NY 11235-3915
P: 347.973.0004
E: info@ReentryEssentials.org
I: www.ReentryEssentials.org

This workbook belongs to:

_____

You may find it helpful to keep important names and phone numbers handy.

Write them below.

Health-care provider

Name_____

Phone_____

Counselor

Name_____

Phone_____

Emergency contact

Name_____

Phone_____

Other important numbers

_____

_____

_____

_____

_____

_____

_____

_____

_____

THIS WORKBOOK CAN HELP YOU MANAGE YOUR ANGER AS YOU RAISE YOUR CHILD.

Being a parent* is a rewarding job! It can also be a very demanding one that brings up strong feelings

We all get angry sometimes.

It's normal for parents to get angry with their children. Getting angry is OK! What really matters is how you express that anger. Parents who don't manage their anger may hurt their children.

Everyone can learn to manage anger better.

It's a skill that involves:

- finding out what triggers your anger
- learning how to calm down
- expressing anger in healthy ways

Improving anger management skills takes time, but it's worth it!

CONTENT

*In this workbook, "parent" also refers to guardians, grandparents and other primary caregivers.

IT'S OK TO FEEL ANGRY.

Anger is a natural emotion. But it's also a very powerful one. Feelings of anger can get very intense. That's why anger needs to be managed.

Being a parent is filled with wonderful moments!

But it can also be very stressful. It is normal for your child to sometimes:

- misbehave
- ignore you
- do the opposite of what you tell him/her
- talk back

These are situations all parents face. But they can bring up angry feelings.

When you get angry, things happen in your body.

Anger is your body's way of getting ready for an emergency. Adrenaline and other chemicals enter your bloodstream. This causes physical changes, such as:

- increased heart rate
- tense muscles
- rapid breathing
- flushed face

You may also sweat or tremble. When you feel angry, it is also hard to think straight.

There are different ways to express anger.

It's important to control your anger and express it in a positive way. This can help you be a more effective parent.

Uncontrolled anger can lead to problems for you and your family.

You might express anger in a negative way—verbally or physically. But these ways of responding to anger solve nothing.

Managing anger effectively has many benefits.

Learning to keep your anger under control can help you:

- stay healthy
- solve the problems that come up when raising a child
- teach your child positive ways to deal with anger
- focus on being the best parent you can be

We can all learn to manage anger more effectively!

WHAT CAUSES ANGER?

Everyone reacts to situations in different ways. Our thoughts and experiences influence, whether or not something makes us angry. But some common causes of anger include:

Stress

Raising a child can be very stressful! It takes a lot of work every day. You may also experience stress related to work, health or money problems.

Frustration

You may get angry if your child misbehaves, or if you feel like you're losing control of a situation.

Fear

At times, you may feel that you are not cut out to be a parent. Or, you may be afraid that your child will stop loving you if you discipline him or her.

Daily hassles

Raising a child can involve a lot of annoyances and irritations. Frequent diaper changes or cleaning up after your child may get on your nerves. Driving your child somewhere can be aggravating if the traffic is bad.

Disappointment

For example, you might be disappointed that your child is not doing better in school. Or, you may have had expectations and desires about parenthood that don't match what it's really like.

Resentment

Raising a child requires a lot of time, effort and commitment. You may have to set aside some of your personal goals. You will probably have less time to spend with friends.

Other people

Someone may say or do something that makes you angry. This person could be a:

- partner
- family member
- friend
- co-worker
- stranger

Think about a time you got angry due to one of the causes listed on this page. What made you angry? Write about it here:

_____

_____

_____

_____

_____

_____

_____

_____

_____

_____

_____

_____

Improving anger management skills can help you deal with many different situations.

ANGER CAN CAUSE SERIOUS PROBLEMS.

Trying to ignore angry feelings and hoping they go away does not work. Uncontrolled anger can lead to:

Health problems

If you don't express anger in a positive way, it can take its toll on your body and cause health problems. These may include:

- headaches
- sleep problems
- digestive problems
- high blood pressure
- heart problems

Poor judgment

When you are angry, it is hard to think clearly. You may have trouble concentrating or make bad decisions. Poor judgment puts both you and your child at risk— for example, if you are driving.

Problems with relationships

You may insult or criticize:

- your partner
- friends
- family members

They may respond with anger or resentment.

Depression

Anger that isn't dealt with can affect your thoughts and feelings. You may lose interest in things you used to enjoy, such as special moments with your child.

Passive-aggressive behavior

If you don't express your anger in a positive way, it will come out in other ways. If you are angry about something else, you might take it out on your child by refusing to allow him or her to go to a friend's house.

Alcohol or other drug problems

Some people may try to deal with anger by using alcohol or other drugs. They mistakenly think substance use will help them:

- dull anger and other strong feelings
- forget about the negative consequences of an angry outburst

But using alcohol or other drugs doesn't solve anything. In fact, it can make things much worse. It can also affect your judgment when you are taking care of your child.

Low self-esteem for your child

Uncontrolled anger can come out in the form of harsh words. Words can be very hurtful to young children. If you yell and criticize often, it may affect the way your child thinks of him or herself. He or she may become insecure or withdrawn.

Emotional problems for your child

If you don't manage your anger well, it's likely your child won't either. He or she may have problems expressing anger in healthy ways. This can affect all of your child's relationships.

Your child may also feel a lot of guilt or shame. A child who is criticized constantly will believe that nothing he or she does is ever good enough.

Behavioral problems for your child

Children learn a lot by watching. Your child sees you losing control of your anger, he or she may think that is what people are supposed to do. This can lead to future problems at home and in school.

Children who do not learn to express anger in positive ways are at higher risk of:

- bullying others
- avoiding social situations
- not doing as well as they can in school
- using alcohol or other drugs
- violence

Improving anger management skills can help you avoid these problems.

Has your anger been causing a problem for you or your child?

Check off any problems that you think are related to the way you manage your anger. Explain your answers below.

- ☐ Health problems
- ☐ Poor judgment
- ☐ Problems with relationships
- ☐ Depression
- ☐ Passive-aggressive behavior
- ☐ Alcohol or other drug problems
- ☐ Low self-esteem (your child)
- ☐ Emotional problems (your child)
- ☐ Behavioral problems (your child)

_____

_____

_____

_____

_____

_____

_____

_____

_____

_____

_____

_____

Contact your health-care provider or a mental health professional if you think anger is currently harming you or your child.

UNCONTROLLED ANGER CAN ALSO LEAD TO ABUSE.

Abuse is any mistreatment of a child that results in harm or injury. It is never OK to be abusive toward a child. Abuse includes:

Physical abuse

This includes:

- hitting
- slapping
- pushing
- kicking
- restraining
- grabbing
- pulling
- burning
- throwing things

Another form of physical abuse is shaken baby syndrome. This is when a baby is shaken violently. It can result in serious brain damage and death.

Verbal abuse

This includes:

- yelling
- criticizing
- insulting
- name-calling
- shaming your child
- trying to make your child feel guilty

Neglect

This happens when a child's basic needs aren't met. Every child needs:

- love
- physical affection
- attention
- food
- shelter
- proper clothing
- supervision
- health care
- education

Sexual abuse

This includes:

- any type of sexual contact with a child
- using a child for sexual films or photographs
- Prostituting a child

The effects of abuse can last a long time.

Children who are abused may feel:

- angry
- ashamed
- guilty
- afraid of adults
- hate for the abuser
- the need for revenge

Victims of abuse have trouble dealing with their emotions and don't trust others. This makes it difficult for them to have meaningful relationships in life.

Abuse also teaches children the wrong lesson.

Children who are abused learn that it is OK to hurt others when they feel angry or frustrated, even people they love. They may also learn to lie or hide things from a parent to escape further abuse. They may even try to run away.

MANAGING ANGER CAN HELP IN MANY WAYS.
It can help you:

Reach goals

You can learn to use anger to motivate you to work harder on your goals, such as completing an exercise session or mastering a skill.

Solve problems

Anger can be a warning sign that something is wrong. When you feel angry, it's time for you to think about your feelings and attitudes about a situation. For example, you may feel angry because you don't think your partner is doing enough to help with household chores. That could be a sign that you both need to talk about responsibilities.

Handle emergencies

Anger sends adrenaline into your bloodstream, giving you a boost of strength and energy. This can allow you to take quick action in an emergency—for example, if you see your child is about to accidentally hurt him or herself.

Communicate

Talking about your anger can help you keep it from building up. This releases tension and allows you to communicate more easily and effectively with your child and other family members.

How can anger help you?

Think of a problem with your child you are trying to solve—one that makes you feel angry. Or, think of a goal you are trying to reach with your child that causes frustration and angry feelings. Write it here:

_____

_____

_____

_____

_____

_____

Describe what happened when you got angry:

_____

_____

_____

_____

_____

_____

_____

_____

_____

As you read the tips in this workbook, think of how you could express your anger in a more positive way that helps the situation. Include this in your plan on page 319.

Find ways to make anger work for you, not against you.

IS ANGER AFFECTING YOUR PARENTING?

Think about how often you get angry and how you handle angry feelings around your child.
Complete the checklists. They can help you decide if your anger management skills could be improved.

Do I get angry a lot?	True	False
I feel tense a lot of the time when I take care of my child.	☐	☐
I have been told I need to learn to stay calm	☐	☐
I get angry with my child quickly.	☐	☐
I stay angry at my child for a long time.	☐	☐
Sometimes it seems that everything my child does makes me angry.	☐	☐
Minor things my child does annoy me more than they annoy my partner or other caregivers.	☐	☐
I often blame my troubles on my child.	☐	☐
When my child misbehaves, I want to punish him or her.	☐	☐
Getting angry makes me feel I am in control.	☐	☐
I am still angry about something my child did in the past.	☐	☐
I get easily frustrated with my child.	☐	☐
I get very upset when my child does even little things wrong.	☐	☐
I am still angry about other things when I am taking care of my child.	☐	☐
My child has commented that I seem to get angry a lot.	☐	☐
If my child disobeys me or misbehaves, I take it personally.	☐	☐

How many "true" responses did you check off?

The more "true" answers you have, the more likely it is that anger is affecting your parenting.
Being aware of your anger is the first step in learning to manage it. On the following pages, you'll learn more about warning signs, which are your body's response to angry feelings.
You will also learn how to identify the things that are triggering your anger.

Now, complete the checklist on the following page to see if you are expressing anger in positive ways.

How do I express my anger?	True	False
I store up my anger until it feels like I'm going to explode.	☐	☐
I try to ignore my anger and hope it goes away.	☐	☐
When I get angry, I say or do things I later regret.	☐	☐

My anger:

	True	False
• frightens me	☐	☐
• frightens my child	☐	☐

When I get angry, I:

	True	False
• yell or scream at my child	☐	☐
• cry in front of my child	☐	☐
• break or throw things	☐	☐
• hurt myself	☐	☐
• hurt my child	☐	☐

	True	False
My anger has resulted in: problems with my partner (or another caregiver), trouble with the law.	☐	☐
I have tried to control my anger and failed.	☐	☐
I use alcohol or other drugs to try to deal with angry feelings.	☐	☐
I have overreacted to something my child has done.	☐	☐
I take out my anger with other people or things on my child.	☐	☐
People have told me I have a bad temper.	☐	☐
My anger with my child seems to follow a pattern.	☐	☐
I feel I make things worse when I express my anger.	☐	☐
I fear anger is negatively affecting my job as a parent.	☐	☐
I want help managing my anger.	☐	☐

How many "true" responses did you check off?

The more "true" answers you have, the more likely it is that anger is harming you and your child. But it doesn't have to be that way. You can learn to manage your anger and stay in control. This workbook includes tips on staying calm and expressing your anger in healthy ways. This can help you communicate with your child, solve problems and be a more effective parent. This workbook also includes tips on positive discipline for your child and dealing with your child's anger.

Remember, getting angry is normal. It's what you do with that anger that counts.

DO YOU KNOW YOUR BODY'S ANGER WARNING SIGNS?

Learning to recognize anger is an important step in improving how you manage it.
But we don't always realize when we are getting angry. Fortunately, our bodies give us plenty of clues.

Your body responds to angry feelings.

You've already learned about some of the changes that take place in your body when you feel angry (see page 292). Your nervous system prepares your body to react to situations that cause anger (or other strong emotions, such as fear or excitement).

Anger helps your body get ready to protect itself by:

- breathing faster to take in more oxygen
- pumping blood to your muscles for more energy
- cooling your body with sweat

It causes other changes, too. Learning about these changes can help you identify angry feelings.

Think about how you feel when you get angry.

Check the warning signs you get. Write in any signs that aren't listed. (If you're not sure, think of something in the past that made you very angry. How did your body react?)

- ☐ tense muscles
- ☐ tight fists
- ☐ clenched jaw
- ☐ sweaty palms
- ☐ racing heartbeat
- ☐ fast breathing
- ☐ trembling or feeling shaky
- ☐ feeling warm or flushed
- ☐ upset stomach
- ☐ loud or mean voice
- ☐ dry mouth
- ☐ _____
- ☐ _____
- ☐ _____
- ☐ _____

Talk with your healthcare provider.

Certain physical and mental health problems, such as brain injury, may increase your anger. Anger may also be part of postpartum depression, which can lead to thoughts of harming your baby, as well as yourself. And anger that is not managed well can lead to other health problems. Talk with your health-care provider about your anger and how it affects you.

Your child probably notices some of your body's anger warning signs, too.

KNOW YOUR TRIGGERS.

Our anger can be triggered by different things. Some possible triggers are listed below. Check the ones that trigger your anger. Use the blank spaces to write down other anger triggers.

I feel angry when I:

- ☐ think too much child-care responsibility falls on me
- ☐ don't feel appreciated
- ☐ feel ignored
- ☐ have to clean up after my child
- ☐ feel I'm not being a good enough parent
- ☐ feel helpless or out of control
- ☐ think about paying bills
- ☐ have to turn down invitations because of my child
- ☐ have to take care of my child when I'm not feeling well
- ☐ try to balance work and home life
- ☐ _____
- ☐ _____
- ☐ _____
- ☐ _____

I feel angry when my child:

- ☐ doesn't pay attention
- ☐ doesn't do what I say
- ☐ has a temper tantrum
- ☐ fights with another child
- ☐ won't help with chores
- ☐ whines or complains
- ☐ doesn't want to go to bed
- ☐ stays on the phone or computer too long
- ☐ doesn't call if he or she will be late coming home
- ☐ does not do well in school
- ☐ complains about something I do
- ☐ hides out in his or her room
- ☐ _____
- ☐ _____
- ☐ _____
- ☐ _____

I feel angry when faced with these situations:

- ☐ changing a diaper
- ☐ cleaning
- ☐ planning meals
- ☐ shopping
- ☐ heavy traffic
- ☐ disagreeing with my partner
- ☐ buying things for my child
- ☐ trying to help my child with homework
- ☐ having an argument
- ☐ not getting enough sleep
- ☐ _____
- ☐ _____
- ☐ _____
- ☐ _____

Knowing your anger triggers can help you change the way you respond to them.

MY ANGER JOURNAL

Use these 2 pages to start an "anger journal."
Over the next several days, keep track of things that trigger your anger.

Date/Time	Trigger	My anger warning signs	My anger rating 1 = Mild 2 = Moderate 3 = Severe	What I did in response	How my child reacted

Date/Time	Trigger	My anger warning signs	My anger rating 1 = Mild 2 = Moderate 3 = Severe	What I did in response	How my child reacted

WATCH OUT FOR HIDDEN ANGER.

If you get angry but you're not sure why, there may be other things going on that bring up angry feelings.

Try not to overreact.

Is your level of anger out of proportion to what triggered it? If your child misbehaves at night after you've had a bad day, you may be letting out all of the angry feelings that have been building up.

Recognize the source of your anger.

You may have angry feelings brought on by your partner or someone else you know, or by something that happened to you earlier that day. If you don't express those angry feelings in a positive way, you may direct them at your child without realizing it.

Learn not to take things personally.

If your child misbehaves, won't listen to you or talks back, it's easy to think your child is trying to hurt your feelings. But your child is just acting the way all children do at times. (Talk to your child's health-care provider if you think your child's behavior issues are more serious.)

Try to break anger patterns.

For example, do you react with anger if your child stubbornly refuses to clean his or her room? Does the same thing happen each time—you ask, your child refuses, you get angry? Look for other ways to approach the problem.

The signs of hidden anger.

When you don't express your anger, it doesn't go away. It can come out in other ways, including:

- putting off doing things you need to do
- sarcastic comments
- being overly polite
- frequent sighing
- difficulty sleeping
- irritability
- loss of interest in things· you usually enjoy
- teeth grinding (especially while sleeping)
- a repeated physical movement, such rolling your eyes
- a chronically stiff neck
- depression

You may not even realize you're angry. But unless you express those feelings, they may come out in ways you don't like.

It's important to express your anger in healthy ways.

TAKE CONTROL OF YOUR ANGER.

The next time you feel yourself getting angry, take steps to stay in control.
The first step is to calm down. Here are some suggestions that might work for you.

Be prepared.

Remind yourself that unexpected things happen all the time when raising a child. For example, if you are feeding a very young child, there's a good chance some of that food will end up on the floor, or on you. Anticipating things that might happen can help you stay in control when they do.

Tell yourself to stop.

If you notice any warning signs of anger and start thinking angry thoughts, tell yourself to stop.

You could say something like:

- "OK, just relax."
- "Calm down."
- "Take it easy."
- "Chill."

Pretend there is a TV camera in the room and you are being watched. How would you want people to see you act?

Try to relax.

Use one of the following methods to calm down:

- Count to 10 (or higher, if needed)
- Get a drink of water
- Take several slow, deep breaths
- Listen to soothing music

Leave the situation, if you can.

If you are angry with your child, take a timeout. If possible, ask someone to watch him or her while you calm down. If that's not possible, step away from your child for a few moments until you feel calm.

Wait until you are calm.

Unless it is an emergency, responding before you have had a chance to calm down is not a good idea. You may do or say something you will regret.

Think about a time you found yourself getting angry, but were able to stay in control. What happened? What did you do to stay calm? Write about it here:

_____

_____

_____

_____

_____

_____

_____

_____

_____

_____

_____

_____

_____

_____

_____

FOCUS ON HEALTHY WAYS TO EXPRESS ANGER.

It's important to express angry feelings in ways that don't hurt anyone.

Think.

After you calm down, think about what happened to make you angry, and the best way to handle the situation. What kind of result do you want?

Identify the problem.

If you are angry with your child, explain what you are angry about calmly and clearly. Be specific about what made you angry. If your child didn't put away his or her toys as agreed, don't say "You never do what I tell you." Say "I am disappointed because you didn't put away your toys like I asked you to." Don't yell or call your child names.

Use "I" statements.

These let your child know how you feel about something without blaming or criticizing. Don't say "You are useless." Instead, say "I feel angry when you don't do the chores you were asked to do."

Identify solutions.

Tell your child what you would like to change or see happen in the future. Try to work out a solution together. For example, if your child is not putting away his or her toys, work out a time to do it, such as before going to bed.

Get help if you need it.

If you are having trouble expressing your anger in healthy ways, talk with your partner, a friend or another family member. Have someone you can call in times of crisis. It should be a person who can help you stay calm and see the situation clearly. A family therapist may be able to help. (See page 317.)

Fill in the blanks below to practice using "I" statements with your child. Use specific situations you have faced recently.

I feel_____ When_____

I feel_____ When_____

I feel_____ When_____

I feel_____ When_____

I feel_____ When_____

I feel_____ When_____

I feel_____ When_____

I feel_____ When_____

I feel_____ When_____

I feel_____ When_____

I feel_____ When_____

I feel_____ When_____

I feel_____ When_____

I feel_____ When_____

I feel_____ When_____

CERTAIN REACTIONS CAN MAKE THINGS WORSE.
If you tend to react to anger in one of the following ways there's something you can do about it.

Holding on to the past

You may still feel angry about events or hurts that happened a long time ago. As time goes by, you may think about those angry feelings a lot.

Things that happened in the past can't be changed. It's best to forgive and move on.

Keeping things bottled up

This will only make you feel worse, and it doesn't address the problem. Your angry feelings will come out eventually, and may come out in a way that hurts your child.

Overgeneralizing

If something your child does makes you angry, stick to that one thing in your response. Avoid using words such as "always" or "never."

Blaming

This doesn't solve anything. If you are having a bad day, that isn't your child's fault. Take responsibility for all of your own feelings and actions.

Not admitting when you're wrong

For example, you may be angry at having to drive your child somewhere on short notice. But your child reminds you that he or she asked for the ride last week. If you are wrong, own up to it.

Using alcohol or other drugs

They do nothing to get rid of angry feelings. They will only cause more problems and make it harder for you to think clearly to find a solution. Alcohol and other drugs may even increase your anger.

If you have a problem with alcohol or other drugs, call the Center for Substance Abuse Treatment's Referral Service at

1-800-662-HELP
(1-800-662-4357).

Think of a time when you reacted to anger in a way that made things worse. What happened? Write about it here:

_____
_____
_____
_____
_____
_____
_____
_____
_____
_____
_____

If faced with the same situation again, how would you handle it?

_____
_____
_____
_____
_____
_____
_____
_____
_____
_____
_____

HEALTHY HABITS CAN HELP.

There's a lot you can do to help you be better prepared to deal with anger.
Here are some tips:

Stay physically active.

Physical activity is a quick and safe way to let out angry feelings. It releases stress and improves your overall health. It will also help you feel better.

Some good choices include:

- walking
- running
- swimming
- tennis
- dancing
- yoga

Even doing household chores counts as physical activity. For more fun, choose an activity you and your child can do together.

Try to get at least 150 minutes of moderate—or 75 minutes of vigorous—physical activity each week. In addition, do muscle strengthening exercises on 2 days. To meet these goals, try replacing some TV or other "screen time" with exercise.

Be sure to consult your Health-care provider before starting an exercise program.

Eat for good health

Eating right gives you the energy you need to raise your child!

- Make a variety of nutrient dense choices from each food group in the right amounts for your calorie needs. Choose items that fit your culture, tastes and budget.
- Vary your choices from each food group throughout the week.
- Make small shifts to healthier choices. For example, switch to fat-free or low-fat dairy products. Choose seafood, lean meats, lean poultry, nuts, seeds and soy products over high-fat meats.
- Fill half of your plate with fruits and vegetables.
- Make at least half of your grains whole grains.
- Limit saturated fat, added sugars and sodium.
- Use vegetable oils (like canola and olive) in place of solid fats like butter, shortening, lard and coconut oil).

Learn more at www.ChooseMyPlate.gov.

NOTE: These guidelines are for adults and for children age 2 and older. Ask a healthcare provider about nutrition for younger children.

Get plenty of rest.

It's not always easy for parents to get a good night's rest, but it's important! Sleep helps refresh and repair your body and mind. Most adults need about 7-9 hours of sleep each day. If you are having trouble sleeping:

- Go to bed at the same time each night.
- Avoid caffeine at least 8 hours before going to bed.
- Don't use alcohol to help you sleep.
- Don't use sleeping aids without consulting your health-care provider first.

Make sure your child gets plenty of rest, too.

Try to find the humor in things.

A good sense of humor helps many people avoid getting angry. Look for the humor in minor troubles and annoyances. Look for opportunities to laugh together as a family.

Meet with friends regularly.

Raising a child limits your social schedule, but you can still find time to catch up with friends. This is a great way to relieve stress.

Take up a hobby.

This can be a productive outlet for tension and energy. It can also be a welcome distraction from angry feelings. A hobby is any activity you enjoy, such as:

- gardening
- cooking
- painting
- playing piano or guitar
- bird watching
- making crafts

You might want to choose something you and your child can do together.

Keep a journal or diary.

Write down your thoughts and feelings. Writing can help you work through problems calmly at your own pace.

Write a letter.

If someone did something to make you angry, explain it in a letter. But you don't have to send it. Simply writing out problems can help you work out your feelings.

Avoid labeling.

Try not to use labels—such as "foolish" or "stupid"—when referring to yourself or your child. And avoid referring to activities as "pointless" or "endless." These kinds of labels make a problem seem worse than it is. They also take away energy you could use toward solving the problem.

Remember that people can't read minds.

Sharing your thoughts and feelings with others will help improve communication.

What changes can you make in your life to practice healthy habits? When could you do these things? Write your thoughts here:

_____

_____

_____

_____

_____

_____

_____

_____

_____

_____

_____

TRY A RELAXATION METHOD.

Being a parent can be stressful! Using one or more of these relaxation techniques regularly can help you reduce stress and stay calm.

Meditation

This can help calm you and clear your mind of anger.

Follow these steps:

1. Find a quiet place. Wear loose, comfortable clothing. Sit or lie down.

2. Close your eyes. Take slow, deep breaths.

3. Concentrate on a single word, object or calming thought.

4. Don't worry if other thoughts or images enter your mind while you are doing this. Just relax and return to what you were focusing on.

5. Continue until you feel relaxed and refreshed.

Deep-breathing exercises

These can help keep anger from getting out of control.

Follow these steps:

1. Sit comfortably or lie on your back.
2. Breathe in slowly and deeply for a count of 5.
3. Hold your breath for a count of 5.
4. Breathe out slowly for a count of 5, pushing out all the air.
5. Repeat several times until you feel calm and relaxed.

Visualization

This technique uses your imagination to help you relax and reduce your anger.

1. Sit in a comfortable chair or lie down.
2. Imagine a pleasant, peaceful scene, such as a lush forest or a sandy beach. Picture yourself in this setting.
3. Focus on the scene. Continue until you feel refreshed and relaxed.

Progressive muscle relaxation

Tense and relax each muscle group, starting at your head and working your way down to your toes. Here's how:

1. Wear loose, comfortable clothing. Sit in a comfortable chair or lie down.
2. Tense the muscles in your face for 5-10 seconds. Then relax them for about 20 seconds.
3. Tense the muscles in the back of your neck for 5-10 seconds. Then relax them for about 20 seconds. Notice the difference in how your muscles feel when relaxed.
4. Move down to your shoulders. Tense and relax the muscles the same way you did in step 3.
5. Repeat the same steps with the other muscle groups in your body—in your hands, arms, chest, stomach, lower back, buttocks, thighs, calves and feet—one at a time.

DISCIPLINE SHOULD NEVER HURT.

Discipline is not about punishment. It's about teaching your child how to respect limits and follow rules. Discipline helps your child:

Stay safe

Teaching discipline involves helping your child learn how to make good choices. This means doing things that are safe for your child and others.

Learn right from wrong

As your child grows, he or she may experience:

• bullying (as a victim, a bystander or the person bullying)

• pressure to do unsafe things, such as use tobacco, alcohol or other drugs

• other types of peer pressure It's important to keep talking about these issues and how to make good decisions with your child.

Develop values

Learning right from wrong helps children develop many positive values.

By sharing your own values with your child, you can help your child think about the kind of person he or she would like to be.

Respect others

Your child learns by watching you. By being respectful in your daily life, you'll teach your child to do the same.

Talk with your child about why you think it's important to show respect to adults and other children at all times.

Build self-esteem

Giving children attention and praise when they behave well helps them feel good about themselves. It also helps motivate them to keep behaving well.

Develop self-control

Discipline involves teaching your child the appropriate way to handle emotions, including anger. Children who learn how to handle emotions are less likely to have outbursts or get into fights.

Understand consequences

Learning that all actions— positive and negative—have consequences helps children make good decisions.

Be successful in school and in life

Positive discipline helps children build good work habits (such as finishing tasks, cleaning up after themselves and helping others). These work habits also help children succeed later in life, in college and in the workplace.

Discipline is an ongoing process.

It begins early in your child's life and changes as he or she matures. The skills and values you teach your child now can benefit him or her throughout childhood, adolescence and adulthood.

Discipline is not always easy, but with patience and determination, you can help your child develop valuable skills.

PRACTICE POSITIVE DISCIPLINE WITH YOUR CHILD.
Having a plan will help you keep angry feelings under control.

Make sure your child knows you love him or her.

Let your child know you will love him or her no matter what. You can:

- Use words—tell your child you love him or her.
- Give your child a hug.
- Show you care by spending time with your child.

Know the causes of misbehavior.

Children often misbehave because they feel:

- tired or hungry
- sick
- angry after not getting what they want
- a certain behavior is acceptable
- afraid (for example, of the dark or of new people)
- jealous (of a brother or sister, for example)
- hurt or disappointed

Understanding the causes of misbehavior can help you choose effective ways of handling it.

Set rules and limits.

Children of all ages need the structure that rules and limits provide. Structure helps children gain independence and learn self-control.

- Make sure your child understands the rules. Make sure all family members and other caregivers know them, too.
- Explain the reasons for the rules—and the consequences for breaking them.
- Remind your child about rules when needed. He or she may test you to see if you're serious about enforcing a rule. Or your child may simply forget a rule from time to time.
- As your child gets older, give him or her more choices, freedom and responsibility.

Be firm.

Say only what's necessary to stop the behavior. Use a firm no with a young child, or say "that's enough" to an older child. Then, let him or her know what is acceptable.

Praise and encourage good behavior.

Be specific:

- Say "Thank you for helping me clean the table," instead of saying "Good job." This way your child knows exactly what you like about his or her behavior.
- Acknowledge when your child stops or admits to inappropriate behavior. You could say, "Thank you for apologizing to me for talking back."

Use timeouts.

This may work if your child has lost control.

- Bring your child to a safe place that has no distractions.
- Have your child stay there until he or she calms down— or for a set length of time (for example, one minute for each year of age).
- Make it clear that the time will be increased if your child comes out too soon.

When the time is up, praise your child for calming down.

Take away privileges.

You could forbid your child to watch TV for a while. Be sure your child understands why you took away the privilege.

Use consequences for inappropriate behavior.

A consequence is an action you take in response to your child's misbehavior. (If a child uses crayons to draw on the wall after being told not to, one consequence can be taking away the crayons.)

Talk to your child about the consequences in terms he or she can understand. In general:

- Respond right away. But always remember to think before you act!
- Fit the consequence to the action. Avoid consequences that are too harsh.
- Be consistent. Always follow through if you say a behavior will have a certain consequence. This helps teach that the behavior really is not OK.

Encourage good behavior as much as possible to keep from using consequences too often. Encouragement works better in the long run!

Use methods that fit your child.

If you have more than one child, be sure to do this for each one. It's important to:

- Keep your child's age in mind. Discipline needs to change as a child grows up.
- Consider your child's personality. Some children are more active or outgoing. Others are more quiet or shy.

Limits that are fair for one child may be too hard for another to follow. For example, a younger or more active child may find it hard to resist touching things in a store.

Ask for help if you need it.

Seek professional help if discipline becomes a problem. Check your phone book for family counseling services, mental health services or social service agencies.

Remember, effective discipline is an ongoing effort. Keep working on it!

POSITIVE DISCIPLINE PLAN

Use this sheet to plan an effective discipline when your child misbehaves. Refer back to it to see what worked.

Date/Time	Misbehavior	Discipline used	How my child reacted	Was this effective?

WHEN YOUR CHILD GETS ANGRY
It's important to learn how to respond to your child's anger, too.

Don't fight back.

If your child gets angry with you, you may be tempted to respond with anger or to be defensive. Instead, stop and listen to what your child has to say.

Try to communicate.

A conflict with your child is an opportunity for each of you to express your feelings. Wait until you are both calm. Be respectful with your child when sharing your feelings. Encourage your child to do the same.

Practice listening.

When your child is angry, it could be about something that happened to him or her. He or she may have had an argument with a friend, for example. Encourage your child to talk about it and listen closely. Don't interrupt. Offer your help if your child needs it.

Don't take it personally.

It's not easy seeing your child angry, and it's natural to think it's because of something you did. But many times, your child's anger may have nothing to do with you.

Dealing with temper tantrums.

Sometimes children lose control and will start screaming or whining in response to something that happens. A timeout may help your child calm down. (See page 313.) Here are some other tips:

- Keep your cool. Don't reward your child's tantrum by paying attention to it in the form of anger or frustration.
- Try to understand the cause of the tantrum. Offer comfort if your child accidentally broke a favorite toy, but not if the tantrum is in response to your child not getting his or her way.
- Ignore the tantrum if there is not a valid reason for it. Pay attention to your child only when he or she starts behaving again.

If you have upset your child and feel you were in the wrong, offer an apology.

TEACH YOUR CHILD HOW TO MANAGE ANGER.

It's a valuable skill your child can use throughout his or her life.

Help your child identify anger.

Teach your child about the warning signs of anger on page 300. Ask your child to look for these warning signs when he or she feels angry.

Teach your child about anger triggers.

Tell your child how important it is to identify what it is that makes him or her angry. (See page 301.)

Teach your child how to calm down.

Share the tips from page 305 that worked for you, such as:

- counting to 10 or higher
- taking slow, deep breaths
- walking away from a situation that makes him or her angry

Show your child healthy ways to express anger.

Encourage your child to find an outlet that works for him or her, such as:

- music, art or another form of creative expression
- a hobby
- a journal or diary
- sports or any other form of physical activity. (Be sure to consult your child's healthcare provider before starting an exercise program)

Make sure your child knows what is not acceptable.

Teach your child that when angry, it is not OK to:

- yell at someone
- hit someone
- throw things

Teach your child problem solving skills

With your child, think of a common conflict (such as a problem at school) and then practice how to solve it. Teach your child these steps:

- Identify the problem. What is it we are trying to solve?
- Brainstorm (come up with many ways to solve the problem). Discuss each idea with your child, focusing on why each one may or may not be effective.
- Pick the best choice to try.
- Try out the solution and check the results. If it doesn't work, explain that he or she can try another solution.

SOURCES OF HELP

Let others know that you want to be a more effective parent by improving your anger management skills. They can provide support and encouragement. You can contact:

Your health-care provider

He or she can suggest relaxation techniques. Your health-care provider may also prescribe medications for any conditions related to your anger.

Mental professionals and mental health centers

They may offer outpatient treatment and support groups for issues related to anger control.

Counselors, family therapists or social workers

They can help you learn ways to manage anger, control stress and solve problems that you will face as a parent.

Hotlines

These can provide emergency counseling to help you control angry feelings if you are concerned for your child. Check your local phone book, or call:

- Childhelp® National Child Abuse Hotline 1-800-4-A-CHILD (1-800-422-4453).

Employee Assistance Programs (EAPs)

These may offer referrals or counseling to help employees deal with family problems.

Friends and other family members

They can be a source of help and support, especially ones who raised children of their own.

Federal agencies

They can provide information on what works in parenting. Contact:

- National Institute of Child Health and Human Development www.nichd.nih.gov 1-800-370-2943.

- U.S. Department of Education www.ed.gov 1-800-USA-LEARN (1-800-872-5327).

Raising a child is a rewarding but challenging job. Help is out there!

MAKE A PLAN TO MANAGE ANGER IN YOUR FAMILY.

You've learned about anger and how to express it in healthy ways.
Now it's time to put it into practice in your own family! Follow these steps:

1. Set positive goals with a time frame.

Your goals should address both a specific response and your reaction. Over the next month, your goal could be to try a new way to calm down when you get angry with your child. Or use the situation you wrote down on page 297.

Set different goals for yourself, but don't try to meet too many at one time.

2. Get support

Tell your partner, your friends and other family members about your goals. They can offer encouragement, advice and support. Have someone you can call if you are feeling overwhelmed by taking care of your child. Or consider seeing a mental health professional.

3. Track your progress.

Consider keeping a daily log or journal. Make notes of times when you handled your anger well in response to something your child did. Seeing improvement can keep you feeling encouraged.

4. Reward yourself.

Treat yourself when you reach a goal or get halfway there. For example, enjoy a special meal. Ask your child to help prepare it!

Anger response checklist.

Use this as a quick reference guide when you get angry (especially with your child or another family member).

1. Calm down.
2. Think about what happened.
3. Identify the problem.
4. Talk about it, using "I" statements.
5. Identify solutions.
6. Call

   _____

   ' if I'm having trouble.

MY ANGER MANAGEMENT PLAN

Goal

_____

_____

_____

_____

My action plan

_____

_____

_____

_____

Target date

_____

Reward

_____

_____

_____

People I can call for help

_____

_____

_____

Improving anger management skills can help you be the best parent you can be!

RELAXATION FOR YOUR HEALTH

REENTRY
ESSENTIALS, INC.

Life Skills Series
Basic Skills for Lifelong Success

Please read:

Talk to your healthcare provider! This workbook is not a substitute for the advice of a qualified health-care provider.

REENTRY
ESSENTIALS, INC.

Reentry Essentials, Inc.
2609 East 14 Street, Suite 1018
Brooklyn, NY 11235-3915
P: 347.973.0004
E: info@ReentryEssentials.org
I: www.ReentryEssentials.org

This workbook belongs to:

_____

You may find it helpful to keep important names and phone numbers handy.

Write them below.

Primary health-care provider

Name_____

Phone_____

Other health-care providers

Name_____

Phone_____

Health plan

Name_____

Phone_____

An emergency contact

Name_____

Phone_____

Child support office

Name_____

Phone_____

Other important numbers

_____

_____

_____

_____

_____

_____

_____

_____

_____

IF YOU'RE INTERESTED IN RELAXATION TECHNIQUES, THIS WORKBOOK IS FOR YOU.

It can help you better understand—and manage— the connection between the stress in your life and your health.

High stress levels are common
in our culture. The daily demands of work, family, community and technology affect most of us to one degree or another.

Many relaxation techniques are available
to help you offset the negative effects of stress. This workbook can help you choose—and use— the ones that are right for you!

CONTENT

STRESS IS PART OF LIFE.

It's your body's reaction to significant changes—negative or positive
(For example, developing a serious illness or landing a great new job).

Stress causes physical responses.

In the face of stress, your body prepares for "fight or flight" — to take on a perceived danger or to run away from it. This involves a series of reactions:

- Your body releases adrenaline and other chemicals into your blood.
- Your heart rate, breathing rate and blood pressure increase.
- Your muscles tense.
- Your digestion slows.
- You may begin to sweat.
- Fats and sugars quickly enter your bloodstream to fuel your body for action.

Some stress is helpful.

Stress can raise your energy level. It can give you that "pumped up" feeling that helps you rise to the challenge of exciting events. Examples include:

- beginning a romantic relationship
- buying a home
- getting a promotion— or landing a new job

Unrelieved stress is a problem.

Ongoing stress can sap your energy and leave you feeling tired.

Is stress a problem for you?

It may be if you are experiencing any of these warning signs:

- development or worsening of certain health problems (see the next page)
- difficulty concentrating or remembering
- changes in appetite
- tendency to drink alcohol or smoke cigarettes more often than usual
- withdrawal from people in your life
- chronic sense of worry or fear
- Loss of sense of humor If you notice these signs, too much stress may be the culprit.

WHAT ARE THE EFFECTS OF TOO MUCH STRESS?

Ongoing stress can be both physically and emotionally taxing.

Physical health problems

caused—or worsened— by stress may include:

- back and neck pain
- headaches
- gastrointestinal problems (such as diarrhea or ulcers)
- heart disease
- high blood pressure
- a weakened immune system (your body's defense against disease)
- skin disorders (such as acne or hives)
- menstrual irregularities
- arthritis
- asthma
- diabetes
- chronic pain

Other problems

related to stress may include:

- trouble sleeping (insomnia)
- depression
- anxiety
- hostility
- loss of sex drive

Unhealthy responses to stress just make matters worse.

Some people may try to cope with stress by:

- overeating or eating a lot of junk foods (see page 348)
- drinking smoking or using other drugs (see page 349)
- sleeping too much
- watching a lot of TV
- making a lot of social plans to avoid facing problems or responsibilities
- repeating tasks over and over unnecessarily
- lashing out at others

The following pages can help you discover healthy, effective ways of dealing with life's stressors.

ASSESS YOUR STRESS.

We all have different stresses in our lives. To get a better idea of your stress levels, place a check next to the stressors that apply to you. Then, write in any other stressors—major or minor—you're experiencing in the lines below each category. Remember that minor stressors can add up to lots of stress!

Family

- ☐ recent or upcoming marriage
- ☐ pregnancy, adoption or birth of a child
- ☐ recent divorce or breakup
- ☐ death of a spouse
- ☐ death of a close family member
- ☐ getting back together with your mate
- ☐ not enough time for loved ones
- ☐ child leaving home, deployment of a family member or loved one to military service
- ☐ Other:

_____

_____

_____

_____

_____

_____

_____

_____

_____

_____

_____

_____

Job/career

- ☐ promotion, demotion or transfer
- ☐ start of a new career
- ☐ job loss
- ☐ retirement
- ☐ more work with less time
- ☐ time conflicts between work and child care
- ☐ trouble getting along with your supervisor
- ☐ trouble getting along with co-workers
- ☐ reorganization/merger
- ☐ Other:

_____

_____

_____

_____

_____

_____

_____

_____

_____

_____

_____

_____

Day-to-day pressures

- ☐ difficult commute
- ☐ getting kids off to school
- ☐ preparing meals
- ☐ household chores
- ☐ running errands
- ☐ transportation hassles
- ☐ finding time to exercise
- ☐ volunteer or other commitments
- ☐ Other:

_____

_____

_____

_____

_____

_____

_____

_____

_____

_____

_____

_____

Health

- ☐ personal injury
- ☐ personal illness
- ☐ illness or injury of a spouse, close family member or friend
- ☐ Other:

_____

_____

_____

_____

_____

_____

_____

Finances

- ☐ sudden financial windfall
- ☐ sudden dip in income
- ☐ new mortgage or major loan
- ☐ mortgage or loan foreclosure
- ☐ Other:

_____

_____

_____

_____

_____

_____

_____

Personal

- ☐ major personal achievement or failure
- ☐ major increase or decrease in your level of participation in recreational activities
- ☐ major change in sleeping or eating habits
- ☐ sexual difficulties
- ☐ relocation or major change in living conditions
- ☐ jail sentence or legal problems
- ☐ starting or finishing schooling
- ☐ Other:

_____

_____

_____

_____

_____

_____

_____

_____

_____

_____

_____

_____

Social

- ☐ decrease or increase in family gatherings
- ☐ vacation
- ☐ major change in social activities (such as having a best friend move away)
- ☐ joining or leaving a religious group
- ☐ Other:

_____

_____

_____

_____

_____

_____

_____

_____

_____

_____

Not all stressors affect us equally. But keep in mind that stress in one area can add to stress in another. Chances are the more items you've checked the more you'll benefit from relaxation techniques!

RELAXATION IS FREEDOM FROM TENSION.

While life's stressors are hard to avoid, learning to control your responses to stress puts you in charge!

It takes practice and commitment.

Like anything worthwhile, the more you put into your relaxation techniques the more you get out of them. That means practicing on a regular basis.

Relaxation can improve your physical health.

Many relaxation techniques have been shown to lower blood pressure. Since high blood pressure can lead to heart disease and other serious health problems, learning to relax may mean helping to prevent these.

Some techniques, such as visualization (see page 337), are also known to lessen pain.

Relaxation has other benefits, too.

These may include:

- enhanced balance and flexibility (if physical techniques are used)
- more energy
- a greater sense of well-being
- increased confidence and courage
- increased motivation, creativity and productivity in your life

What does relaxation mean to you?

Write down the first thoughts that come to mind when you hear the word "relaxation":

_____

_____

_____

_____

_____

_____

_____

Now, write about what you hope to achieve by learning relaxation techniques—or in what ways you think these techniques will help you:

_____

_____

_____

_____

_____

_____

_____

_____

RELAXATION TECHNIQUES CAN BE USED IN MANY SITUATIONS.

For example, you can practice relaxation:

As part of your daily or weekly schedule

Simpler techniques, such as breathing exercises (see pages 334-335), may require only a few minutes per session. For skills requiring regular practice, such as meditation, you'll eventually want to devote about 45 minutes to each session. This means you will probably need to set aside time in your schedule. (Keep in mind that these skills are the ones that will give you deeper, longer-lasting benefits.)

On an "as needed" basis

For example, once you've learned how to do breathing exercises, you can use them just about any time you feel pressured or tense. Try them when you:

- are caught in traffic
- need to interact with or have just interacted with a difficult person
- are about to enter a job interview, make a presentation or do something else that may be nerve-wracking to you
- feel like you need a break

Depending on where you are and how much time you have, other techniques—such as visualization and progressive muscle relaxation (see page 336)—may also be useful in "spontaneous" situations.

It's important to set aside time for daily practice.

When creating a relaxation schedule, you may want to consider some basic questions:

- Are you a morning, afternoon or evening person?

_____

- What times of day are best for you to practice undisturbed?

_____

_____

- Is a friend or family member willing to practice with you or help you remember your schedule? If so, who?

_____

- Can you link your relaxation practice to other daily activities—for example, as you cool down after exercising (see page 345)?

_____

_____

_____

Try not to skip sessions. If something comes up, try to reschedule.

MEDITATION

involves calming your thoughts by completely focusing your mind on one thing.

What does it do?

Meditation helps your body relax and recover from the effects of stress. It may also help:

- lower heart rate and blood pressure and relax breathing
- increase energy levels
- boost self-confidence
- relieve headaches
- curb anxiety and depression
- promote creativity

How do you do it?

It requires concentration. For example, you may choose to focus on:

- a sound—such as recordings of the ocean, bird songs or flute music
- an image—for example, of a favorite tree, work of art or scene in nature
- a word or phrase (called "mantra" meditation)— "peace," "one" or "love," for example
- your breathing

Simple mindfulness: getting the full experience

At the core of meditation techniques is the concept of "mindfulness"—being fully aware of a task at hand. For example, next time you reach for a piece of fruit:

- Notice the color and texture of its skin.
- Breathe in its aroma. Try to describe it in your mind.
- Think about where it came from and how it got to you.
- As you bite into it, think about how it affects your senses. How does the bite sound? Feel? Taste?

Practicing simple mindfulness can help you live in the moment—a key to inner peace and calm.

LEARNING TO MEDITATE TAKES TIME.

Start by meditating for short periods (5 to 15 minutes at a time). With daily practice, you'll be able to lengthen your meditations. Here are some meditation basics:

Choose an approach that feels comfortable to you.

For example, you might choose to concentrate on a mental image of a flower or on a word or phrase you can repeat easily to yourself.

Situate yourself.

You will want to:

- Wear comfortable clothes.
- Sit or lie in a comfortable position.
- Choose a place that's quiet and free of distractions.

Try to relax and focus.

As you concentrate on the object of your meditation:

- Close your eyes.
- Relax your muscles.
- Breathe in through your nose and out through your mouth. Keep your breathing slow but natural.
- If your focus is on a word or phrase, repeat it silently as you exhale.

Refocus when your mind wanders.

Simply return your thoughts to the object of your meditation. But remember that a passive attitude is important when meditating. Don't worry about how you are doing. Your mind is likely to go off in many different directions. With practice—you'll learn to stay focused!

Helpful reminders to get you going

My daily meditation space(s):

_____

_____

_____

_____

_____

My daily meditation time(s):

_____

_____

_____

_____

_____

_____

_____

My reasons for practicing meditation:

_____

_____

_____

_____

_____

_____

_____

_____

STRETCHING
is a good way to keep muscles flexible—and help you relax.

Why stretch?

Stretching feels good! Along with aiding in relaxation, stretching can help:

- relieve tension in your head, neck and shoulders— the muscle groups most affected by stress
- keep your muscles less prone to injury (when exercising, for example)
- strengthen your joints

What are the basic rules of stretching?

- Go slow. Start with easier stretches, and never hold painful stretches.
- Don't stretch cold muscles. Take a short walk or do some easy warm-up exercises first (such as jumping jacks).
- Hold stretches for about 5-15 seconds. Don't bounce!

"Office" stretches are great tension busters!

Here are a few examples:

- shoulder rolls—sit straight and shrug your shoulders. Roll them forward making big circles. Do the same thing going backward. Repeat 5 times in each direction.
- neck stretch—tilt or tum your head toward one shoulder. Hold the position for 15 seconds, then relax. Repeat the exercise, tilting or turning your head toward your other shoulder. Stretch each side 3 times.
- mid-back stretch—sit up straight and extend your arms in front of you. Interlock your fingers and turn your palms face out. Turn your shoulders to the right, back to the center, then left and back to center.

HERE ARE SOME POPULAR STRETCHES
that will help you keep loose and relaxed!

Side stretch

Stand straight. Keep your feet hip-width and your knees slightly bent. Extend your right arm over your head and lean to your left. Hold for 5-8 seconds, then repeat on your other side.

Calf stretch

This is a good warm-up stretch to do before walking or jogging. Stand with your left leg extended behind you. Point your left foot forward and keep it hip-width apart from your right foot. Keep your right knee bent and put your hands on it as you drop the heel of your left foot to the floor. Hold for 5-8 seconds, then repeat on the other side.

Lat stretch

This helps stretch the muscles along your sides and in your upper back and shoulders. Kneel on the floor and extend both arms straight out in front of you touching the floor. As you do this, lower your chest to the floor and your knees. Hold for 15 seconds.

Hamstring stretch

This stretches the muscles in the backs of your thighs. Stand with one leg straight out in front of you and the other slightly bent beneath you. Plant the heel of your straight leg on the floor, pointing your toes upward. Slowly bend forward from your hips (not your waist) you can help ensure this by keeping your back as straight as possible. Hold the position for a few seconds, then relax. Repeat on the other side.

Toe touch

Sit on a flat surface with your legs out in front of you, slightly bent. Extend your arms straight out in front of you. Slowly bend forward at the hips, reaching toward your toes. Keep your back straight as you bend. Hold for a few seconds, then relax.

DEEP BREATHING
can help quiet the mind, relax the body and ease pain.

Chest breathing

is shallow breathing that's often accompanied by anxiety, depression and hyperventilation (rapid breathing that can lead to fainting). This type of breathing can reduce oxygen flow in the body and increase heart rate and muscle tension.

Abdominal breathing (deep breathing)

is the relaxed breathing we enjoy during sleep. It is the goal of most breathing exercises. Abdominal breathing involves contracting and expanding the diaphragm (the large muscle between the lungs and abdomen) to allow air deep into the lungs.

Proper breathing has many benefits.

It can help people who are experiencing:

- anxiety/panic attacks
- depression
- anger
- headaches
- fatigue

Abdominal breathing has also been shown to slow heart rate, which, in turn, can lower or stabilize blood pressure.

A difference you can see

Choose someone in your household, such as your spouse or child. Subtly observe the way he or she breathes when:

- sleeping
- awake and relaxed
- awake, and nervous or excited

Describe your observations on the lines below. What differences do you notice among the three observations? Breathing can help quiet the mind, relax the body and ease pain.

_____

_____

_____

_____

_____

_____

_____

_____

_____

_____

_____

_____

_____

_____

_____

A NUMBER OF BREATHING EXERCISES
are based on the principles of deep breathing.

First, find out how you breathe now.

Put one hand on your chest and the other on your stomach. Breathe the way you usually do. The hand that moves the most will tell you if you're a chest breather or a deep breather.

Then, make deep breathing part of your daily ritual.

1. Lie down on your bed or a comfortable rug.
2. Place one hand on your stomach and the other on your chest.
3. Inhale slowly and deeply through your nose and let your stomach expand (your chest should only move a bit).
4. Purse your lips and exhale slowly through your mouth (make a slight whooshing sound).
5. You can use the hand on your stomach to push gently on your abdomen during exhales.
6. Practice for 5 or 10 minutes twice a day. Extend your breathing exercises to 20 minutes once you get the hang of it.

Before and after

How did focusing on the way you breathe make a difference in the way you feel? After a deep-breathing session, fill in the blanks below.

Before the session, I felt:

_____

_____

_____

_____

_____

_____

_____

_____

_____

_____

After practicing deep breathing for _____ minutes, I felt:

_____

_____

_____

_____

_____

_____

Progressive Muscle Relaxation (PMR)

is based on the idea that in order to relax you need to be aware of how it feels to be tense.

When can you do it?

You can practice PMR on a daily basis or as needed when stress and tension build up. As a first step, find a place where you can comfortably sit or lie down.

Choose a muscle group to start with.

Make those muscles tense and tight, and then relax them. For example, if you start with your hands:

- Clench your fists for 5-10 seconds—focus on the feeling of muscle tension.
- Relax your fists completely for 20-30 seconds—notice the difference between muscle tension and muscle relaxation.

Repeat the exercise throughout your body.

Tense and relax the muscles in your:

- lower and upper arms
- face and jaw
- neck and shoulders
- chest
- stomach
- back
- buttocks
- thighs
- calves
- feet
- toes

Try to move systematically through the muscle groups. For example, if you started with your hands, you might move upward to your arms, shoulders, neck and head, then start downward.

Personal observation log

In which muscle groups do you notice the most tension?

_____

_____

_____

_____

In what daily situations do you notice greater—or less—muscle tension?

_____

_____

_____

_____

What effects does PMR have on your body, your emotions and your energy?

_____

_____

_____

_____

VISUALIZATION

uses mental images—or stories—to help you relax, reduce pain and sleep better.
Visualization is also known as guided imagery.

How do you do it?

Visualization is another relaxation technique you can do on your own. The basic idea is to use the power of your imagination to shape your mood.

Visualization happens in steps.

Here's a basic approach for helping to relieve pain:

- Lie down in a quiet place and close your eyes.
- Scan your body and relax any muscles that feel tense.
- Imagine the pain in your knee (for example) is a kite stuck on the ground.

In your mind, tie a string to the kite and launch it into the air. As the kite goes higher, imagine your pain fading away. Finally, let go of the string and watch the kite float out of sight.

Describe a scene

you find safe and relaxing. Use it while practicing visualization.

_____
_____
_____
_____
_____
_____
_____
_____
_____
_____
_____
_____
_____
_____
_____
_____
_____
_____
_____
_____
_____
_____
_____
_____

MASSAGE THERAPY

releases muscle tension, promotes relaxation and helps with pain relief.

Self-massage

is a simple, inexpensive way to relieve pain and tension in your muscles. Consider taking a class (available in many communities) that teaches self-massage techniques.

Informal massage

can be done by a friend, relative or other trusted person. Basic techniques include:

- gliding the hands across the skin
- kneading the muscles
- gentle pressure
- percussion (using gentle chopping or pounding motions)

Professional massage

Can bring about deep relaxation. It may also be used as therapy for certain physical problems such as muscle strains, pulled ligaments and repetitive motion injuries. Massage therapy may also help:

- reduce blood pressure
- boost the immune system
- improve joint flexibility

My massage appointments with

_____

Day and date:

_____

_____

_____

_____

_____

_____

_____

_____

_____

Time:

_____

_____

_____

_____

_____

_____

_____

_____

_____

AROMATHERAPY
involves the use of essential oils (essences of various plant and flower fragrances) to balance mind and body.

What are the benefits?

Aromatherapy may help:

- promote relaxation
- provide relief from insomnia
- relieve pain (headache, joint and menstrual pain, for example)
- enhance mood
- combat allergies

Essential oils may be used in several ways.

For example, they may be applied through:

- massage oils
- compresses
- warm baths
- lightly scented linens

Check it out.

Put a check next to the aromas that may help you:

- ☐ lavender—calming, sinusitis, depression, muscle pain
- ☐ chamomile—relaxation, allergies, joint swelling
- ☐ marjoram—menstrual cramps, muscle spasms
- ☐ eucalyptus—stimulant, decongestant

The scent of relaxation
What natural scents do you find soothing? Describe them here:

_____
_____
_____
_____
_____
_____
_____
_____
_____
_____
_____
_____
_____
_____
_____
_____
_____
_____
_____
_____
_____
_____

PETS CAN HELP YOU RELAX, TOO!
Pets can offer:

Emotional rewards

For example, having a pet may help you:

- reduce loneliness
- relieve stress and depression
- boost your self-esteem
- adjust to major life changes

A physical boost

Research has found many positive effects of pet ownership on human health. Some of these include:

- lower blood pressure
- fewer colds, flus and backaches
- fewer visits to healthcare providers
- lower cholesterol
- more exercise

Make sure pet ownership is right for you!

Before becoming a pet owner, consider both the pros and cons (for example, the type of pet that's right for you based on costs, time commitment, lifestyle, possible allergies, etc.).

Type of pet

1 _____

2 _____

3 _____

Pros

1 _____

2 _____

3 _____

Cons

1 _____

2 _____

3 _____

LAUGHTER IS GOOD FOR YOUR HEALTH.

It can have positive physical effects.

For example, laughter can help:

- relieve pain
- reduce muscle tension
- boost the immune system
- exercise the heart
- reduce blood pressure and improve circulation

It's also good for your emotions.

There's nothing like a good laugh to help:

- improve self-confidence
- create a sense of control
- release pent-up feelings
- minimize anger and other negative emotions
- shape a positive outlook

Make humor part of your life.

- Spend more time enjoying playful activities with others, especially children.
- Watch humorous videos.
- Post humorous comics, greeting cards, photos or other items in your home and workspace.
- Learn a new skill or try doing something you're used to in a new way—laugh at yourself as you expand your horizons.
- Look for humor in daily situations. This is where it often hides!

Laugh log

Don't take a good laugh for granted—take note of what made it happen! Over the next week, notice the humorous things in your life. Describe your top 3 laughs below.

1. _____
   _____
   _____
   _____

2. _____
   _____
   _____
   _____
   _____

3. _____
   _____
   _____
   _____

RATE YOUR SUCCESS.

Fill out the chart on the next page based on the relaxation techniques you've already learned.

Use this rating scale for the chart on the next page.

As you fill it in, describe yourself as:

- 1—completely relaxed
- 2—fairly relaxed
- 3—slightly relaxed
- 4—fairly tense
- 5—extremely tense

How—and when—does stress affect you most?

Use this chart—or one like it—to keep track of the daily stressors in your life.

Symptoms of stress include headaches, irritability, muscle tension, etc.

Day/Date/Time	Stressful Event	Symptom(s) of Stress

Week of:	Pre-Session Rating	Post-Session Rating	Relaxation Technique(s) Used	Remarks/Notes
Sunday				
Monday				
Tuesday				
Wednesday				
Thursday				
Friday				
Saturday				

IT'S NO SURPRISE—YOU RELAX WHEN YOU EXERCISE

How does exercise help reduce stress?

When you're physically active your body releases endorphins—natural chemicals that:

- improve your mood and overall sense of well-being
- improve your ability to cope with stress

Exercises that involve repetitive movement, such as walking, running and rowing, can be especially beneficial.

Exercise offers many health benefits.

For example, regular exercise can help:

- relieve muscle tension
- boost energy and stamina
- lower blood pressure
- improve sleep
- relieve pain
- treat or ward off depression
- raise metabolism
- keep you fit and active as you age
- reduce the likelihood of injury
- protect the immune system
- prevent obesity and related diseases (such as diabetes)

It helps in other ways, too.

Through exercise, you can:

- clear your mind and improve concentration
- enhance self-confidence and self-image
- develop a more positive outlook—and motivation to make other positive changes

TIPS TO HELP MAKE EXERCISE WORK FOR YOU

Talk to a health-care provider before starting an exercise program.

Get enough physical activity.

- Get at least 150 minutes of moderate—or 75 minutes of vigorous—physical activity each week.
- For greater health benefits, get at least 300 minutes of moderate—or 150 minutes of vigorous—physical activity each week.
- Try to spread your activity throughout the week, going at least 10 minutes at a time.
- In addition, do muscle strengthening exercises at least 2 days each week.

In general, one can talk during moderate physical activity—but can only say a few words at a time during vigorous physical activity.

Choose activities you enjoy.

If the idea of a daily jog sounds tedious, consider dancing, biking, walking, swimming—even regular yard-work. Exercising with a friend may help you stay motivated.

Warm up.

Spend 10-15 minutes doing basic movements similar to your chosen activity. Remember to stretch your muscles after you warm up.

Cool down.

Slow your pace before finishing an activity. For example, end a brisk run by jogging, then walking. Stretching exercises are also a great way to cool down before you hit the shower.

Play it safe.

Wear appropriate clothing, footwear and safety gear for chosen activity. For example, always wear a helmet when biking. Make sure the helmet is certified by the U.S. Consumer Product Safety Commission (CPSC). Look for a label that states it complies with U.S. CPSC safety standards. To learn more, contact the CPSC at 1-800-638-2772 or www.cpsc.gov.

Take it slow.

Don't try to do too much too fast. A slow, steady start will help reduce your risk of injury and increase the chances that you will stick with your plan.

Hidden fitness: daily activities as exercise

Being active doesn't have to seem like exercise. In the list below, check off any activities which you engage regularly. Count them as forms of fitness!

- ☐ walking to school, work or the bus stop
- ☐ climbing flights of stairs
- ☐ dancing
- ☐ playing actively with children or pets
- ☐ Other _____

  _____

- ☐ Other _____

  _____

- ☐ Other _____

  _____

AN EXERCISE LOG

can help you keep track of the activities you like best and their impact on your physical and emotional health.

Week of:	Activity and Duration	Location	Time of Day/ Conditions	Remarks/Notes
Sunday				
Monday				
Tuesday				
Wednesday				
Thursday				
Friday				
Saturday				

A HEALTHY DIET CAN HELP
offset the effects of stress.

Prolonged stress may rob the body

of important nutrients such as protein, calcium, vitamin C, potassium, zinc and magnesium.

Supplements can help,

especially during times when it's hard to eat a balanced diet. But don't depend on them for your nutritional needs. Check with your health-care provider before taking supplements (including herbal supplements). Also, let him or her know what supplements you are taking any time he or she is prescribing medications for you.

Create a healthy eating pattern.

Make smart choices from each food group every day— and try not to skip meals. This is the best way to maintain your energy and control your weight.

- Know how many daily calories are right for your gender, age and activity level. Having more calories will lead to weight gain.
- Find out what's in your food and drinks—check Nutrition Facts labels and other sources. Limit items high in calories, saturated or trans fats,* sodium, cholesterol and added sugars.
- Choose more whole grains.
- Build a healthy plate—fill half with fruits and vegetables. Drink more low-fat or fat-free milk*
- Choose lean cuts of meat. Eat seafood at least twice a week.
- Limit sweetened drinks and alcohol to help cut calories.
- Cook more at home so you are in charge of what's in your food. Use small amounts of vegetable oils, when needed, in place of butter or other solid fats. And add little salt or sugar.
- Avoid oversized portions, and don't eat in front of the TV you'll eat more.
- Handle food safely to help avoid illness.

* Ask a health-care provider about your child's nutrition. Don't restrict fat for those under age 2 (unless directed to) or give cow's milk to those under age 1.

Learn about an eating pattern that fits your calorie needs at www.ChooseMyPlate.gov.

EATING THE WRONG FOODS
can make you more vulnerable to stress—even though they may help you feel relaxed at first.

Limit sodium and added sugars.

Sodium can contribute to high blood pressure in some people. Added sugars have little nutritional value and can become a crutch for handling stress.

Avoid fast foods and junk foods.

For example, try to steer clear of pizza, sweets and fried foods. These tend to be high in calories, saturated and trans fats, cholesterol, sodium and added sugars—and low in nutrients.

Watch your caffeine intake.

Caffeine is a stimulant found in coffee, colas, teas and chocolate. Too much caffeine (over 200 mg a day, or the amount in 10 oz. of regular brewed coffee) can result in irritability, nervousness and poor sleep.

Nutrition Facts

Serving Size 1 cup (228g)
Servings Per Container 2

Amount Per Serving

Calories 260   Calories from Fat 120

	% Daily Value*
Total Fat 13g	**20%**
Saturated Fat 5g	**25%**
Trans Fat 2g	
Cholesterol 30mg	**10%**
Sodium 660mg	**28%**
Total Carbohydrate 31g	**10%**
Dietary Fiber 0g	**0%**
Sugars 5g	
Protein 5g	

Vitamin A 4%	•	Vitamin C 2%	
Calcium 15%	•	Iron 4%	

*Percent Daily Values are based on a 2,000 calorie diet. Your daily values may be higher or lower depending on your calorie needs.

Source: U.S. Food and Drug Administration

Stress test

If stress tends to send you running for the fridge or pantry, you may be making things worse. For the next week, assess whether some of your urges to eat are actually reactions to stress. If they are, try doing something else instead—for example, practice a relaxation technique or call a friend. At the end of the week, assess how resisting "stress eating" ultimately made you feel. Write about it below.

_____

_____

_____

_____

_____

_____

_____

_____

_____

_____

_____

_____

_____

_____

UNHEALTHY HABITS

do not help with long-term relaxation or pain reduction even though they may seem to aid relaxation in the beginning. If your goal is to be a healthier, more relaxed person:

Avoid tobacco products.

The idea that tobacco use helps relieve stress is not true. Nicotine is a stimulant, not a sedative. Also, the need to constantly light up or dip to avoid nicotine withdrawal actually raises stress levels. Smoking also causes heart disease, cancer and other serious health problems.

If you smoke, get help to quit. You can get help from:

- your health-care provider
- a mental health professional

Or try a smokers' help line, such as 1-800-QUITNOW (1-800-784-8669).

Limit alcohol—or don't drink at all.

Drinking too much lowers your ability to handle stress and increases your risk of chronic health problems, such as depression. If you choose to drink, do so in moderation.

This means no more than:

- 2 drinks per day for men
- 1 drink per day for women or anyone age 65 or older

People who should not drink at all include recovering alcoholics, people under 21, people taking certain medications and women who are pregnant or trying to get pregnant.

Don't use illegal drugs.

Illegal drugs, such as marijuana and cocaine, are harmful to your health and should be avoided. (Your health-care provider may prescribe prescription or over-the-counter medications for relief of pain, anxiety, depression and other problems associated with stress. Use these exactly as directed by your health-care provider.)

Note: According to the FDA (U.S. Food and Drug Administration), those taking some antidepressants should be on the lookout for worsening depression or thoughts of suicide. Fully discuss all risks and benefits of any medication you are considering with your health-care provider.

If you become more depressed or suicidal while taking antidepressants, get medical help right away. If you are already taking antidepressants, never increase or decrease the dose, or stop taking them, except as directed by your health-care provider.

Breaking unhealthy habits is a great way to help reduce stress and improve relaxation.

HELP IS AVAILABLE.

Reaching out is a sign of strength—not weakness. Resources for handling stress and learning relaxation techniques include:

Your health-care provider

He or she can offer advice and information on diet, exercise and other strategies to improve relaxation.

Your local hospital or Veterans

Administration hospital. Many hospitals offer classes on stress management.

Libraries and bookstores

Many offer books, articles, DVDs and CDs on relaxation.

Mental health centers

These offer counseling, classes and a variety of services, including referrals.

Employee Assistance Programs (EAPs)

Free counseling and referrals are available to many people through their employers.

Pain management clinics

These specialize in helping people cope with chronic pain through relaxation and other strategies.

Open your body and mind to relaxation—and breathe a deep sigh of relief!

LEARNING HEALTHY RELAXATION TECHNIQUES TAKES TIME.

By now you have probably come across a few ideas that will help you meet your relaxation goals. Write down the ones that suit you the best and make a plan to start practicing them. Good luck!

Relaxation Goal	Action Plan	Target Start Date
_____	_____	_____
_____	_____	_____
_____	_____	_____
_____	_____	_____
_____	_____	_____
_____	_____	_____
_____	_____	_____
_____	_____	_____
_____	_____	_____
_____	_____	_____
_____	_____	_____
_____	_____	_____
_____	_____	_____
_____	_____	_____
_____	_____	_____
_____	_____	_____
_____	_____	_____
_____	_____	_____

People who can help:_____

_____

Reward for meeting my goal(s):_____

_____

SUCCESSFUL MONEY MANAGEMENT

REENTRY
ESSENTIALS, INC.

Life Skills Series
Basic Skills for Lifelong Success

Please read:

Talk to a professional! This workbook is not a substitute for the advice of a qualified expert.

Reentry Essentials, Inc.
2609 East 14 Street, Suite 1018
Brooklyn, NY 11235-3915
P: 347.973.0004
E: info@ReentryEssentials.org
I: www.ReentryEssentials.org

This workbook belongs to:

_____

You may find it helpful to keep important names and phone numbers handy.

Write them below.

Bank

Name_____

Phone_____

Other important numbers

_____

_____

_____

_____

_____

_____

_____

_____

_____

_____

_____

_____

_____

_____

_____

_____

_____

_____

_____

_____

YOU CAN GET WHAT YOU WANT OUT OF LIFE.

Whether you're supporting yourself for the first time or you've supported a family for years, you can learn good money-management skills.

CONTENT

Good money-management skills are important for everyone.

They help you:

- provide for and protect yourself and your family
- plan for the future
- reach your goals

Getting started is the hardest part.

Maybe you haven't known where to start. Or, maybe you've been avoiding it. Either way, learning how to manage your money is mostly about:

- deciding what you want to do with your money
- making a plan and sticking to it

Even if you think you're doing OK, you can learn how to make your money go further.

Get everyone involved.

If you have a spouse or partner, plan your finances together. It's easier to work toward goals you both agree on. Also, it'll help him or her know how to handle expenses if you can't.

This workbook can also help you avoid common mistakes.

Some of the most common ones include:

- not having a spending plan (budget)
- thinking that you don't have enough money to save
- borrowing too much money

Start learning about money management now. Use this workbook to help take control of your money—and your future.

SET GOALS FOR YOURSELF.
This is an important step in managing your money.
It gives you a clear direction for making a spending plan later.

What do you want out of life?

Your goals could include buying a car, getting out of debt or planning for a comfortable retirement. Make creating an emergency fund of at least 3 months' worth of expenses a high-priority goal. (See page 380.) This will help cover you in case of unexpected expenses or income loss.

Use the worksheet on the next page to help you organize your goals.

When do you want to reach your goals?

Divide your goals into:

- short-term goals (within a year or two)
- medium-term goals (within about 5 years)
- long-term goals (5 years or longer)

How much will each goal cost?

Get as much information as you can. Write down the estimates. (Keep in mind that the costs of long-term goals may change over time.)

Make a payment plan for yourself:

- Set a deadline for each goal.
- Divide the cost by the number of months until the deadline. This is what you need to save each month.

Interest earned on savings or money made through other investments will help your savings grow faster. (See pages 382-383.) And, some investments can lose money. Adjust your plan as needed.

Don't be discouraged.

Add up the payments for all your goals. You may see that this is more than you can realistically save each month. But you've already taken the first step toward getting what you want.

Now set priorities.

You may have to rethink some of your goals. Which ones are really important? Which can wait a little longer? Look at your goals again with this in mind. Your goals may change as you learn more about managing money and as time passes. Review them regularly.

Pay yourself first.

Once you've fine-tuned your payment plan for reaching your goals, make it a regular "bill." Pay it first. Learn how to meet your other expenses with the money you have left.

GOALS WORKSHEET

Priority	Goal	Deadline	Cost		# Months to Deadline	Savings Per Month

Short-term goals (1-2 years)

Priority	Goal	Deadline	Cost		# Months to Deadline	Savings Per Month
#____	_____	_____	$____	÷	_____	$_____
#____	_____	_____	$____	÷	_____	$_____
#____	_____	_____	$____	÷	_____	$_____
#____	_____	_____	$____	÷	_____	$_____
#____	_____	_____	$____	÷	_____	$_____
#____	_____	_____	$____	÷	_____	$_____

Medium-term goals (within 5 years)

Priority	Goal	Deadline	Cost		# Months to Deadline	Savings Per Month
#____	_____	_____	$____	÷	_____	$_____
#____	_____	_____	$____	÷	_____	$_____
#____	_____	_____	$____	÷	_____	$_____
#____	_____	_____	$____	÷	_____	$_____
#____	_____	_____	$____	÷	_____	$_____

Long-term goals (5 years and beyond)

Priority	Goal	Deadline	Cost		# Months to Deadline	Savings Per Month
#____	_____	_____	$____	÷	_____	$_____
#____	_____	_____	$____	÷	_____	$_____
#____	_____	_____	$____	÷	_____	$_____
#____	_____	_____	$____	÷	_____	$_____
#____	_____	_____	$____	÷	_____	$_____

FIGURE YOUR NET WORTH.
Now that you know what you want to accomplish, figure out where you stand.

Your net worth equals what you own minus what you owe.

This is where you'd be if you had to pay off all your debts (everything you owe others) today.

Use the worksheet on the next page to figure your net worth.

Make a list of your assets.

These are things that belong to you. They are accounts you have and the things you could sell if you had to. Examples include your car, appliances, house and savings.

Write down how much each item is worth.

Use the amount that someone would pay for the item today, not what you paid for it.

Make a list of your liabilities.

These are the debts you owe. They could include loans for your car or education, credit card balances and mortgages. Don't leave anything out.

Add up each list.

Total the values of what you own. Do the same for what you owe.

Subtract your liabilities from your assets.

This amount is your net worth

Don't get discouraged.

If you're not happy with what you see, make a plan to improve things. Add it to your goals. Even if you're pleased with your situation, planning can help you make sure you stay on track.

Track your net worth over the years. It will help you see the progress you're making on the road to financial security.

NET WORTH WORKSHEET

Assets	Value		Assets	Value
Financial			**Loan balances**	
Cash	$ _____		Mortgage	$ _____
Checking accounts	$ _____		Auto	$ _____
Savings accounts	$ _____		Bank	$ _____
Savings bonds	$ _____		Student	$ _____
Certificates of deposit (CDs)	$ _____		_____	$ _____
Stocks/Mutual Funds	$ _____			
Pension	$ _____		**Credit care/department store balances**	
Life insurance cash value	$ _____		_____	$ _____
_____	$ _____		_____	$ _____
_____	$ _____		_____	$ _____
			_____	$ _____
Personal property			_____	$ _____
Appliances	$ _____		_____	$ _____
Automobile	$ _____		**Taxes due**	
Home furnishings	$ _____		Home	$ _____
Furniture	$ _____		Social Security	$ _____
Jewelry	$ _____		Federal	$ _____
Sound system $	$ _____		State	$ _____
TV and vide	$ _____		Excise	$ _____
Computer	$ _____		Real estate	$ _____
	$ _____			
	$ _____		**Other debts**	
Real estate			_____	$ _____
Home	$ _____		_____	$ _____
_____	$ _____			
_____	$ _____		Total	$ _____
Total	$ _____			

Total asset - Total liabilities = Net worth

$ _____ - $ _____ = $ _____

PRACTICE GOOD BOOKKEEPING.
It makes managing your money easier, and it saves you time in the long run.

Create an easy filing system.

Keep all your important records in one place and in order. For example, use different folders for different items. You might have folders for your:

- bank statements and canceled checks
- credit card receipts and statements
- income tax returns and related forms
- insurance policies
- loan statements
- personal documents (birth certificate, passport, etc.)
- receipts for major purchases
- retirement plan statements
- will and power of attorney

Use a regular bill-paying system.

Put all bills to be paid in one place. Set aside the same days each month to pay them.

If you pay your bills online, be sure to keep a record of your payments.

Also, be careful to prevent identity theft. Keep your username and password in a private and safe place.

Know what to keep and what to throw away.

In general:

- Keep tax forms and any related receipts or canceled checks for 7 years.
- Keep bank statements and canceled checks for a minimum of 1 year, longer if they support your taxes or show payment for valuable goods or property (such as real estate, vehicles or other investments) that you still own.
- Keep insurance policies, warranties, deeds, etc., until they expire or you no longer have the item.
- Keep receipts as long as needed for your tax return and warranties. For charges, keep receipts at least until you check them against the credit card statement.
- Keep credit card and loan documentation for as long as you have the account.
- Throw away bills for phone, utilities, cable, etc., after you pay them and record them in your budget (unless you'll need them later—for example, to compare phone rates).

Know how to read your pay stub

It includes information you can use to make your spending plan and balancing your checkbook:

- gross pay (this is what you earn before taxes and other deductions)
- automatic deductions that you've arranged, as well as taxes
- net pay (after taxes and other deductions)
- amounts deposited directly into bank accounts (if you've arranged for any)

MAKE A BUDGET.

A budget is a plan for spending money.
It's your plan for making sure you get exactly what you want out of life.

Start by tracking your spending.

Before you start budgeting, find out where your money's been going. Keep a diary of spending in a pocket notebook for a couple of weeks. Include everything, even money spent at vending machines— it can really add up.

Next, use the budget worksheet on pages 362-363.

Your pay stub, financial records and spending diary will help. Use whole dollar amounts (not cents) to make your math easier.

1. Budget an amount for each expense.

Expenses are divided into different types:

- Fixed expenses are those that are generally constant.
- Variable expenses are those that you may be able to change. Use the last few months' bills and spending diaries to figure average variable expenses.
- Savings expenses are your way of reaching your goals and preparing for financial emergencies. Pay yourself first!

2. List your income.

Use your pay stub, bank statements, etc. Don't forget to include other sources of income.

3. Balance your budget.

Your total expenses and income should match. If they don't, reassign the amounts budgeted for expenses until they do. For example, trim your entertainment budget or try to cut transportation costs (But don't cut savings.)

4. Track the money you actually spend.

At the end of the month, use your records to track what each expense actually costs. Use:

- bills
- checks you wrote
- receipts for cash purchases

If you're spending more than you budgeted, look for ways to cut back. Pages 364-367 can help.

5. Review your budget regularly

This will help you see how well you're meeting your goals and where you need to make changes.

Budget worksheet

Expenses	Budgeted Amount	Actual Amount Per Month (write in month)					
FIXED EXPENSES							
Rent/mortgage	$_____	$_____	$_____	$_____	$_____	$_____	$_____
Insurance	$_____	$_____	$_____	$_____	$_____	$_____	$_____
Automobile payments	$_____	$_____	$_____	$_____	$_____	$_____	$_____
Loan payments	$_____	$_____	$_____	$_____	$_____	$_____	$_____
Taxes	$_____	$_____	$_____	$_____	$_____	$_____	$_____
Alimony (paid)	$_____	$_____	$_____	$_____	$_____	$_____	$_____
Child support (paid)	$_____	$_____	$_____	$_____	$_____	$_____	$_____
Child/Elder care	$_____	$_____	$_____	$_____	$_____	$_____	$_____
Child's allowance	$_____	$_____	$_____	$_____	$_____	$_____	$_____
Credit card installments	$_____	$_____	$_____	$_____	$_____	$_____	$_____
Other:	$_____	$_____	$_____	$_____	$_____	$_____	$_____
VARIABLE EXPENSES							
Groceries	$_____	$_____	$_____	$_____	$_____	$_____	$_____
Utilities	$_____	$_____	$_____	$_____	$_____	$_____	$_____
Transportation	$_____	$_____	$_____	$_____	$_____	$_____	$_____
Telephone	$_____	$_____	$_____	$_____	$_____	$_____	$_____
Medical or dental	$_____	$_____	$_____	$_____	$_____	$_____	$_____
Clothing	$_____	$_____	$_____	$_____	$_____	$_____	$_____
Personal hygiene	$_____	$_____	$_____	$_____	$_____	$_____	$_____
Pet care	$_____	$_____	$_____	$_____	$_____	$_____	$_____
Entertainment	$_____	$_____	$_____	$_____	$_____	$_____	$_____
Other:	$_____	$_____	$_____	$_____	$_____	$_____	$_____
SAVINGS							
Savings account	$_____	$_____	$_____	$_____	$_____	$_____	$_____
Credit union	$_____	$_____	$_____	$_____	$_____	$_____	$_____
Other:	$_____	$_____	$_____	$_____	$_____	$_____	$_____
Total expenses and savings	$_____	$_____	$_____	$_____	$_____	$_____	$_____

Income	Estimated Amount	Actual Amount Per Month (write in month)					
Job #1	$_____	$_____	$_____	$_____	$_____	$_____	$_____
Job #2	$_____	$_____	$_____	$_____	$_____	$_____	$_____
Government support	$_____	$_____	$_____	$_____	$_____	$_____	$_____
Spouse or partners income	$_____	$_____	$_____	$_____	$_____	$_____	$_____
Alimony (received)	$_____	$_____	$_____	$_____	$_____	$_____	$_____
Child support (received)	$_____	$_____	$_____	$_____	$_____	$_____	$_____
Interest/Dividends	$_____	$_____	$_____	$_____	$_____	$_____	$_____
Other	$_____	$_____	$_____	$_____	$_____	$_____	$_____
	$_____	$_____	$_____	$_____	$_____	$_____	$_____
	$_____	$_____	$_____	$_____	$_____	$_____	$_____
Total income	$_____	$_____	$_____	$_____	$_____	$_____	$_____
Total expenses	$_____	$_____	$_____	$_____	$_____	$_____	$_____

Compare total expenses to total income.

Your budget is balanced when they match. If they don't, reassign expenses until they do. (Remember not to cut into your savings if you can avoid it!)

Amount to reassign	$_____	$_____	$_____	$_____	$_____	$_____	$_____

GET YOUR SPENDING PLAN IN SHAPE.

If you're having trouble balancing your budget, take another look at your spending.

Keep your spending in line.

Your spending will depend on your needs and those of your family. But try to keep your spending within these percentages of your take-home pay:

- housing—no more than 30%
- food—15-30%
- utilities—4-7%
- transportation—6-20%
- installment loan payments— less than 20%
- savings—at least 10%

For example, if you take home $2,500 a month, try to keep your rent or mortgage to no more than $750 (2,500 X 30% = 2,500 X .30 = 750).

Are your fixed expenses set too high?

These may not be as "fixed" as you think. For example, could you:

- move to a less expensive apartment or get a roommate?
- adjust the amount taken from your paycheck for federal income tax so you don't overpay?

Avoid reducing payments on your debts. Paying less now could leave you paying more in the long run.

Trim your variable expenses.

Use the tips for cutting costs on pages 366-367 to help with these.

Savings.

Try not to touch this. Cutting back here will mean having to wait longer to reach your goals.

SOME TIPS ON BUDGETING

You may not get your budget right the first time. But keep at it. Here are some ideas:

Pay yourself first.

Make your savings a regular bill. Pay it first. Plan to meet your other expenses with what's left.

Make budgeting a family affair.

Making your budget work may take the help of everyone in your family. Explain what you're doing and how each household member can help.

Plan for big expenses.

For example, set aside a small amount each month for holiday gift giving. That way, you'll avoid overspending— or overcharging— when holidays arrive.

Be flexible.

Be prepared to change your budget when needed. For example, plan what to do if you have to pay for a sudden car repair.

Use unexpected money wisely.

Use raises, bonuses, extra money, etc., to get ahead on your financial plan or invest in a necessary purchase. For example, put the extra income from a raise into savings.

Don't forget to budget "fun" money.

You don't have to deny yourself every pleasure to manage your money well. Just be sure the spending is part of your plan.

Consider using direct deposit and payments.

- If your job offers direct deposit, you can have your paycheck electronically deposited into different bank accounts. This lets you put money directly into a savings account before you get tempted to spend it.
- Some businesses, such as electric utilities, allow you to make electronic payments from your bank account so you don't have to write checks.

TRIM UNNECESSARY EXPENSES.

Here are some tips:

Shopping

- Don't shop when you're hungry or bored— you may spend more.
- Compare prices on items both within the store and at different stores. Try discount or thrift stores.
- Take advantage of sales. But don't buy things you don't need or items of poor quality.
- Use coupons and rebates for additional savings on items you need to buy.
- Don't buy on impulse. Think things over to be sure you really need the item.
- Make a list of what you need. Buy only what's on it.
- Compare unit prices to find the best deals. For example, it may be a better deal to buy an item in a larger quantity.
- Keep in mind that nonfood items may be more expensive at supermarkets.
- Rent tools and equipment you won't use often instead of buying them.
- Beware of sales gimmicks. Don't lose sight of what you need.
- Buy generic or store brands when you can. They're usually cheaper.

Food

- Plan meals so you can shop with a list.
- Use cheaper cuts of meat than a recipe calls for or substitute a less expensive type of meat.
- Buy the fruits and vegetables that are in season.
- Be careful when buying prepared foods. They may be faster, but they're usually more expensive.
- Pack your lunches and snacks instead of buying them.
- Eat out less.

Clothing

- Take advantage of offseason sales.
- Avoid dry cleaning bills by buying only machine-washable clothes.
- Consider buying from used-clothing stores.

Transportation

- Use public transportation when possible. Ask if reduced fares are available. For example, you may be able to buy a pass for several trips instead of paying for each trip separately.
- Consider buying a used vehicle that's in good shape instead of a new one to keep monthly payments lower.
- Have regular maintenance done on your vehicle to avoid costly repairs.
- Use the lowest octane gas recommended by your car manufacturer.
- Compare fares on different airlines before purchasing tickets.

Entertainment

- Look into free events for adults and children offered around town. Your local chamber of commerce may have more information.
- Rent a movie or go to a matinée—instead of paying full price.
- Visit your local library. It may sponsor events for adults and children. And, you can check out books—and in some cases videos and other materials for free.

Phone service

- Shop for the best long-distance calling plan. Look into using prepaid discount phone cards, too.
- Get rid of phone services you don't use often, such as call waiting, if there's an extra charge for them.
- Limit your long-distance calls, and call when rates are lowest.

Housing

- In warm weather, raise the thermostats of air conditioners when no one's home and at night when it's cooler.
- In cold weather, lower the heat when no one's home.
- Look into energy-saving devices, such as energy-saving light bulbs and temperature control devices that will automatically turn your heat or air conditioning on and off at specific times.
- Learn to make repairs yourself to save money. Follow all safety recommendations and local building codes.
- Lower your water heater temperature to 120°F. (If you have a dishwasher, check the owner's manual to ensure that this is adequate.)

CHECKING ACCOUNT BASICS
Find the best checking account for you, and manage it well.

Know your checking patterns.

This can help you comparison shop for the best checking account. Review your bank statements, or estimate your needs if you don't have a checking account.

- How many checks do you normally write each month?
  _____

- How many times do you use an ATM each month?
  _____

- How much money do you normally keep in your account?
  $_____

Know your checking account fees.

Read each bank's fee disclosure statement. It tells you the fees and conditions of the account. Common ones include:

- a monthly fee
- a per-check fee
- ATM fees
- a "bounced check" fee (for writing checks you don't have enough money to cover)
- a fee for falling below a minimum balance

Which fees are you charged each month? How much do they amount to?

$_____

Match your patterns to a checking account.

Look for a checking account that charges the least for the services you use the most. Shop around for the best deal. Ask if you can get a better deal by also opening a savings account.

For example, Bank A charges you a $3 monthly fee, but there's no charge for the checks you write. Bank B has no monthly fee but charges you $.15 per check. If you usually write 25 checks each month, it would cost you $3.75 a month to have an account with Bank B (25 checks x $.15 = $3.75).

Read the fine print on "free" checking accounts.

There may be hidden fees or restrictions. For example, you may be required to keep a minimum balance, or there may be fees for using your ATM card.

Consider joining a credit union, if you can.

Credit unions often offer good deals on many different types of banking services.

Find out how the daily balance is calculated.

If possible:

- Choose an account that uses the average daily balance formula. (This computes the average balance of all days in the statement period.)
- Avoid accounts that use a minimum daily balance formula. If you fall below the minimum even one day, you could be charged fees.

Choose a bank that offers direct deposit.

This allows your paycheck to be deposited into your account electronically.

ABOUT ATM AND DEBIT CARDS:

Know what it costs to use your ATM card.

Some banks have fees for using ATM cards. For example, there may be a fee for:

- each time you use your card
- each time you use your card at another bank's ATM
- each different transaction you make (for example, checking your balance, withdrawing money, etc.)

Beat ATM fees.

For example:

- If you can avoid the temptation to spend money in your wallet try making only 1 large withdrawal instead of several small ones if your bank charges you each time you use your ATM card.
- Use only your bank's ATMs if you get charged for using other banks' ATMs.

Know that a debit card isn't a credit card.

Some banks offer debit cards that may double as ATM cards. They look like credit cards and can be used where credit cards are accepted. But, like traditional ATM cards, they deduct money directly from bank accounts. Debit cards do not give credit. Ask about any debit card fees at the bank.

KEEP YOUR ACCOUNT IN CHECK.
Balance your checking account regularly.
This is an important part of keeping your financial affairs in order.

Keep track of your account.

Record:

- the check number and amount on your register or stub before you write the check
- every ATM/debit card withdrawal, purchase or fee as it happens
- all automatic deductions
- all deposits

Keep a running balance so you'll know at a glance how much money you have.

Check your balance against your bank statement.

- Go through your bank statement and make sure all cleared checks, deposits, ATM/debit card usage and fees, etc., match your register. Put a checkmark in your register by the checks that have cleared.
- Add or subtract any charges, fees or interest you didn't already record in your register.

Use the worksheet on the next page to check your balance against your bank's, If they don't match, check your math. Also, check that you recorded the correct amounts for your charges and deposits.

Report mistakes right away.

If your statement has an error, contact your bank.

Other checking tips:

- When endorsing a check for deposit by mail, write "For deposit only" above your signature on the back of the check. Nobody else can cash it if you do that.
- Be careful not to "bounce" checks. You'll be charged high fees, it could hurt your credit record, and it's illegal!
- Find out if your bank offers overdraft protection.
- Give checks you deposit time to clear before trying to use that money. Read your bank's policies on how long that takes.
- Before closing a checking account make sure that all the checks written against it have cleared.

Keep track of your savings account, too!

BALANCED CHECKBOOK WORKSHEET

This worksheet will help you match your balance to your bank's records.
Make sure that you've properly recorded every charge and credit to your account.

Part I:

1. Enter the balance from your checkbook register: $_____

2. Subtract any fees from your statement not already recorded in your register: - $_____

3. Add any Interest reported In the statement: $_____

4. Your checkbook balance is: $_____

Part II:

5. The ending balance on your statement Is: $_____

6. Subtract the sum of all the checks and ATM/debit card transactions that haven't cleared yet:

Check/Transaction	Amount
_____	$_____
_____	$_____
_____	$_____
_____	$_____
Total	$_____

                                                                      - $_____

                                                                         $_____

Add deposits not credited on statement: + $_____

This amount should match #4: $_____

GIVE YOURSELF CREDIT.

Using credit has its advantages. But if you're not careful, buying now and paying later can leave you paying for a long time and paying more for your purchases.

Credit is very convenient.

It comes in many forms, including credit cards, bank installment loans and store charge accounts.

Managed wisely, credit can help you:

- make large purchases by letting you pay for them over time
- handle emergencies
- buy things over the phone or online

You pay for the convenience of credit.

When you use credit you commit to paying back what you've borrowed—usually plus interest and fees. Those are the costs of credit, and they can add up quickly.

Can you afford credit?

Credit isn't a way to live beyond your means. Overestimating the amount you can pay back is a quick way to get into money trouble. Before you apply for credit, check your budget. Can you balance your budget after including another payment?

Build a good credit history.

A possible lender will want to know how you've handled credit in the past. To build a credit history:

- Open checking and savings accounts.
- Get a secured credit card. (You keep a certain amount of money on deposit with a bank in exchange for credit.)

Manage all your accounts responsibly.

LEARN THE LANGUAGE OF CREDIT.

Know how to talk the talk. Here are the basics:

Credit history

This is your record of credit use. It can include personal information about you, your payment history, the amount of credit you have, etc.

Credit bureau

This is a company that puts together reports on your credit history. There are 3 main credit bureaus. (See page 383.)

Interest

This is the cost of borrowed money. It's figured as a percentage of the amount borrowed and added to what's owed.

Annual Percentage Rate (APR)

This is the percentage of yearly interest charged for the money you borrow. Divide your APR by 12 to find out the monthly interest charged.

Finance charge

This is what the money you borrow actually costs each month. It's based on the APR and your balance. But balances can be calculated different ways. The way your creditor does it can make a big difference in what you end up paying.

Grace period

This is the time you have to pay your balance in full before getting charged interest. If there's no grace period, you can be charged from the moment you use your credit card.

Annual fee

This is like a membership fee for having a credit card. Some cards charge fees, some don't.

Other fees

A credit card may have other fees for things like late payments, going over your credit limit, getting a cash advance, etc.

FIGURE OUT FINANCE CHANGES.

The amount of interest you owe is figured using your balance. But a creditor can calculate your balance in any one of these ways:

Adjusted balance method

This is usually the cheapest method. It takes the balance you owe from the last billing period and subtracts any payments you make during the current period. The amount left over is your balance.

Average daily balance method

This is the most common method. It totals up each day's balance, minus any payments you make. That total is then divided by the number of days in the billing period to get an average.

For example:

Your billing period is 30 days. For half the month, you carry a balance each day of $200 ($200 x 15 days = $3,000).

Then you send in a payment of $100. So for the second half of the month, your balance is only $100 each day ($100 x 15 days = $1,500).

So, your average daily balance would be: $3,000 + $1,500 = $4,500 + 30 days = $150.

Previous balance method

This is usually the most expensive method. It uses the balance owed from the last billing period without subtracting the payments you made this period.

The interest equals your balance multiplied by the monthly interest rate.

For example, if your APR is 18%, that would mean you'll be charged interest at a rate of: 18% + 12 months = 1.5% each month.

On a balance of $150, the interest charged would be: $150 x .015 = $2.25

So, your new balance, not including any other fees, would be: $150 + $2.25 = $152.25

MASTER THE CREDIT CARD GAME.

Find the best credit. Once you get it, keep it clean.

Review your credit reports before applying.

Lenders use credit reports to decide when to extend credit. Review the reports on your credit history. Get reports from the 3 credit bureaus (see page 383) through www.annualcreditreport.com.

The reports may not all contain the same information. Notify the credit bureau in writing immediately if you find any mistakes. You have the right to receive one free report per credit bureau per year. You also have the right to a free report if:

- you've been denied credit in the past 60 days
- you are unemployed and looking for work or you are on welfare
- you believe your credit is inaccurate due to fraud

Shop for the best deal.

Compare and understand the terms of different credit cards before you accept one. For example, shop for the lowest:

- annual fee—especially important if you'll be paying the entire balance regularly, since the annual fee may be as much as the interest you avoid by paying in full (some cards don't have a fee)
- APR—especially important if you plan to pay only a part of your balance each month since it tells you how much interest you will pay on the balance each month

Remember—paying off the entire balance is best.

Don't get more credit than you need.

Limit yourself to 1 credit card, if possible. And try not to use your entire credit limit. (Make sure you cancel and properly dispose of credit cards you won't be using.)

Here are some tips:

- If you don't have the cash, don't charge it. Charge only items you can pay for in full when the bill comes due.
- Always pay on time. This will keep finance charges down. Plus, it will help keep your credit history spotless.
- Avoid cash advances. These may carry higher interest rates and fees.
- Compare your statements to your charge receipts. Be sure you know how many days you have to point out mistakes. Put everything in writing and save copies for yourself.
- Report address changes promptly. You're responsible for making payments even if you don't get a bill.

MORE ON MANAGING CREDIT.

Know when to use credit.

Try to limit using credit to:

- purchases of items that may increase in value
- large, necessary purchases
- emergencies
- purchases that can be made only with credit cards

Mind the 20% limit.

Keep your debt payments (not including mortgage or rent) below 20% of your take-home pay.

Know the results of bad credit.

Late payments or accounts turned over for collection can stay on your record for 7 years. That can affect your chances of getting loans or even employment and housing. And, payment for unpaid debts may be taken straight from your paycheck (garnished).

"Beat the interest" is the name of the game.

This is why staying ahead is important:

Say you saved $50 by shopping around for a sound system that was on sale. You charged $500 for it. But you decide to make only the minimum payment of $25 each month to spread out the cost. Good idea? Maybe not. Here are the hard facts:

- You'll end up paying a total of $588 for that system. That means $88 in finance charges (with an 18% APR—1.5% a month— using the adjusted balance method, the cheapest one).
- It'll take you 2 years to pay it off.

So much for the sale. And remember—this is just 1 purchase!

Pay more than the minimum due.

Interest can really add up.

Paying more than the minimum helps you stay ahead of it and avoid penalty charges. For example, by paying just $50 each month, you could have paid off that system in 11 months and saved $51 in interest.

STAY OUT OF THE HOLE.

The best way to avoid debt and credit problems is to take control of the situation now. Know your limits. And know what to do if you run into trouble.

Get away from high-interest debt.

If you have high-interest debt, consider:

- paying this debt off first (then paying the next highest and so on)
- transferring this debt to a credit card or loan with a lower interest rate
- asking your creditor for a better rate

Know the warning signs.

These are some signs that you could be in debt trouble:

- You don't know how much you owe.
- You're skipping paying some bills so you can pay others.
- You're using cash advances from credit cards to pay off other bills.
- Your accounts have been turned over to collection agencies.
- You're having to borrow so you can pay off old debts.
- You have no money for emergencies.
- You're over the 20% limit (see page 376).

If you're having problems, you should:

Talk to your creditors.

Let them know if your payment will be late or if you need to make payment arrangements. They may be able to help.

Get help.

There may be local nonprofit consumer credit help in your area. (See page 383 for details.)

Consider using your savings to pay off your debt.

Keeping your credit healthy may be worth a setback in savings. But avoid using your emergency fund, if possible.

Avoid services that claim to fix your credit for you.

They charge for a service that offers little or no help.

Make sure your bad credit history is erased.

Don't assume that the credit bureaus will erase your bad credit after its time has expired. Check your report to make sure.

Look into a secured credit card.

This is a good option if you can't qualify for a credit card because of past problems and you're not overspending anymore. It may also help you rebuild your credit history. (See page 372.)

LEARN ABOUT LOANS.
Knowing what lenders look for can help you get the loan you need.

Loans can help you reach some of your goals.

But make sure the reason you're borrowing is worth the extra drain on your finances.

- Is the item a "need" or just a "want"?
- Can you afford the extra payment?
- Will the new payment put you over the 20% debt limit?

Check your budget to find out.

Know what lenders look for.

Most lenders will consider:

- stability—the amount of time you've been at the same residence and job
- • your credit history—the amount of credit you can afford based on your income and current expenses

Consider low-cost borrowing options.

Before you go to a lender, think about borrowing from yourself.

- Savings: Using your savings might make more sense if you really can't afford more debt. Or you could use your savings as collateral for a loon.
- Insurance policy: You may be able to borrow against your life insurance. If you don't finish paying this back, the loan is subtracted from the policy value.
- Retirement plan: You may be able to borrow against your retirement plan. There may be fees involved. You'll have to pay the loan back to avoid penalties.

Keep in mind that while interest rates on loans from your retirement plan or insurance policy may be low, you're using money that could be earning money for your future.

Be prepared.

Before you apply for a loan, gather your information. It will help you answer questions. It also shows that you've really thought about your request.

- Make a list of all your debt. Include the amounts, account numbers, balances and amounts of your payments.
- Take a list of credit references with you.
- Know how much you can afford to pay in installments for a new loan.
- Know how long it will take to pay it back.
- Detail how much you need and what you need it for.
- Don't withhold information on your application.

Shop for the best loan terms. Have the loan officer explain them, especially how the interest will be calculated.

TIPS ON BUYING

There are many things to consider when making a major purchase.
But keep these tips in mind when financing and buying:

A car

- Try to avoid dealer financing—unless they're offering a very low rate. Get a pre-approved loan from a credit union, bank, etc.
- Credit unions may offer the best rates on car loans.
- A bigger down payment may mean a lower interest rate.
- Make payments into savings starting several months before you buy. This helps you save for a down payment and see if you can afford the car.
- Make the biggest monthly payments you can afford. Extending your payments only means that the car will cost more in the long run.
- Comparison shop for the best deal.
- Choose a car that's economical and fits your needs.
- Consider special options carefully. Don't get talked into added expenses, such as extended warranties that aren't worth the cost.
- Sell your old car yourself, if possible.
- Negotiate the lowest price before telling the salesperson you have a trade-in.

A home

- Start cleaning up your credit at least 6 months before applying for a loan. Check your credit reports, pay your debt down as much as possible and don't apply for any new credit.
- Get pre-qualified for a loan. A lender can help you figure out all the costs, what you can afford, etc.
- Shop for the best mortgage deal you can find. You may get a better deal at a bank where you're known.
- An adjustable-rate mortgage (ARM) may be a good deal if you don't have the money for a big down payment or closing costs and you don't plan to have the home for more than a few years. But be sure you understand all the loan terms before deciding.
- The Federal Housing Administration (FHA) may help you get a mortgage with a low or no down payment. If you are a veteran, the Veterans Administration (VA) may also offer benefits.
- Renting may be the better deal for you if you can't come up with a big down payment or you don't have the money for upkeep.

Consider the complete cost of ownership before you buy—insurance, maintenance, taxes, etc.

FINANCIAL SECURITY

Are you ready for your retirement? For your child's college tuition?
Being financially secure means being able to handle your expenses now. It means planning for your future expenses, too.

Make sure you have an emergency fund.

This should be your first step for savings. Have at least 3 months' worth of expenses ready for emergencies. You should keep this money in an account that's easy to get at such as a savings account.

Create a savings system that works for you.

If you don't see the money, you'll be less tempted to spend it. For example, consider having money put automatically into a savings account, retirement account etc., each month. You can do that with direct deposit.

Aim to save at least 10% of what you earn.

This includes all savings for retirement, other goals, etc. Save more if you can. It may seem hard, but putting aside even a little bit every month can add up.

For example, if you save $100 a month, you'll have $2,400 in only 2 years. You'll have $36,000 in 30 years—and thousands more in interest. Your money could earn even more if you invest wisely in a retirement account.

Make sure you're well insured.

Comparison shop for the best insurance deals, too.

- The amount of life, health and disability insurance you need depends on the needs of your family. Review your policies often.
- In general, term life insurance should meet your needs and be a better buy than whole life insurance.
- You should get auto and renter's or homeowner's insurance if you don't have it already.

Do you have health insurance?

It's easy to put off worrying about health care. But without insurance, a serious illness could push you into serious debt. Insurance also makes regular checkups more affordable so you can prevent problems or catch them early, when they're easier—and cheaper—to treat.

Invest in health insurance for yourself and your family. If you can't get health insurance through your employer and you can't afford it on your own, see if you or your children qualify for Medicaid.

Are you planning for retirement?

You need to plan to make sure that your retirement years are taken care of. Social Security may not be enough to let you live comfortably. Putting away retirement money in a savings account now is one thing you could do.

Creating a retirement account is another option. It lets you invest pre-tax income. (See page 382.)

The earlier you start planning, the easier it will be to reach financial security.

MAKE MONEY ON YOUR MONEY.

When investing, consider your goals, the risk and when you'll need the money. Talk to a reputable financial planner for advice.

Savings accounts

Savings accounts are reliable and safe, your money is easy to get at and they don't usually require a big deposit. But interest rates are low. That means your money will grow very slowly.

Money Market Accounts (MMAs)

These are like savings accounts. But, they require you to keep a high minimum balance, you can write a limited number of checks on them, and they may pay slightly higher interest rates.

Don't confuse MMAs with money market funds. Those are types of mutual funds, and you can lose money on them. (See Stocks, bonds and mutual funds.)

Certificates of Deposit (CDs)

CDs pay higher interest rates than bank accounts and are generally safe and reliable. But you can't withdraw your money for a certain amount of time (a "term"). Terms can be several months or years long. There's a penalty for withdrawing your money early. When shopping for a CD:

- Ask the bank to explain what a CD will earn in actual money, not percentages.
- Find the best CD term by comparing annual percentage yields (APYs). The APY is the amount you earn on your money in a year.
- Check CD rates at credit unions, too.

Stocks, bonds and mutual funds

These investments can give you a bigger return on your money. But they're riskier. Talk to a financial planner for advice.

Retirement accounts

Consider investing as much as you can in a traditional Individual Retirement Account (IRA) or a Roth IRA. Or invest in a 401(k) plan or pension plan, if these are available to you or your spouse.

Many accounts offer investment options that may include CDs, stocks, bonds or mutual funds. Different types of retirement accounts have different features and advantages— ask a financial planner to discuss the options with you.

But in general, the money you invest in retirement accounts isn't taxed until you start drawing money off them—neither is the interest. That means that you earn much more in interest. The sooner you start, the better.

Remember— always shop around to make sure you're getting the best deal. And make sure you understand all the details before committing.

SOURCES OF HELP AND INFORMATION.

Make note of the local phone numbers for the resources listed below for your future reference.

Local consumer services

Call the National Foundation for Credit Counseling at 1-800-388-2227. You'll get the number of a local nonprofit office that can help you budget and negotiate a payment plan with your creditors. There is little or no fee for this service.

Employee Assistance Programs (EAPs)

Some employers have EAPs that may offer financial counseling. Check with your job's human resources department to find out if your job offers one.

Government and community services

Look under the Community Services section of your phone book for listings of government and community organizations that may be able to help.

Credit reports

To get free copies of your credit reports, contact:

- www.annualcreditreport.com
  1-877-322-8228

You can buy extra copies, if needed, by contacting each credit bureau separately:

- Experian
  www.experian.com
  1-888-397-3742

- Equifax
  www.equifax.com
  1-800-685-1111

- TransUnion
  www.transunion.com
  1-800-916-8800

Don't wait until you're in money trouble to ask for help.

Make note of financial phone numbers.

Bank/Credit Union:

_____

_____

_____

Local Consumer Service:

_____

_____

_____

EAP:

_____

_____

_____

Other:

_____

_____

_____

Other:

_____

_____

_____

SELF-ASSESSMENT
Use the information you've put together in your worksheets and your records to complete these sections.

After completing them, review your answers They can help you see the big picture—where you stand financially and where you're going. If you're not satisfied with what you see, use the skills you've learned in this workbook to make changes.

Record keeping

Are your record keeping skills helping you or slowing you down? Put a check mark by, or write the answer for, the items that apply to you.

1. ☐ I know how to read my pay statement.

2. ☐ I've created automatic pay deductions to pay these people or organizations each month:

_____

_____

_____

_____

_____

3. ☐ I never bounce checks—I always know what my checkbook balance is.

4. ☐ I record every ATM and debit card withdrawal and deposit in my checkbook register.

5. ☐ My checkbook balance is currently $ _____

6. ☐ My checkbook balance regularly matches my bank's records.

7. ☐ I have a regular system for paying my bills.

8. ☐ I regularly record the bills I've paid in my budget so I can see if I'm on track.

9. ☐ My system for filing important records works like this:

_____

_____

_____

_____

_____

10. ☐ My spouse understands and can handle our finances if I'm not able to.

BUDGETING
How good are your budgeting skills?
Will your budget help you reach your goals? Fill out the following items.

1. These are my short-term goals: _____
   I need to save a total of $_____ to reach them.

2. These are my medium-term goals:_____
   I need to save a total of $_____ to reach them.

3. These are my long-term goals:_____
   I need to save a total of $_____ to reach them.

4. My net worth is $_____ I plan to improve it by:

   _____

   _____

   _____

5. My total yearly income is $_____

6. I've budgeted a total of $_____ a month to reach my goals. I will pay myself first.

7. My total monthly expenses are now $_____

8. I plan to cut my expenses further by doing these things:

   _____

   _____

   _____

9. I've budgeted $_____ for fun money.

10. I plan to improve these areas of my budgeting:

   _____

   _____

   _____

DEBT MANAGEMENT
Are you headed for debt trouble?
Use this form to see how close your debt is to the 20% limit.

1. 1List the totals you owe each month on credit cards, store charge cards, etc.:

Card #1 $_____

Card #2 $_____

Card #3 $_____

_____ $_____

_____ $_____

_____ $_____ $_____   **Total monthly CREDIT payments**

Total: $_____

2. List the monthly payment for every loan you have (not including mortgage): $_____   **Total monthly loan payments**

Auto loan $_____

Student loan $_____ $_____   **Total monthly debt payments**

        $_____

        $_____

Total: $_____

3. Total monthly debt payments $_____

4. List your monthly income (after taxes) $_____

5. Total monthly debt payments ÷ monthly income (after taxes) = Debt as a percentage of income

$_____ ÷ $_____ = $_____

This figure should be
less than .20 (20%).

Take steps immediately to reduce your debt if it's close to or over 20%.

FINANCIAL SECURITY

How prepared are you?
Take a look into tomorrow by completing these items.

I'm saving $ _____ each month. This is _____ % of my paycheck.

I have an emergency fund of $ _____ right now.

I plan to create a fund of $ _____ by _____ / _____ (month/year).

My life insurance pays $ _____ .

Based on current expenses, this should cover my family for _____ years.

Yes/No   **I'm fully enrolled and understand**
             my health-care and disability benefits.

Yes/No   **I have complete auto and renter's**
             or homeowner's insurance.

When I retire, my Social Security, military retirement, other retirement etc.,
will give me an income of $ _____ a year.

I plan to save a total of $ _____ for my child's education.
I am saving $ _____ each month.

Remember:

- Save at least 10% of your paycheck each month.
- Create an emergency fund of at least 3 months' worth of expenses.
- Have enough insurance to provide for you and/or your family in case of illness, disability, disaster or death.
- Look into an Individual Retirement Account (IRA), for example, if you're not satisfied with your retirement income.
- Get qualified financial advice if you have questions about your insurance needs, retirement needs, etc.

YOU AND YOUR HEALTH

REENTRY
ESSENTIALS, INC.

Life Skills Series
Basic Skills for Lifelong Success

Please read:

Talk to your health-care provider! This workbook is not a substitute for the advice of a qualified health-care provider.

Reentry Essentials, Inc.
2609 East 14 Street, Suite 1018
Brooklyn, NY 11235-3915
P: 347.973.0004
E: info@ReentryEssentials.org
I: www.ReentryEssentials.org

This workbook belongs to:

_____

You may find it helpful to keep important names and phone numbers handy.

Write them below.

My health-care provider:

Name_____

Phone_____

Emergency contact:

Name_____

Phone_____

Pharmacy phone number:

Name_____

Phone_____

Health insurance Company:

Name_____

Phone_____

Other important numbers

_____
_____
_____
_____
_____
_____
_____
_____
_____
_____
_____
_____
_____
_____
_____
_____
_____

IF YOU WOULD LIKE TO IMPROVE YOUR EATING AND EXERCISE HABITS, THIS WORKBOOK IS FOR YOU.

It will help you:

Think about the benefits

of eating healthier and being more active. They include:

• reducing the risk for—or managing—a health problem (such as heart disease, stroke, high blood pressure, high cholesterol, diabetes, arthritis and certain types of cancer)

• having more energy and managing stress better

• losing weight to feel and look better

Chart your course for making healthy changes.

To help you stay motivated:

• Keep reminding yourself of the benefits.

• Make a plan that helps these changes become a normal part of your day.

• Set realistic goals and track your progress.

Work with your health–care provider to make a plan that's right for you.

You may also want to ask about working with a dietitian or nutritionist, or a personal trainer.

Eating healthier and being more active are keys to feeling your best—physically and mentally!

Note: Sources of information used in the creation of this workbook include www.ChooseMyPlate.gov and the 2015-2020 Dietary Guidelines for Americans (U.S. Department of Agriculture and U.S. Department of Health and Human Services).

CONTENT

EATING BETTER FOR BETTER HEALTH
Start by knowing what's part of a healthy eating pattern.
In general, healthy eating involves:

Balancing portion sizes with physical activity

You'll gain weight if you take in more calories than you burn off with activity. Being overweight puts you at risk for health problems.

Check the calories and ingredients in foods and drinks. Track your daily intake. Make adjustments to stay within your calorie needs.

Eating the right amounts of different foods

- Eat more vegetables and fruits at each meal. Drink more low-fat or fat-free milk.
- Eat seafood at least twice a week. When you eat meat, choose lean cuts.
- Choose fewer items high in calories, saturated or trans fats, sodium and added sugars.

Taking other healthy steps

- Make smart choices from each food group every day. Think variety.
- Limit alcohol—or don't drink at all. People who should not drink at all include women who are pregnant or may be pregnant, and people recovering from alcoholism. Ask your health-care provider what's best for you.

Nutrient	Good Sources Include:
Carbohydrates	Whole grains, potatoes, fruits, vegetables and whole-grain cereal and pasta
Protein	Lean meats and poultry, seafood, eggs, low-fat or fat-free dairy products, beans, soybeans and nuts
Vitamins	Vegetables, fruits, low-fat or fat-free dairy products, beans and whole grains
Minerals (such as calcium and iron)	Low-fat or fat-free dairy products, green vegetables, lean meats and poultry, beans and dried fruits
Fats	Most liquid vegetable oils, nuts and some seafood
Water	Water, low-fat or fat-free milk, 100% fruit juice, and nonalcoholic and caffeine-free beverages

Ask yourself:

How happy am I with my eating habits? What do I do well? What would I like to change? Would tracking what I eat for a few days help me see what I need to change? Start by knowing what's part of a healthy eating pattern. In general, healthy eating involves:

_____

_____

_____

_____

_____

_____

_____

_____

_____

_____

_____

See pages 396-401 for more on making healthy food choices.

DIFFERENT PEOPLE HAVE DIFFERENT NUTRITION NEEDS.
Know about any special needs you may have.

Your daily calories

The right number of calories for you depends on different factors. These include your age, gender and level of activity. (See page 396.)

Ask your health-care provider or a dietitian or nutritionist how many calories are right for you.

Also, ask about any other special nutrition needs (such as for supplements). Recommended calories per day: _____ .

Other recommendations:

_____

_____

_____

_____

_____

_____

_____

_____

_____

Women

Ask your health-care provider about folate and folic acid. In general:

- Women who are capable of becoming pregnant need 400 micrograms of folic acid daily, plus folate-rich foods.
- Pregnant women need 600 micrograms of folic acid and folate.

Getting enough folate and folic acid can help lower the risk of certain birth defects, especially in the first few weeks of pregnancy. Good sources include:

- leafy green vegetables
- beans
- citrus fruits
- foods fortified with folic acid (such as whole-grain breads and cereals) and/ or folic acid supplements

Iron supplements are also often recommended during pregnancy. Ask your health-care provider.

Older adults

Older adults generally need fewer calories than when they were younger. But nutrient needs stay the same—or may increase in some cases, such as for vitamin D. So it's important for older adults to:

- choose foods that are low in calories and high in nutrients
- ask a health-care provider about the need for any supplements
- ask how to get the right amount of calories and nutrients if a health condition or medication affects your appetite

Feelings of thirst may decline with age. But getting enough water is still important for good health. Older adults should ask their health-care providers about how much water they should drink.

See pages 396-397 for more information on the food groups.

PEOPLE WITH CERTAIN HEALTH CONDITIONS

may also have special nutrition needs. Talk with your health-care provider or a dietitian or nutritionist about your needs.

People who have high blood pressure

need to:

- lose weight, if they are overweight
- get less sodium per day (see page 399)
- follow other dietary advice from their healthcare provider, such as cutting back on fats

Some people may also need medication.

People who have diabetes

need to:

- lose weight, if they are overweight
- follow the meal plan they develop with their health-care provider (including when to eat)

Some people may also need insulin or other medication.

People who have high cholesterol

need to:

- lose weight, if they are overweight
- limit saturated fat to the same general amounts recommended for everyone (see page 399), or to lower amounts in some cases (for example, to help manage heart disease)
- limit trans fat-found in baked goods, margarine, fried foods, snack foods and other processed foods that contain "partially hydrogenated" oils
- work with a dietitian or nutritionist, in some cases

Some people may also need medication.

If you have another health condition, be sure to talk with your health-care provider or a dietitian or nutritionist about any special nutrition needs.

HAVING A HEALTHY WEIGHT IS A KEY TO YOUR GOOD HEALTH.

It can help reduce your risk for future health problems.
Talk with your health-care provider about what's a healthy weight for you. He or she may:

Figure out your body mass index (BMI)

BMI is figured by a special formula that relates weight and height. For most adults, a BMI of:

- less than 18.5 means underweight
- 18.5–24.9 means healthy weight
- 25.0–29.9 means overweight
- 30.0 and up means obese

You can also calculate your BMI by visiting the Centers for Disease Control and Prevention Web site at www.cdc.gov/ healthyweight/assessing/bmi.

Note: The BMI figures above don't fit everyone, especially children, pregnant or breastfeeding women, and very muscular people.

Measure your waist

- This can help tell how much fat is around your abdomen—too much is a health risk.
- Health risks increase if a man's waist is over 40 inches or a woman's waist is over 35 inches.

Recommended steps to losing weight, if you are overweight

Keep in mind:

- Making permanent, healthy changes in your eating and exercise habits helps you lose fat, not needed muscle. Having healthy muscles helps your body be leaner and burn more calories—and be healthier overall.
- Losing weight slowly (about 1-2 pounds a week) is generally best. Avoid crash or fad diets (for example, high–protein diets). These can be dangerous to your health. And any weight loss is usually regained.

Focus on having good health—not on having an "ideal" body size or shape.
That size or shape may be unrealistic or unhealthy for you. Ask yourself:

How happy am I with my weight, and my body size and shape? _____

What changes, if any, would I like to see? _____

Does my health-care provider see these changes as realistic? _____

What weight, and ways to reach or maintain it does my health-care provider recommend for me?

_____

_____

_____

EAT FOR GOOD HEALTH.
What you choose to eat over time creates a pattern.
Make it a healthy one by:

Making healthy choices consistently

No single meal will make or break your health. But when you make mostly healthy food and beverage choices, it helps you:

- achieve and maintain a healthy weight
- get the nutrients your body needs
- lower your risk of chronic disease

It's important to stay within your calorie needs. Calorie needs change with age and activity levels. To find out what's right for you, visit www.supertracker.usda.gov

NOTE: These guidelines are for adults and for children age 2 and older. Ask a health-care provider about nutrition for younger children.

Starting with small shifts

For example:

- shift to fat-free or low-fat dairy
- choose whole fruits over juice
- make at least half of your grains whole grains
- choose seafood, lean meats, lean poultry, nuts, seeds and soy products over high-fat or processed meats and poultry

Focusing on nutrients, variety and amount

- Nutrients—Look for foods and beverages that are high in vitamins and minerals and low in solid fats, added sugars, refined starches and sodium.
- Variety—Have meals that include various food groups (see the next page). Vary choices within each food group, too. (For example, get a range of red, dark-green, orange and starchy vegetables, plus beans and peas, throughout the week.)
- Amount—Balance portion sizes with physical activity to manage your weight.

Limiting saturated fat, added sugars and sodium

- Limit saturated fat to 10% of your daily calories.
- Limit added sugars to 10% of your daily calories.
- Get less than 2,400 mg of sodium per day.* (Avoiding processed foods helps.)

*American Heart Association recommendation for adults

Write down any special needs you may have for how much of a food to eat. Ask your health-care provider or a dietitian or nutritionist for help.

_____

_____

_____

_____

_____

_____

_____

_____

_____

_____

Make healthy choices from each food group every day. Vary your choices within each group over the week. Here are some examples of healthy eating patterns for 2,000 daily calories:

U.S.-style

- Vegetables*—2½ cups
- Fruits—2 cups
- Grains—6 ounces
- Dairy—3 cups
- Protein foods*—5½ ounces

(aim for at least 8 ounces of seafood each week)

Vegetarian

(more plant proteins and whole grains; no meat, poultry or seafood)

- Vegetables*—2½ cups
- Fruits—2 cups
- Grains—6½ ounces
- Dairy—3 cups
- Protein foods*—3½ ounces

Mediterranean

(more seafood and fruit, less dairy)

- Vegetables*—2½ cups
- Fruits—2½ cups
- Grains—6 ounces
- Dairy—2 cups
- Protein foods*—6½ ounces (aim for 15 ounces of seafood each week)

*Most beans and peas can count as either a vegetable or a protein. Green peas and green beans count only as vegetables.

A note about measuring amounts of food

In some cases, different amounts of food count as 1 cup or 1 ounce.

For example:

- 2 cups of leafy greens count as 1 cup of vegetables
- 1 egg, ¼ cup of cooked beans and ½ ounce of nuts each count as 1 ounce of protein

Use your personal and cultural tastes to help build a healthy pattern. Learn more at www.ChooseMyPlate.gov.

READING THE NUTRITION FACTS LABEL

Can also help you make healthy food choices. It can help you quickly compare different foods before buying them. The format of labels may vary somewhat. But in general, you can check them for:

Serving size and number of servings per container

—size is given in household measures, such as cups, and metric measures, such as milligrams (mg) or grams (g).

The number of calories in a serving

and how many calories come from fat. (Depending on your calorie needs, you may want to eat less than a full serving size.)

How much of certain items a food contains

—for example, this food contains 660 milligrams of sodium.

Nutrition Facts

Serving Size 1 cup (228g)
Servings Per Container 2

Amount Per Serving		
Calories 260		Calories from Fat 120
		% Daily Value*
Total Fat 13g		20%
Saturated Fat 5g		25%
Trans Fat 2g		
Cholesterol 30mg		10%
Sodium 660mg		28%
Total Carbohydrate 31g		10%
Dietary Fiber 0g		0%
Sugars 5g		
Protein 5g		
Vitamin A 4%		Vitamin C 2%
Calcium 15%		Iron 4%

*Percent Daily Values are based on a 2,000 calorie diet. Your daily values may be higher or lower depending on your calorie needs.

	Calories	2,000	2,500
Total Fat	Less than	65g	80g
Sat. Fat	Less than	20g	25g
Cholesterol	Less than	300mg	300mg
Sodium	Less than	2,400mg	2,400mg
Total Carbohydrate		300g	375g
Dietary Fiber		25g	30g

Calories per gram:
Fat 9   Carbohydrate 4   Protein 4

Percent (%) Daily Value

—to see how the food fits into a diet of 2,000 calories a day. (Ask your health–care provider how many calories you need.) In general, 5% or less is low and 20% or more is high.

Daily Values footnote

—for the suggested daily intake of certain nutrients. For example, your total fiber intake should be at least 25 grams if you're on a 2,000–calorie diet.

Conversion information

—for example, there are 4 calories in each gram of protein and 5 grams of protein in a serving of this food, so 20 calories per serving come from protein.

Different sodium levels may be recommended in some cases. See page 399.

Ask yourself:

Do I usually read nutrition labels? _____

If yes, how do they help me? _____

If no, what's stopping me? _____

Reading the Nutrition Facts label may be new to you. If it is, practice by comparing labels on some foods you have at home.

YOU CAN USE THE NUTRITION FACTS LABEL TO KEEP TRACK OF ITEMS YOU SHOULD LIMIT.

You can also use it to help track any items you may need to eat more of (vitamins or minerals, for example).

Recommended limits for most people are:

- 20-35% or less of daily calories from total fat
- less than 10% of daily calories from saturated fat
- less than 10% of daily calories from added sugars
- no more than 2,400 mg of sodium per day. People who can't lower their intake to 2,400 mg should try to reduce it by at least 1,000 mg. Getting only 1,500 mg per day can have even greater health benefits

(No daily limit has been established for trans fat, but you should avoid it, when possible.)

Remember, these guidelines apply to foods eaten over the course of a day—not to a single food or meal.

Every so often, check to see if you are eating the right amounts.

To do this, compare your recommended amounts with the amounts you actually eat. (Use the Nutrition Facts label to help add up the amounts you eat.)

Use the chart below to learn how many grams of fat you need each day. If the amount of calories you need (from page 393) is not listed, ask your health-care provider to help you figure out your fat needs.

	Total Calorie Level		
	1,600	2,200	2,800
Total Grams of Fat	36-62	49-86	62-109
Total Grams Saturated Fat	18	24	31

Ask your health-care provider if you need any special limits, or if there are any items you need to eat more of than you do now. Write them here:

_____

KNOW HOW TO MAKE HEALTHY FOOD CHOICES IN EVERY SITUATION.

Follow the tips below. And ask your health-care provider or a dietitian or nutritionist for other tips. Write them in the spaces below.

Shopping

Healthy choices for meals and snacks include:

- fruits and vegetables—fresh, frozen or canned (no added salt, sauce or syrup)
- whole-grain bread, oatmeal, pasta and brown rice
- fat-free or low-fat (1%) milk and other fat-free or low-fat dairy products
- meats labeled "lean" or "extra lean," fresh fish, skinless poultry, light tuna packed in water, soy products (such as tofu), beans and nuts

Eating fast food

- Order a salad (with dressing on the side) or a baked potato (plain, or with low-fat toppings).
- Choose a small, plain burger or order skinless chicken (grilled, roasted or baked).
- Avoid added cheese or bacon, fried sandwiches, French fries, mayonnaise and high-fat sauces.

Eating out

- Avoid high–fat foods (those that are crispy, fried, creamed or "au gratin").
- Ask how food is prepared. Request a healthier cooking method (such as steaming vegetables or leaving out salt). Choose restaurants that prepare food to order.
- Skip dessert or order a low-fat treat, such as fresh fruit or sherbet, or fat-free frozen yogurt.
- Share a meal or take some home.

Cooking

- Trim fat from meat and remove the skin from poultry. Eat less meat, and more grains and vegetables.
- Cook with vegetable oil spray. Use oils high in unsaturated fat (such as olive, canola, corn or soybean).
- Flavor with parsley or other herbs instead of butter, sauces or salt.
- • Poach, steam, roast, broil or grill instead of frying.

_____

_____

_____

_____

_____

_____

_____

_____

_____

_____

Eating Chinese food

• Choose steamed foods (such as vegetables or rice) and stir-fried dishes cooked in a small amount of oil.

• Avoid fried foods (such as egg rolls and fried rice), sweet-and-sour dishes, duck and foods with monosodium glutamate (MSG) added.

Eating Italian food

• Choose whole—wheat pasta with marinara (tomato) sauce or pizza with vegetables and low-fat cheese.

• Avoid dishes made with cream sauces, high-fat meats (such as sausage) or cheeses (such as Parmesan dishes).

Eating Mexican food

• Choose rice and beans, gazpacho, salsa and soft tacos or tortillas.

• Avoid refried beans cooked in lard, fried tortilla or nacho chips, sour cream and cheese dishes.

If you eat a vegetarian diet, follow the tips on these pages for the foods you eat. Ask your health-care provider or a dietitian or nutritionist for other advice to ensure that all your nutrition needs are met.

Eating your favorite foods

Talk with your health-care provider or a dietitian or nutritionist about ways to make your favorite food choices healthier—for meals and snacks. (You may want to keep a food diary for several days to help you do this. Write down what and how much you eat.)

_____

_____

_____

_____

_____

_____

_____

_____

_____

_____

SOME QUESTIONS AND ANSWERS

Shouldn't I take vitamin and mineral supplements even if I have no special needs?

Most people should aim to meet their nutritional needs by eating a variety of healthy foods. Certain people (pregnant women, for example) may be exceptions. Be sure to always consult your health-care provider for advice before taking any supplement. Tell all of your health-care providers about any supplements you take.

I keep hearing about antioxidants. What should I know about them?

Antioxidants are nutrients that may play a special role in reducing the risk of cancer, heart disease and other chronic health conditions. Research is being done to learn exactly how they work.

- Antioxidants include vitamin C, beta-carotene (which forms vitamin A), vitamin E and some minerals.
- They are found in plant foods, such as fruits, vegetables, grains and some nuts. Seafood and black or green tea are also good sources.

As with other vitamins and minerals, it's best for most people to get needed antioxidants by eating a variety of healthy foods.

You may have other questions.

Write them here and talk about them with your health-care provider or a dietitian or nutritionist.

_____

_____

_____

_____

_____

_____

_____

_____

_____

_____

_____

WHAT'S KEEPING YOU FROM EATING HEALTHIER?

Write down what you want to gain from eating healthier. Then think about what may be keeping you from doing it. Read some of the common barriers listed, and write your own. Talk with your health-care provider about ideas for change. Use these to help make your plan (see page 404).

Benefits

I would like to eat healthier, to help me...

_____

_____

_____

_____

Barrier	Possible change
I don't have time to sit down and eat a meal.	Pack easy-to-carry foods, such as fruit, carrot sticks and crackers with low-fat cheese.
I live alone—preparing a healthy meal isn't worth it	Prepare extra to freeze for other meals.
I eat to relieve stress.	Take a walk or talk to a friend instead.

_____   _____

_____   _____

_____   _____

_____   _____

_____   _____

_____   _____

_____   _____

_____   _____

_____   _____

SET YOUR PERSONAL GOALS

for healthier eating. Ask your health-care provider or a dietitian or nutritionist to help you plan 1 or 2 changes to try each week. Use your notes from pages 401 and 403.

Sample	Instead of... Drinking whole milk	Try... Low–fat or fat–free milk	Notes I got used to the new taste.
WEEK 1			
WEEK 2			
WEEK 3			
WEEK 4			

TRACK YOUR PROGRESS

toward healthier eating. Especially in the first month or so, recording your successes and any benefits you notice can help you stay motivated. You may also find it helpful to note any problems reaching a goal, and other ideas to try.

	I Succeeded In	I Had Trouble With	Notes
WEEK 1			
WEEK 2			
WEEK 3			
WEEK 4			

BEING MORE ACTIVE—ANOTHER KEY TO BETTER HEALTH

Be sure to talk with your health-care provider before starting or changing an exercise program. In general, a healthy exercise plan involves:

Keeping the benefits in mind

Most people can improve their health and quality of life through a modest increase in physical activity. People of all ages can benefit from regular physical activity. Especially early on, keep reminding yourself that physical activity can:

- help control weight and reduce the risk of health conditions (such as heart disease, high blood pressure, colon cancer and diabetes)
- help muscles, bones and joints stay healthy
- improve energy levels, mental health and the ability to manage stress

Getting enough physical activity

In general:

- Get at least 150 minutes of moderate—or 75 minutes of vigorous—physical activity each week.
- You may need more activity to lose weight or keep off the weight you've lost (up to 300 minutes or more of moderate—or 150 minutes or more of vigorous—activity each week).
- Try to spread your activity throughout the week, getting at least 10 minutes at a time.
- In addition, do muscle-strengthening exercises at least 2 days each week.

See pages 410-411 for examples of all types of exercise.

Making physical activity a part of daily life

This doesn't have to mean making major changes. Keep in mind that there are many ways to fit physical activity into your day. And every little bit counts. Say your goal is 150 minutes of physical activity in a week. If you did yard work for 30 minutes on 2 days, took a 15-minute walk to the post office on 4 days and rode your bike for 30 minutes on 1 day, you've reached your goal!

Also, substitute exercise for some TV or other "screen time."

SOME PEOPLE MAY HAVE SPECIAL EXERCISE NEEDS.

Know what special needs you may have.

Keep in mind that most people can benefit from being more active. But your health-care provider may have special advice about how to do this, for example, if you:

- are pregnant or have recently given birth
- have certain disabilities
- are a man over age 40, especially if you have not been active
- are a woman over age 50, especially if you have not been active
- need to manage heart disease (or reduce your risk for it), diabetes, arthritis or another chronic health condition

Talk with your health-care provider.

Discuss any special exercise needs you may have. Write them here.

Use the information to help you complete the charts on pages 415-417.

_____

_____

_____

_____

_____

_____

_____

_____

_____

_____

_____

_____

_____

_____

_____

_____

_____

_____

_____

MAKING AN EXERCISE PLAN THAT WORKS FOR YOU

To help make a plan that you're likely to stick with, try to:

Incudes a variety of activities that you enjoy.

This can help keep you interested. Consider these examples:

- walking
- swimming
- bicycling
- dancing
- yard work or gardening
- a group sport, such as soccer or basketball

Think about how you can fit some physical activity in every day.

For example:

• Could you set aside a regular time, such as when you get up in the morning or get home from work?

• Could you do smaller amounts of exercise throughout the day? For example, walk to work or take a walk at lunchtime? Or make a habit of using stairs instead of elevators, or parking at the far end of the parking lot when shopping?

(Be sure to keep personal safety in mind at all times.)

Set realistic goals.

This can help you:

• prevent injury

• avoid becoming discouraged

Especially if you have not been very active, it's important to start slowly (exercising for short amounts of time, for example). It's also important to build up gradually, at a rate that's right for you. (See pages 412-413 for ways to monitor your exercise intensity.)

ASK YOURSELF: WHAT ACTIVITIES WOULD I LIKE TO INCLUDE?

Answer these questions to help you get ideas.

Do I prefer to exercise alone, or with a friend or group?

What activities have I tried before?

How did I enjoy them?

What activities do I do now (including things such as housework or yard work)?

Would I rather be outdoors or indoors (for example, playing tennis or using an exercise video)?

What time of day works best? Would I rather set aside one time or shorter blocks of time?

What smaller changes can I make (for example, walking to the store)?

Is money a factor? Do I prefer not to spend much money on exercise? Do I want to try joining a fitness center (see page 414)?

Will planning nonfood rewards (such as new exercise clothes) help me?

_____
_____
_____
_____
_____
_____
_____
_____
_____
_____
_____
_____
_____
_____
_____
_____

Ask your health-care provider to help you plan your first month of exercise. Use the chart on page 416.

INCLUDING AEROBIC EXERCISE IS IMPORTANT.

Aerobic activities make your heart beat faster and make you breathe harder.
They involve constant movement of large muscle groups (such as the legs).

Benefits of aerobic activity

include:

- strengthening your heart and lungs
- increasing your endurance
- burning calories

Some examples of aerobic activities

include:

- brisk walking
- bicycling
- active dancing
- swimming

How much energy (calories) do different activities use?

Here are some examples of activities that use 150 calories:

- washing windows or floors for 45-60 minutes
- gardening for 30-45 minutes
- bicycling 5 miles in 30 minutes walking 2 miles in 30 minutes
- playing basketball for 15-20 minutes
- jumping rope or stair walking for 15 minutes

Source: Centers for Disease Control and Prevention, Division of Nutrition and Physical Activity.

My health-care provider recommends:

_____

_____

_____

_____

_____

_____

_____

_____

_____

_____

_____

_____

_____

OTHER TYPES OF EXERCISE ARE ALSO IMPORTANT.

Ask your health-care provider for advice about including these in your exercise plan, and to suggest exercises for each type. You may want to ask about activities such as yoga, too.

Warming up and cooling down

Each time you exercise, it's important to warm up before and cool down after. This can help prevent soreness, stiffness and injury. (Doing your main exercise at a lower intensity is one way to warm up and cool down.)

Stretching

This helps improve flexibility, prevent injury and reduce tension. Be sure to warm up before stretching.

Ask yourself: What things could I do more easily if I were more flexible?

Strengthening

Do strength-training exercises at least 2 days each week in addition to your physical activity routine. These exercises help keep muscles and bones strong. They also help burn calories. Strengthening improves balance and helps with daily activities.

Ask yourself: What things could I do more easily if I were stronger?

My health-care provider recommends:

_____
_____
_____
_____
_____
_____
_____
_____
_____
_____
_____

MONITORING THE INTENSITY OF YOUR EXERCISE

can help you make sure you're exercising hard enough, but not too hard. It can also help you see your progress as you become more fit. Here are some ways to monitor exercise intensity:

Using the talk test

Try talking out loud while exercising. Keep these general guidelines in mind:

- You should be able to carry on a conversation while exercising. If you can carry on a conversation without difficulty, you're exercising at a moderate intensity. If the conversation is difficult or broken, you're exercising at a vigorous intensity.
- If you can sing, you're only exercising at a light intensity. Try to speed up or work harder.
- If you are unable to speak, you're working too hard and should slow down.

Rating how hard you feel you're exercising

This involves paying attention to how your whole body feels while exercising. One way to rate how hard you feel you're working is to ask yourself if it feels like you are:

- doing no activity
- doing very light activity
- working somewhat hard
- working hard
- working very, very hard

In general, stay in the middle range to improve endurance.

Ask your health-care provider for more information about what range to aim for.
Ask about warming up, cooling down and different types of exercises (such as strengthening).
You may also want to ask for ideas about activities to help you stay within that range

_____

_____

_____

_____

_____

_____

_____

_____

_____

_____

_____

_____

Knowing your target heart rate

This is how fast your heart needs to beat each minute during exercise for you to get the most benefit. Many beginners may want to aim for a target heart rate that is 50-60% of their maximum heart rate. (Your maximum heart rate is the fastest your heart can beat. Never exercise at this rate.)

Ask your health-care provider to help you figure out your target heart rate.

Use these steps:

1. Subtract your age from 220 to find your maximum heart rate.

220 – _____ = _____ .
       (age)   (max. heart rate)

2. Multiply your maximum heart rate by the correct percentage to find your target heart rate. (Your health-care provider can tell you what percentage is right for you.)

_____ x _____ = _____
(max.)   (percentage)   (target)

Example for a 40–year–old with a recommended target heart rate of 60%:

1. 220 – 40 = 180.
2. 180 x .60 = 108 beats per minute.

Taking your pulse

This is a way to monitor your target heart rate during exercise. You may also want to take your pulse before and after you exercise. Here's one method for taking your pulse:

1. Lightly place your index and middle fingers on the underside of your wrist, below the base of your thumb.
2. When you feel a steady beat, count the number of beats in 15 seconds.
3. Multiply the number of beats by 4 to get the number of beats per minute.

Ask your health-care provider for help taking your pulse if you need it.

It may also help to practice when you're not exercising. And ask what your pulse should be at other times, such as during rest (about 60-100 beats per minute is usually considered normal).

Notes:

_____

_____

_____

_____

_____

_____

Exercising for more time at a lower level of intensity is just as helpful as exercising for less time at a higher level.

TAKE OTHER STEPS TO EXERCISE PROPERLY.

It's important to:

Wear the proper gear.

For example, you may need:

• walking shoes or other special footwear

• safety gear, such as a bicycle helmet, or reflective tape or clothing

• clothing that's right for the weather, such as the proper layers and types of fabric

• sunscreen, sunglasses and a hat to protect your skin and eyes from the sun

Exercise indoors in hot, cold or stormy weather.

Drink enough water.

Drink water before, during and after exercising, especially in hot weather. Don't wait until you feel thirsty.

Ask your health-care provider about any special advice for getting enough water.

Know when to stop exercising.

For example, stop right away if you:

• injure yourself or feel pain (including chest or neck pain)
• feel dizzy, nauseated or extremely tired— or sick in any way

Ask your health–care provider what to do in these cases and about other signs to watch for. Also ask about exercising if you're not feeling well (for example, if you have a cold).

Write the instructions below:

If you're thinking about joining a fitness center, buying home equipment or using a personal trainer, be sure to:

• Ask about staff certifications.
• Ask about equipment safety and about training to use it.
• Learn about all your options. Ask if there's a trial period to see how you like the equipment or service.
• Consider convenience. For example, how busy is a center when you want to use it? Is it near enough that you're likely to keep going?

_____

_____

_____

_____

_____

_____

_____

_____

WHAT'S KEEPING YOU FROM BEING MORE ACTIVE?

Write down the benefits you want from being more active. Then think about what may be keeping you from doing it. Read some of the common barriers listed, and write your own (if time is a barrier, see page 408 for some ideas). Talk with your health-care provider about ideas for change. Use these to help make your plan (see page 416).

Benefits

I would like to eat healthier, to help me...

_____

_____

_____

Barrier	Possible change
Exercising costs too much.	Focus on activities with little or no cost, such as walking or gardening.
I get bored when I exercise.	Make exercise a social time, by including my family or friends.
I might get hurt.	Try an easier activity, such as walking, and build up gradually.
I'm too tired most of the time.	Try a small amount when I wake up or during lunch. Track my energy level, to see if I notice an improvement.
_____	_____
_____	_____
_____	_____
_____	_____
_____	_____
_____	_____
_____	_____
_____	_____

SET YOUR PERSONAL GOALS

for being more active. Ask your health-care provider to help you plan the first 4 weeks of your exercise program. (Make copies of this chart.)

Week of: _____	Activity	When	How Long	Notes
Sunday				
Monday				
Tuesday				
Wednesday				
Thursday				
Friday				
Saturday				

TRACK YOUR PROGRESS

toward being more active. Help yourself stay motivated during your first month of exercising. Record successes and any benefits you notice, any problems reaching a goal and other Ideas to try.

	I Succeeded In	I Had Trouble With	Notes
WEEK 1			
WEEK 2			
WEEK 3			
WEEK 4			

LEARN MORE

about how you can make healthier eating and exercise habits part of your life. Contact these sources:

Food and Nutrition Information Center
1-301-504-5414
http://fnic.nal.usda.gov

Weight–control Information Network (WIN)
1-800-860-8747
www.win.niddk.nih.gov

Center for Nutrition Policy and Promotion
www.cnpp.usda.gov

Academy of Nutrition and Dietetics
www.eatright.org

American Heart Association
1-800-AHA–USA-1
(1-800-242-8721)
www.heart.org

Shape Up America!
www.shapeup.org

Notes

_____

_____

_____

_____

_____

_____

_____

_____

_____

_____

_____

_____

_____

_____

_____

_____

_____

_____

_____

_____

Remember to visit **www.ChooseMyPlate.gov** or talk to your health-care provider to learn about an eating pattern that fits your needs!

YOU CAN MAKE HEALTHY CHANGES FOR A HEALTHIER YOU!

Work with your healthcare provider to help make eating and exercise plans that work for you.

Build healthier eating habits by making changes a little at a time.

Increase your physical activity at a rate that's right for you, doing activities you enjoy.

Track your progress to help you stay motivated and make any needed changes.

Enjoy your efforts and your results!

YOUR RESUME AND YOU

REENTRY
ESSENTIALS, INC.

Life Skills Series
Basic Skills for Lifelong Success

This workbook belongs to:

_____

You may find it helpful to keep important names and phone numbers handy.

Write them below.

Local career center

Name_____

Phone_____

Address_____

Networking contacts

Name_____

Phone_____

Name_____

Phone_____

Name_____

Phone_____

Name_____

Phone_____

Other important numbers

_____

_____

_____

_____

_____

_____

_____

_____

Reentry Essentials, Inc.
2609 East 14 Street, Suite 1018
Brooklyn, NY 11235-3915
P: 347.973.0004
E: info@ReentryEssentials.org
I: www.ReentryEssentials.org

A GOOD RÉSUMÉ CAN HELP OPEN DOORS.

Even in a challenging job market, a well written résumé can get you noticed.

A résumé is an important tool in your job search.

It lets employers know that you have the skills and experience necessary to do the job.

Your résumé should help you stand out.

A well-written résumé should highlight your skills and experience in a way that is clear, concise and easy-to-read.

There's a lot you can do to create a résumé that is more effective.

This workbook can teach you how to:

- present your skill and experience
- set the right tone
- prepare your résumé for electronic formats

Create the résumé that gets you your next job!

CONTENT

WHAT IS A RÉSUMÉ?

It's a brief history of your accomplishments that can help you get your next job.

Your résumé is your introduction to an employer.

It gives the employer a brief summary of your:

- education
- skills
- experience

You want it to show the employer why you should be considered for a job.

The goal of a résumé is to get you an interview.

An employer is looking for people with certain qualifications for the job being offered. A hiring manager will look through résumés for candidates who have those qualifications. Those candidates will then be invited to interview for the job.

Once you have an interview, you have an opportunity to sell yourself and convince the employer you are the best candidate to hire.

A well-written résumé can help you stand out from the crowd.

Hiring managers usually have to sort through many résumés for each job opening—sometimes hundreds. As a result, a hiring manager is likely to give each résumé a quick scan first to see if a person seems to have the qualifications the employer is seeking. He or she will immediately set aside the résumés that don't seem to meet those qualifications.

So a résumé needs to catch the hiring manager's attention at first glance. It's important to know how to help yours get noticed.

Your résumé needs to make a good first impression.

A hiring manager should be able to take one look at your résumé and decide whether you are a candidate he or she should consider.

Your first job is to create a more effective résumé.

This is something you can do yourself. There are many services that offer to write your résumé for you. But some are quite expensive, and there is no guarantee you will be happy with the results. Also, nobody knows about your background and abilities better than you! This will take some time and effort. But you're worth it! And remember, your effort is going to pay off with a new job.

Your résumé will also change over time.

For example, you can add to it as you:

- work different jobs
- get promotions
- continue your education
- learn new skills

You can also customize your résumé for a specific job you are applying for. (See page 438.) This means changing your résumé to give more emphasis to certain skills and abilities you have that match what an employer is seeking.

What are your job goals?

Think about the career fields you'd like to work in, and the kinds of jobs you would be interested in. What skills do those jobs generally require? Write them below.

Field(s) you want to work in:

1._____

2._____

3._____

Jobs you would consider:

1._____

2._____

3._____

Skills needed for those jobs:

1._____

_____

2._____

_____

3._____

_____

WHAT TO INCLUDE

Depending on your background and the job desired, your résumé should include:

A heading

This usually includes your:

- full name
- complete address
- personal telephone number
- personal e-mail address

Work experience

This can include any full or parttime, seasonal or volunteer work. For each job listed, provide:

- names and locations of employers
- dates of employment
- job titles
- major responsibilities and accomplishments

In general, leave out experience that's very old unless it relates to the job you are seeking.

A job objective or professional profile

- An objective lets the employer know what type of position you are looking for. If you are a new graduate, have varied experience or are changing careers, including an objective can help focus your résumé. Avoid being vague. But don't be so specific that you eliminate yourself from other positions that may interest you.
  Poor: "A challenging position that uses my education and creativity."
  Good: "A sales position in a growing retail organization."

- A professional profile or qualifications summary gives the employer a summary of the skills and experience you would bring to the job. It highlights your key skills and achievements.
  Poor: "Knowledge of many areas of public relations."
  Good: "Creative, detailoriented public relations specialist with over two years' experience in strategic planning and media relations."

Education/training

This section may contain:

- names and locations of schools or programs
- dates of attendance
- degrees, certificates or licenses awarded
- major honors, awards, scholarships or elective offices

If you are a recent graduate, you may also want to include:

- Your grade-point average, if 3.0 or above
- Coursework related to the job you want

Activities/special skills

You may want to mention:

- interests and activities that demonstrate job-related skills (such as leadership and organization)
- personal accomplishments (for example, "paid my own way through college")
- special abilities, such as specific computer skills or knowledge of a foreign language

Your Résumé Information

Refer to the information you write below when you create your résumé.

Work Experience

_____

_____

_____

_____

_____

Job Objective or Professional Profile
(See pages 431 and 433.)

_____

_____

_____

_____

_____

Education/Training

_____

_____

_____

_____

Activities/Special Skills
(See page 435.)

_____

_____

_____

_____

_____

THE CHARACTERISTICS OF A GOOD RÉSUMÉ
Your résumé should be:

Brief

Limit your résumé to no more than 1-2 pages. Remember, a hiring manager does not have a lot of time to read through résumés, so it's best to get straight to the point.

Easy-to-read

Make sure your résumé is pleasing to the eye, and not too text-heavy. This means making good use of:

- fonts
- headings
- bullets
- whitespace

(See page 436 for tips on formatting a résumé.)

Honest

Never lie on your résumé. A skillful interviewer will be able to spot any exaggeration or false information. Also, employers often verify information in résumés and applications.

Customized

Employers will advertise the skills they are looking for in job candidates. On your résumé, emphasize your skills and accomplishments that make you a good fit for the position. This can help you get the attention of the hiring manager.

Specific

When possible, use numbers to describe your accomplishments. For example, a résumé could include:

- the number of employees you managed
- the size of a budget you were responsible for
- quarterly or annual sales figures
- the amount of money you saved an employer on a project

Action-oriented

When describing your experience and skills, use the active voice. For example, begin sentences with words such as:

- accomplished
- budgeted
- supervised
- operated
- guided
- persuaded

Complete

It's OK to leave out experience from early in your work history if it's not related to the job you are seeking. But otherwise, be sure your work and education history is complete. One thing employers generally do not like to see is gaps in work history. These raise questions, and hiring managers may decide to consider another candidate instead.

When possible, include the reason for any gap in your work history. (For example, you went back to college, volunteered, etc.)

AVOID COMMON MISTAKES.

These mistakes can hurt your chances for being considered for employment.

Don't use gimmicks.

For example, don't use photographs, unusual formats or brightly colored paper. Some people think these will help attract attention to their résumé. And they will—but not in a good way.

Don't include salary requirements.

If you are asked for this information, include it in your cover letter. Otherwise, this shouldn't be discussed until after you receive a job offer. (The Occupational Outlook Handbook has salary ranges for different types of jobs. See page 450.)

Don't use personal pronouns.

When describing skills and accomplishments, don't use "I" or "me." Save those words for your cover letter.

Don't use abbreviations.

For example, don't use an abbreviation for the college you attended or a company you worked for. Spell out the full name.

Don't include unnecessary personal information.

The employer needs to know some of your personal information, such as where you live and how to get in touch with you. But the employer does not need to know your:

- race
- religion
- political affiliation
- hobbies
- height or weight
- age or date of birth
- marital or parental status
- reasons for leaving a previous job

Don't emphasize skills and job activities you no longer want to do.

This is especially important for job seekers who want to change careers. (See page 444.) For example, you may have worked in sales but now want to get a different type of job. Emphasizing your skills as a salesperson is going to work against you.

Don't emphasize older experience.

If you have been in the workforce a long time, put emphasis on skills and work experience you've had within the past 15 years.

Don't use job-description language for skills.

Job descriptions use phrases like "duties include" and "responsible for." Avoid these phrases when describing your skills and accomplishments. Use action-oriented words instead. (See page 428.)

A CHRONOLOGICAL RÉSUMÉ IS THE MOST COMMON TYPE.

The format emphasizes your experience.

A chronological résumé gives a timeline of your work history.

It starts with your most recent job, then goes backward. This highlights your work history for employers.

A chronological résumé lets employers easily see:

- how long you worked at each job
- the skills and experience you gained at each job
- if you have any gaps in your work history

How is a chronological résumé organized?

It often lists:

- a job objective or professional profile
- a summary of your skills and other accomplishments
- your professional experience, from your most recent job to your earliest job
- your education

Who should use a chronological résumé?

Consider using this format if you are:

- looking for a similar position in your current field
- trying to advance in your current field
- proud of your most recent position

Give a clear picture of your work history.

For each job you list, include:

- the years you worked at that company
- the company name
- the company location (city and state)
- your job title(s) while you worked there
- a brief list of your accomplishments during that time

If you have a gap in your work history, you can fill it with an activity relevant to the job you are seeking—for example, an internship or volunteer work.

Advantages

- This format gives a clear picture of where you have worked and what you have accomplished.
- It's logical and easy to follow.
- Many employers prefer this format.

Disadvantages

- Limited experience or gaps in employment may stand out in this format.
- This format works against job seekers who are changing careers.
- • If you've changed jobs often, that will stand out.

Juan M. Hernandez

(555) 222-8888
jmdez@abcmail.com

55 Spencer Ave.
Pine Grove, CT 12345

PROFILE

Enthusiastic professional with over 8 years of experience in commercial and retail technology sales. Proven success in increasing sales and developing new business.

PROFESSIONAL EXPERIENCE

2008–present

Senior Sales Representative
Tel-Com Business Solutions, Manderly, CT

Develop leads and present technology solutions to meet commercial customers' telecommunication and computing needs.

- Increased prior year sales 27% over goal.
- Ranked in the top 10% of sales representatives for total profit.
- #1 in customer retention 3 years running.

2004–2007

Assistant Retail Sales Manager
ENZ Computers, Westham, MA

Assisted retail customers in choosing computer systems and related equipment.

- Leader for total sales in 2006 and 2007.
- Suggested changes in point-of-sale system that resulted in yearly savings of over $12,000.
- Helped manage and schedule a sales team of 5 full-time and 7 part-time employees.

A.S., Computer Science, 2004
Westham Community College, Wes

Professional

Write your professional profile.

Your profile is a description of you in your working life. It is usually one sentence and describes some of your skills and experience. For example:

"Creative, detail-oriented public relations specialist with over two years' experience in strategic planning and media relations."

Practice writing your own professional profile. Look over some of your skills to get some ideas. Try to find words that best describe what you do.

_____

_____

_____

_____

ANOTHER TYPE IS THE FUNCTIONAL RÉSUMÉ.
This format emphasizes your skills.

A functional résumé gives a listing of your relevant job skills.

It lets employers easily see all of your major skills and accomplishments in different areas. For example, you may have skills in:

- organization
- leadership
- sales
- writing
- software
- dealing with people

How is a functional résumé organized?

It often has:

- a job objective or professional profile
- a complete listing of your major skills
- a brief summary of your work history
- your education

Who should use a functional résumé?

Consider using this format if you:

- are changing careers
- are a parent who is reentering the workforce
- have been unemployed for a long time
- had the same responsibilities for years and years at multiple job sites
- have experience and skills as a volunteer
- are an older job seeker who wants to emphasize skills or experience from earlier in your work history

List all the skills you think can help you get the job you are seeking.

Look through the employer's ad for the job. It should list the skills they want candidates to have. Be sure to list all the skills you have that match.

Advantages

- This format highlights your skills and accomplishments while placing less emphasis on your work history.
- This format can benefit job seekers who are changing careers or don't have much experience.

Disadvantages

- Some employers may be suspicious of this format and wonder if you are trying to hide something.
- This format doesn't link your skills with specific jobs in your work history.

ANNE E. BATES
16 East Street
Kingston, Minnesota 06006
(333) 555-5555
aebates@anyprovider.net

JOB OBJECTIVE   To obtain a position as a full-time reporter
for a major daily newspaper.

KEY SKILLS & ACCOMPLISHMENTS

Interviewing
- Regularly interview local officials while covering political events.
- Conducted on-the-scene interviews for local TV news team.
- Strong interpersonal and communication skills.

Writing
- Report on local politics for city newspaper with a daily circulation rate of over 25,000.
- Wrote local news pieces for evening TV news broadcast reaching over 30,000 viewers daily.
- Wrote feature articles for college newspaper.
- Able to translate and write in Spanish.
- Skilled in use of word processing and office software.

Editing
- Edited articles for features section of college newspaper.
- Provided editing services as college writing tutor.

WORK HISTORY
The Kingston News, Kingston, Minnesota (2012–present)
Alexandria College News, Alexandria, Minnesota (2009–2011)
WXL Channel 52, Ashland, Minnesota (Summer 2009)

EDUCATION
B.A., Communications, June 2011
Alexandria College, Alexandria, Minn.
Journalism Award, 2011
Cumulative GPA: 3.75

Write a job objective.

What kind of job do you want? What kind of company do you want to work for? Think about your goal for your next job and practice phrasing it as a job objective. Write it below.

If you're having trouble coming up with a job objective, look over ads for jobs you are interested in.

_____

_____

_____

_____

A COMBINATION RÉSUMÉ IS ANOTHER TYPE.
It combines the chronological and functional formats.

A combination résumé focuses on your skills and experience.

It combines:

- the work history timeline in the chronological résumé
- the listing of major skills in the functional résumé

This allows you to link the major skills you have with each job you've held. Employers can compare the skills they are looking for with the skills you have used in the past.

How is a combination résumé organized?

In order, it often lists:

- a job objective or professional profile
- a summary of your qualifications
- your work history, with a list of major skills used for each job
- your education

Who should use a combination résumé?

Consider using this format if you are:

- a student or recent graduate with little work experience
- a worker with a long, consistent work history (no gaps)
- changing careers
- re-entering the workforce

A combination résumé gives you some flexibility.

You can structure it in a way that works best for you. It allows you to:

- emphasize your strongest skills in a summary of your qualifications
- go into detail about skills you used at specific jobs in a chronological work history

Advantages

- This format gives your work history in a chronological order, which some employers may prefer.
- This format links your skills with specific jobs in your work history.

Disadvantages

- It may be repetitive if you list similar skills in different positions.
- This format may be longer than résumés in a chronological or functional format.

Jill Epstein

114 White Street
Portland, OR 97211

(503) 555-5555
jepstein@netmail.com

PROFILE

A highly organized and friendly professional, able to establish long-term, positive relationships with clients, co-workers and outside resources.

QUALIFICATIONS

- More than 10 years of administrative experience in diverse business settings.
- Skilled in working independently and as an enthusiastic team player.

PROFESSIONAL EXPERIENCE

Administrative Assistant
The Webster Agency, Portland, OR   2008–present

Organization & Administration
- Coordinated master calendar of personal and professional engagements, acting as liaison between authors, publicist and booking agent for national appearances.
- Oversaw coordination of national book and television tours, performing troubleshooting, research and follow-through to ensure smooth scheduling.

Communication & Client Relations
- Responded to high volumes of telephone inquiries with friendliness and professionalism, referring callers to Web site and other appropriate resources.
- Worked to ensure on-time delivery of press releases and promotional materials.

Office Manager
Northwest Dental, Beaverton, OR   2002–2008

- Prepared office for daily appointments, including office opening, chart setup, financial arrangements and adequate supplies for staff and clients.
- Balanced daily revenue and expense sheets, issued monthly

What are your key skills?

Think about the jobs you do well. What skills do these involve? Start a list.

Next, think about each job you have had. What did you do there? What skills did you use? Add those to the list. If you are having trouble, visit www.careeronestop.org and www.bls.gov for a list of skills in different types of jobs.

_____

_____

_____

_____

MAKE YOUR RÉSUMÉ PLEASING TO THE EYE.

Here are some tips for designing a résumé that is easy for employers to read.

Make good use of white space.

Use at least one-inch margins on your résumé. Leave some blank space between sections and paragraphs so your résumé doesn't seem dense or text-heavy.

Limit the fonts you use.

Word processing software comes with a lot of different fonts. It can be tempting to use many of them to try to get an employer's attention. But the more fonts you use, the less readable your résumé will be. Limit yourself to two. For example, use one font for the headings and another for the body text.

Use boldface and italics.

Boldface and italics can help certain parts of your résumé stand out. For example, you can use boldface or italics for:

- section headings
- subheadings
- job titles

But don't use them too much. Avoid underlining.

Emphasize skills and accomplishments with bullet points.

This makes it easier for employers to quickly scan your résumé for your skills. Bullets help grab the reader's eye and lead him or her to key points.

Be consistent.

For example, if you use boldface for your first job title, use boldface for all job titles you list. If you center one section title, center all section titles. Being consistent helps make your résumé easier to read and follow.

Consider using a template.

Word processing software often includes different templates for creating résumés. These templates are already formatted with headings and selected fonts. Choose one that looks appealing to you.

SETTING THE RIGHT TONE

Let your résumé show that you are a dynamic individual with a lot to offer!

Be confident.

Your résumé should give the impression that you are proud of your skills and accomplishments. An employer wants to hire someone who is confident in his or her abilities.

Emphasize the positive.

Sell your strengths. Focus on the positive contributions you have made to your employers, your school and your community. Omit any negatives—such as being fired or having a low grade-point average.

Highlight accomplishments.

List your most important qualifications first. If you are a recent graduate, list education before experience since that is your most important qualification.

Avoid wordiness.

- Use keywords and phrases instead of complete sentences.
- Use the active voice. (See page 428.)
- Be direct.

Poor: "I staged a large campaign to cut costs and increase overall profits from fund–raisers by 10% in the course of one year's time."

Good: "Increased profits from fund-raisers by 10% in one year."

Use familiar terms.

Use language appropriate to the type of job that interests you. But, be sure you are clear and easily understood.

Be neat.

Make sure there are no coffee stains, smudges, errors, corrections or anything else that detracts from the résumés appearance.

List some of your accomplishments here.

Use the active voice.

_____

_____

_____

_____

_____

_____

_____

_____

_____

_____

_____

_____

_____

_____

_____

CUSTOMIZING YOUR RÉSUMÉ
Tailoring your résumé to each employer can increase your chances of getting hired.

Research the employer.

Visit the employer's Web site, if there is one. Do an online search for more information about the company, as well. Look for press releases or news stories.

- What does the company do?
- How does the job being advertised fit with the company's mission?
- What is the company philosophy? Goals?
- Who are the company's customers?
- Who are the company's competitors?

This information can help you customize your résumé and cover letter to explain how your skills and experience can help the company.

Research the job being offered.

Learn all you can about the responsibilities that usually come with that job title. Look up the job description in:

- the Occupational Outlook Handbook www.bls.gov/ooh
- Career One Stop www.careeronestop.org
- ads for the same position from other companies
- job-finding Websites

Make it clear which job you are interested in.

If you use a job objective, state the job title. If you use a professional profile, include relevant skills used in the job being advertised. Or include them in a summary of qualifications.

Highlight relevant skills and experience.

List the most important and relevant skills and accomplishments first. This can help your résumé stand out.

Remove information that is not directly related to the job.

For example, leave out work experience and skills that are not relevant to the job you are seeking. If doing so will leave a gap in your work history, you can list non-relevant jobs, but don't provide further details.

Look for keywords.

An employer's ad will use certain words and phrases to describe the skills the employer is looking for in job applicants. For example:

- "work closely with others" means you work well as part of a team
- "communication skills" means verbal and written skills, effective listening and taking direction
- "multitasking" means you can organize and prioritize several activities
- "problem-solving skills" means you can identify, prevent and solve any problems that come up as part of your work

Employers often use software to scan résumés to search for keywords. So be sure to identify keywords in ads and use them in your résumé, if appropriate.

Read an ad for a job that interests you.

Can you spot any keywords? Write them below.

_____

_____

_____

_____

_____

_____

_____

_____

_____

What skills and accomplishments do you have that match those keywords? Write them below. Highlight these in your résumé.

_____

_____

_____

_____

_____

_____

_____

_____

_____

_____

_____

_____

THE FINISHING TOUCHES
Use this checklist.

Final read-through

- ☐ Résumé is focused, and it's clear what type of job you're looking for.
- ☐ The order of the sections makes sense.
- ☐ It seems easy to read.
- ☐ Action words are used to describe skills and accomplishments.

Feedback

Ask someone to read through your résumé for no longer than 20 seconds.

- ☐ Can he or she easily see what your skills and accomplishments are?
- ☐ Is there anything that is confusing or unclear?
- ☐ Is there anything that raises questions?
- ☐ What does the person remember most about your qualifications?

Proofreading

- ☐ I proofread my résumé carefully.
- ☐ Someone else also proofread my résumé carefully.

Printing

- ☐ Type is neat and clean.
- ☐ Paper is high quality with matching envelopes. (White or off-white is best.)

Or:

- ☐ I had my résumé professionally printed.

ESTABLISH AN ONLINE PRESENCE.

Use the Internet to have your résumé reach as many potential employers as possible.

Post your résumé on employment Web sites.

These are sites where employers put job postings. You can keep an electronic version of your résumé on the site and send it to employers in response to certain job postings.

These sites usually have a large client base in a wide range of industries. You can also sign up to be alerted if jobs you might be interested in are posted.

Use social networking sites.

These are sites where people can maintain professional contacts. They can also be used to connect hiring managers with qualified job candidates.

These sites usually ask you to create a profile, where you can post your:

- career history
- education
- skills

You can also upload an electronic version of your résumé.

Respond to job postings on company Web sites.

If there is a company you would like to work for, visit its Web site. Many allow you to upload your résumé and apply for specific positions online.

Create your own Web site.

This is a place where you can:

- demonstrate your knowledge and skills in your career
- provide a snapshot of your abilities
- give a brief bio
- keep a copy of your résumé for potential employers

Consider creating a professional blog.

You can use it to discuss your work experiences in the industry. This is a good way to show employers that you keep up with changes and developments in your field.

Online résumé

Research employment, social networking and company Web sites. Write down the URLs for sites you would like to post your résumé on.

_____

_____

_____

_____

_____

_____

_____

_____

_____

_____

_____

_____

_____

_____

CREATE AN ELECTRONIC VERSION OF YOUR RÉSUMÉ.
It can be an important part of your job search!

General tips

• Save your e-friendly résumé as a plain-text file. E-mail it by pasting it into an e-mail. (Only use other file types and attachments if an employer says it's OK.)

- Don't list your street address when posting a résumé online.
- List your cell phone number.
- If you e-mail or upload your résumé, take a printed copy of your résumé to an interview, too.
- If an employer asks you to fax or mail a scannable version of your résumé, Use 8½" x 11" plain white paper. Print on one side only. Don't fold or staple it. Mail it flat in a large envelope.

Content

Be sure to include keywords related to the skills and experience you have that employers in your field are looking for. Look for those used in their job ads, for example. Screening software may search for these. (You can include keywords as a separate section. Or you can incorporate them into your existing résumé.)

Saving

In some cases, you can save your résumé in a file that keeps formatting intact, such as a PDF. You can then send it to an employer or upload it to their site.

Plain text

In other cases, you will be asked to fill out fields with your:

- name
- phone number
- e-mail

Then you are asked to paste a plain-text version of your résumé into another field.

Creating a plain–text version of your résumé

To create this:

- Remove all special formatting, such as indents, tabs, bullets, graphics, boxes, shading and horizontal or vertical lines.
- Align text to the left.
- Remove any underlining, italics or boldface. (You can replace them with asterisks, hyphens, and standard quotation marks.)
- Use capital letters for section headings.
- Use a basic font (such as Arial), 10-14 points in size.
- Place your name on the top line. Your street address, city and state, phone number and e-mail address should each go on a separate line.

ANNE E. BATES
Kingston, Minnesota 06006
(333) 555-5555
aebates@anyprovider.net

PDF

JOB OBJECTIVE   To obtain a position as a full-time reporter
for a major daily newspaper.

KEY SKILLS & ACCOMPLISHMENTS

Interviewing
- Regularly interview local officials while covering political events.
- Conducted on-the-scene interviews for local TV news team.
- Strong interpersonal and communication skills.

Writing
- Report on local politics for city newspaper with a daily circulation rate
  of over 25,000.
- Wrote local news pie[...] [...] over 30,000 viewers[...]
- Wrote feature articles[...]
- Able to translate and[...]
- Skilled in use of wor[...]

Editing
- Edited articles for fea[...]
- Provided editing ser[...]

WORK HISTORY
The Kingston News, Kin[...]
Alexandria College New[...]
WXL Channel 52, Ashla[...]

EDUCATION
B.A., Communication[...]
Alexandria College, Ale[...]
Journalism Award, 201[...]
Cumulative GPA: 3.75

Plain text version

ANNE E. BATES
Kingston, Minnesota 06006
(333) 555-5555
aebates@anyprovider.net

JOB OBJECTIVE
To obtain a position as a full-time reporter for a major daily newspaper.

KEY SKILLS & ACCOMPLISHMENTS

Interviewing
* Regularly interview local officials while covering political events.
* Conducted on-the-scene interviews for local TV news team.
* Strong interpersonal and communication skills.

Writing
* Report on local politics for city newspaper with a daily circulation rate
  of over 25,000.
* Wrote local news pieces for evening TV news broadcast reaching over
  30,000 viewers daily.
* Wrote feature articles for college newspaper.
* Able to translate and write in Spanish.
* Skilled in use of word processing and office software.

Editing
* Edited articles for features section of college newspaper.
* Provided editing services as college writing tutor.

WORK HISTORY
The Kingston News, Kingston, Minnesota (2012–present)
Alexandria College News, Alexandria, Minnesota (2009–2011)
WXL Channel 52, Ashland, Minnesota (Summer 2009)

EDUCATION
B.A., Communications, June 2011
Alexandria College, Alexandria, Minnesota
Journalism Award, 2011
Cumulative GPA: 3.75

CHANGING CAREERS
Create a résumé that shows you are ready to hit the ground running in your new chosen field.

Highlight your transferable skills.

Many skills can be used for different jobs and careers. Learn about which of your skills are transferable by reading job descriptions (such as those found in the Occupational Outlook Handbook at www.bls.gov/ooh).

Consider using a functional résumé. This will allow you to put more emphasis on the relevant skills and accomplishments from your previous career.

Include all experience you have in your new career.

This includes:

- volunteering
- internships
- part-time work
- classes or workshops
- conferences
- industry events

Do some research.

Learn all you can about:

- your new field
- companies in that field
- jobs at those companies

In your résumé and cover letter, show employers that you have done your homework and are ready to contribute.

Don't sell yourself short.

It's normal to feel nervous about starting a new career. But don't let your employer get that idea from your résumé! Project confidence in your abilities, skills and achievements, even though they were in your old career.

Talk to people working in your desired field.

Ask them to review your résumé and to offer any suggestions for changes.

ENTERING THE WORKING WORLD
Here are some tips for writing a résumé if you are a new graduate.

Don't oversell yourself.

Be sure to emphasize any related skills and experience you gained from:

- internships
- school projects
- training programs
- certifications
- previous jobs

But don't exaggerate your qualifications. If you're applying for an entry-level position, hiring managers will pay more attention to your aptitude and potential.

Don't ignore the job requirements.

You may apply for a job that asks for some qualifications you don't have. And there's nothing wrong with that. Sometimes, employers will hire candidates who don't have all the qualifications they asked for. But don't ignore those qualifications, either. For example, in a cover letter, you can explain how you are working toward fulfilling those requirements (for example, by taking a class).

Emphasize your academic accomplishments.

For example, point out:

- any honors (such as dean's list or Phi Beta Kappa)
- your grade point average, if it is 3.0 or above
- any coursework relevant to your major and career objective

Emphasize the skills you've used in previous jobs.

Even if you've worked only part-time jobs, you've still gained some skills and experience. For example, if you were a cashier at a supermarket, you handled cash transactions and provided friendly customer service. If you mowed lawns over the summer for different clients, you ran a lawn-care business.

Include any relevant extracurricular activities.

This could be related to:

- clubs
- social groups
- sports

For example, if you ran a charity fundraising event for a school club, that could impress an employer.

Consider including a job or career objective.

For example, if you want to work in the banking field, you could list "entry-level management position in the banking industry" as your objective.

IF YOU ARE UNEMPLOYED

Keep your résumé up-to-date, even if you aren't working right now.

Stay busy.

If you are out of work for some time, there will be a gap in your employment history. But you can fill this gap by:

- volunteering
- taking a class
- tutoring
- consulting
- doing temp work
- doing freelance work

This shows potential employers that you have been actively using and improving your skills.

Highlight any new skills or accomplishments gained in those roles. For example, if you volunteered to run a fundraiser, stress your organization of the event and include the amount of money you were able to raise.

Cover up smaller gaps in employment by leaving out months.

For example, you may have lost a job in January and started a new one in November of that same year. But if you only include the years in your start and end dates, it won't look like there is a gap in your work history.

Consider using a functional résumé.

This will put more emphasis on your skills and accomplishments than on your work history. Or use a combination résumé. (See pages 432-435.)

Be honest.

Offer a brief explanation for any gaps in your résumé or cover letter. For example, if you lost your job during a layoff, tell that to your potential employer, no matter how much time has passed.

TAKING AGE OUT OF THE EQUATION
Older job seekers can take steps to reduce the risk of age discrimination.

Keep it recent.

Only include your skills and accomplishments from the last 15 years. Employers are interested in what you have done recently to help the companies you've worked for.

Include older experience if it's relevant.

But don't mention the dates associated with it. For example, you can include highlights of this older experience in the summary of your qualifications. Or you can include it at the end of your résumé in a section titled "additional experience."

Share some of your work history, but not all.

For example, you might have had different job titles at the same company for 20 years. Instead of including your entire history at that company, you can begin with the start date of your most recent position.

Leave the date off your education listings.

Including the year you got your college degree may be a tip-off to your age, so leave it out. But be consistent. If you leave the date off of your education, leave it off for all degrees and training.

Consider a functional or combination résumé.

This lets you put more focus on your skills and accomplishments, and less on our work history.

Highlight your achievements.

This will show an employer how hiring you is in their best interests. Highlight:

- decisions you made that had positive results
- money you saved a company
- problems you solved

Be careful with phrasing.

Avoid descriptions that indicate you are an older worker. For Example, you don't want to point out that you have "over 20 years of experience" in a career field.

Remember, it's about getting an interview.

That's where you can really sell yourself to the employer. Being confident, knowledgeable and enthusiastic will help convince an employer you are the right person for the job.

ALWAYS INCLUDE A COVER LETTER WITH YOUR RESUMÉ.

It will be the first thing a potential employer reads.

A cover letter is your introduction to the employer.

It is where you provide some information on your qualifications and persuade the employer to consider you for a job by taking a closer look at your résumé. Check career reference books and Web sites for help with writing your cover letters. Most cover letters include:

- your name, address and phone number
- the date
- the contact and organization name
- your purpose for writing (the specific position you are interested in and where you learned about the position)
- your background and skills as they pertain to the job
- your specific qualifications for the job
- when and how you will follow up
- strong action words and phrases that will grab the attention of the reader

Follow these tips for writing a cover letter.

- Use the full and correct name and title of the contact person. Call the organization to find out the correct address and spelling. If possible, avoid addressing your letter "to whom it may concern."
- Do your research. If possible, mention specific aspects of the organization that interest or impress you.
- Explain how your specific skills and experience connect to the position. Highlight how you could benefit the organization and help them meet their goals.
- Check the letter carefully for errors and misspellings.
- Keep the letter to one page in length, and print it on high-quality white or off-white paper that matches your résumé.

There are 2 types of cover letters.

- Some are written in response to an advertisement. When you see a specific job advertised, you can tailor your résumé and cover letter to the needs of the job. Send your résumé and cover letter very soon after you see an advertisement. Some jobs are only listed for a few days before the employer has already lined up several interviews.
- Other cover letters are written with hopes that an organization may have unlisted job openings. This is a type of "cold" contact. You may send a cover letter and résumé to inquire about available positions and show your interest in an organization. State in your cover letter what types of position(s) you are interested in and qualified for. It may also help to write that while you understand there may not be any current openings, you would still appreciate meeting with someone to learn more about the organization.

KEEP A LIST OF REFERENCES.

An employer may ask for a list of references after you send your résumé.

Who to include

Choose at least 3 references. If possible, at least one should be a former manager or supervisor. Other choices include:

- a former co-worker
- someone you worked for at an internship or volunteer job
- a teacher or someone who trained or certified you in specific skills

What to include

For each reference, list the person's:

- name
- affiliation
- work address
- e-mail address
- phone number

Print your reference list on white or off-white paper and include your name at the top.

Getting the most from your references

Your references can really make you stand out as a candidate, so choose wisely. Pick references who know your work skills well and can talk about you in a positive way. (Always ask permission before using a reference.) You should also talk to each reference about the skills you want him or her to highlight and the type of job you want. For example, you wouldn't want your former supervisor to only discuss your computer skills if you are applying for a management position.

Keeping in touch with references

Make sure you always have their current addresses and phone numbers. Follow up often—ask them to let you know when they've been contacted by an employer. Knowing how many phone calls they receive will help you know how your job search is going. Don't forget to thank all of your references (especially after you get a job)!

List potential references here.

Include each person's name, affiliation, address, e-mail address and phone number.

_____

_____

_____

_____

_____

_____

_____

_____

_____

_____

_____

_____

_____

_____

_____

_____

RESOURCES

You can learn more about creating a more effective résumé from:

Your local career center

Find the American Job Center closest to you by visiting www.servicelocator.org. Ask about résumé workshops and other resources.

A career placement service

Review samples of résumés and cover letters. Ask about current trends in employer preferences for résumé styles and formats. If possible, set up a placement file (a collection of copies of documents, such as references).

Your library

Check for sources that list job titles and the skills needed for those jobs. The Occupational Outlook Handbook (also available Online) and professional journals are good examples.

People who have written résumés

Counselors, professors, coworkers, friends and others who have had experience in writing résumés and searching for a job can be valuable sources of help.

The Internet

A wealth of career information is available on the Web. For starters, check out:

- the online version of the Occupational Outlook Handbook at www.bls.gov/ooh/
- O*NET (The Occupational Information Network) at www.onetonline.org
- CareerOneStop www.careeronestop.org

Computer resources and Internet access are available at most schools, colleges, libraries and employment agencies.

Other sources

These may include:

- college career centers
- job search fairs
- professional associations

START CREATING A WINNING RÉSUMÉ TODAY!

An effective résumé can help you make a good first impression on employers. This will bring you closer to the job you want.

Assess your skills and experience.

Identify the skills and accomplishments that you want a potential employer to know about.

Choose the format that works best for you.

This could be a résumé that is:

- chronological
- functional
- a combination

Prepare an electronic version of your résumé.

Most employers prefer to receive résumés this way. You also post this version on job sites or your own Web site.

Put your résumé to work.

Send your résumé to employers who have job openings you are interested in. Customize your résumé and cover letter as needed to point out how you would be a good fit for the position.

Write your own job success story!

CONGRATULATIONS!

Your completion of this material demonstrates an ongoing commitment to personal growth and development.

CERTIFICATE
OF ACHIEVEMENT
THIS CERTIFICATE IS HEREBY AWARDED TO

Your Name Here

FOR SUCCESSFUL COMPLETION OF THE _____ HOUR
EVIDENCE-BASED RECIDIVISM REDUCTION PROGRAM ENTITLED,

Program Title Here

ISSUED AND VARIFIED BY REENTRY ESSENTIALS.
THIS CERTIFICATE ATTESTS TO YOUR KNOWLEDGE AND UNDERSTANDING OF THE CONCEPTS AND
THEORIES EXPLORED DURING THIS COURSE OF STUDY.

AWARDED ON THIS _____ DAY OF _____, 20 ___.

Certificate verification available online at,
www.reentryessentials.org or via email at
certificate@reentryessentials.org

Ms. Michaiah
Director of

DEMONSTRATE REHABILITATION

Each of our unique Evidence-Based Recidivism Reduction (EBRR) Programs and Productive Activities (PA) include a transcript and certificate of achievement issued by Reentry Essentials. Ideal for demonstrating rehabilitation to a parole board, case manager, probation officer, judge, potential employer or even your family and friends.

REQUEST YOUR TRANSCRIPT AND CERTIFICATE TODAY!

Simply follow the below instructions based on how your materials were purchased and we will do the rest. We make receiving your certificate and transcript quick and easy!

- **Individual Purchase**
  Materials purchased by you directly or on your behalf by family or friends.
  Written requests should be submitted to the address below. All requests must include full committed name, inmate number and mailing address. Requests will be verified against our customer purchase history. Please allow 2 - 3 weeks for processing.

- **Organizational Purchase**
  Materials purchased by a government agency, nonprofit organization or community service provider. Please contact your program administrator for assistance. Program administrators may forward official requests for certification to, info@reentryessentials.org.

 Reentry Essentials, Inc., 2609 East 14 Street, Suite 1018, Brooklyn, NY 11235-3915
347.973.0004 info@reentryessentials.org www.reentryessentials.org

Made in the USA
Columbia, SC
15 July 2024

38636651R00274